BY GERALD T. DUNNE

Monetary Decisions of the Supreme Court
Justice Joseph Story and the Rise of the Supreme Court
Hugo Black and the Judicial Revolution
Grenville Clark: Public Citizen

Grenville Clark

GRENVILLE CLARK
PUBLIC CITIZEN

Gerald T. Dunne

FARRAR · STRAUS · GIROUX
New York

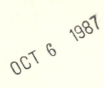

Copyright © 1986 by The Grenville Clark Fund at Dartmouth College, Inc.
All rights reserved.
Published simultaneously in Canada by Collins Publishers, Toronto
Printed in the United States of America
First edition, 1986
Designed by Roxana Laughlin

Library of Congress Cataloging-in-Publication Data
Dunne, Gerald T.
Grenville Clark, public citizen.
Bibliography: p.
Includes index.
1. Clark, Grenville, 1882–1967.   2. Lawyers—
United States—Biography.   I. Title.
KF373.C53D86   1986   349.73'092'4 [B]   85-29912
347.300924 [B]

For Nancy

Who shall find a valiant woman?
Far above rubies is the price of her.

—Proverbs 31:10

Contents

Illustrations

Foreword

This is the story of a man and his life. It is one worth telling for many reasons. It concerns material success: first-name acquaintance with Presidents, in a transit that began as a millionaire twice over and closed as one eight times over. It tells of power and the paths to power, followed not by conventional political action, but by singular application of will and moral force. It is a story of successful achievement in several planes of effort: decisively defending American constitutionalism and vindicating the ethos of America's oldest university. It is also a story of failure, or at least of lack of immediate success, in saving the human race from itself—an engagement whose outcome is yet to be seen.

But most of all, it is the story of a complex and arresting personality and a process of personal development. It is a case study of the failure of social conditioning and an illustration that a birthright of privilege and power need not produce a commitment to the status quo, and that the aging process need not entail defensiveness and conservatism, but can engender a responsible liberalism, open-mindedness, and humanity.

Grenville Clark was a remarkable man who, as a private citizen, made contributions to public causes which were of fundamental importance to his fellow citizens, his country, and the world. In this biography, I have endeavored to tell the story of his life and his achievements in such a way as to do justice to the man and to the public causes to which he gave dedicated and effective leadership.

These public causes included national defense (creating the Plattsburg Camps in World War I and the Selective Service Act in World War II); good government (leading the successful opposition to President Franklin D. Roosevelt's attempt to "pack" the United States Supreme Court); academic freedom and civil rights in general; individual rights, including the protection of the people from arbitrary governmental action and the elimination of discrimination against blacks and other ethnic minorities; and, most important of all, a valiant, determined and long-continued effort to prevent World War III, culminating in the writing and worldwide dissemination of a monumental book, *World Peace Through World Law*. This extraordinary book contained a specific, detailed, and comprehensive plan to prevent another global war, and was translated into Russian, Chinese, French, German, Italian, Spanish, and various other languages. Although little progress has been made, as yet, toward adoption and implementation of the Clark peace program, there is reason to believe that eventually, and possibly in the not too distant future, *World Peace Through World Law*, and the universal attention and recognition it has attained, could have a profound influence on the destiny of mankind.

In my effort to tell the story of Grenville Clark and the public causes he embraced, I have had much help. Most of it came, posthumously, from Clark himself and the sinewy, vigorous prose that fairly leaped out at me from three and a half tons of collected letters and papers at Dartmouth. I was thereby enabled to follow the paradigm of all biographers, James Boswell:

> Indeed I cannot conceive a more perfect mode of writing a man's life than not only relating all the important events of it in their order, but interweaving what he wrote and said; by which mankind are enabled

as it were to see him live and "to live o'er each scene as he actually advanced through the several stages of his life...."

My obligations are immense: first and foremost, to my wife, Nancy O'Neill Dunne. I greatly appreciate the intellectual and logistical support of my generous superior, Dean Rudolph Carl Hasl of the St. Louis University School of Law, where I am professor of law; the expert word processor ministrations of Stephanie (Mrs. Richard) Haley; and the long-suffering competence of the law faculty secretaries. I must also acknowledge the help of those whom Clark's life touched in its own inimitable way: Judge Henry Friendly, Robert Reno, and Samuel Spencer, to list but a few. Two names must be included in any list of acknowledgments: Leo Gottlieb, whose sense of decency and fair play saved me from a number of judgmental turns of phrase, and Carol McKeown, whose unremitting insistence on clarity and precision made this a better book and me a better writer. If in the classroom I can transmit but a fraction of what they taught me, my students—as both lawyers and human beings—will be their beneficiaries. Above all, this book owes its existence to the assistance of Clark's older daughter, the late Mary Clark Dimond, who was every inch her father's child, and in a sense this is her book, too. To her I am grateful for the chance to tell the Grenville Clark story and perhaps to have some small share in the great work to which he set his hand. For, as Julian Benda wrote so well in *The Betrayal of the Intellectuals:* "Peace, if it ever exists, will not be based on the fear of war, but the love of peace. It is not the abstaining from an act, but the coming of a state of mind. In this sense, the most insignificant writer can serve peace where the most powerful tribunals can do nothing."

Gerald T. Dunne

St. Louis, Missouri
Independence Day, 1985

Mr. Clark has been a lawyer in the grand tradition, dedicated to the public service and the uplifting of our legal ideals, fighting for freedom, against our enemies abroad in time of war and against those at home who would have undermined our Bill of Rights.

—*The New York Times*, August 31, 1959

Grenville Clark

Birth and Bloodline

*Had he been born in Jerusalem under the shadow
of the Temple and circumcised in the Synagogue by
his uncle the high priest under the name of Israel Cohen,
he would scarcely have been more distinctly branded.*

—Henry Adams, *The Education of Henry Adams*

A Change of Name

The newborn left home Sidney and came back Grenville, a
turnabout that foreshadowed a later, larger reversal, whereby
intellect and will would overcome massive social programming.
The revision of name had been effected, not in the courts, but in
a hasty christening-party conference within the carriage that had
clopped down Fifth Avenue, turning at the site of the future
Flatiron Building and thence down Broadway to Grace Episco-
pal Church, where the ancient Anglican baptism had been duly
performed. The motive of the name changers had been sound
enough: familial deference to the pre-emption of the name Sidney Clark by a baby cousin in Philadelphia.

The name changers had written straight with crooked lines, for
Grenville (plucked, so to speak, out of the cold Manhattan air
and borne by no known relative or family friend) had a euphony
far superior to the sibilance of Sidney and was most appropriate
for the man the baby would become. More than this, Grenville
was, in its own right, historically superb. For one thing, *grand
ville* fit like a glove on a ninth-generation Manhattanite born
November 5, 1882; for another, a French name nicely caught the

baby's Huguenot inheritance. By rights, the christening party could have pressed on to the little Eglise de Sainte Esprit, where French Calvinist exiles had first worshipped on the island of Manhattan; indeed, the eight generations intervening from them to the newly christened Grenville Clark were studded with names like LeGrand, Bouton, deForest, and the like, all far more significant than the bluff Anglo-Saxon Clark in symbolizing a Calvinist heritage (doubtless fortified by a grandmother named Crawford who came from Scotland via Putney, Vermont). The Huguenot strain blended nicely with the Anglo-Saxon one springing from William Clarke, who came from England in 1630 to become an "inhabytante" of Northampton, Massachusetts. That combined heritage was to find special expression in the newborn's future style and personality. It embodied the conviction (expressed by R. H. Tawney in *Religion and the Rise of Capitalism*) that those who have the courage to turn the world upside down are those who are convinced that, in a higher sense, such effort is disposed for the best by a power of which they are the humble instruments.

That belief had been strikingly exemplified by the baby's grandfather, LeGrand Bouton Cannon, charter Republican and Lincoln supporter, who, just twenty-one years before the christening, had marched up the same Broadway in the turbulent spring of 1861 to rally Copperhead Manhattan almost single-handedly for the Union cause. And it was to the LeGrand Cannon house at 311 Fifth Avenue that the christening party returned when the liturgical rites were completed. Cannon was a remarkable person, who was pleased to live with his favorite daughter and her husband, the newborn baby's parents. Naturally enough, he provided an intellectual and genetic influence on Clark's personality. The railroad-building son of an ironmaster from Troy, New York, Cannon was David Riesman's "inner-directed man" incarnate. Proto-Republican, abolitionist, social Darwinist before the term was coined, Cannon had served as a colonel in the Union Army, in which military experience served only to reinforce his fiercely held moral convictions.

Indeed, the combination of the Fifth Avenue town house and the fashionable church suggested the possible applicability of Henry Adams's reflection on such a *rite de passage:*

> Had he been born in Jerusalem under the shadow of the Temple and circumcised in the Synagogue by his uncle the high priest under the name of Israel Cohen, he would scarcely have been more distinctly branded. . . . Probably no child born in that year held better cards than he.

But there are cards and cards, and different ways of playing them, and the discontinuities between Grenville Clark and Henry Adams are even more impressive than the similarities. Notwithstanding an endowment that included every social and intellectual advantage his age had to offer, Adams lived out his life in baleful reflections upon the upstarts who had come to power in the places where his ancestors had ruled. Clark would turn the accidents of birth and endowment to account, take his world as he found it, and notwithstanding his distinct branding as a child of both the Gilded Age and fundamentalist Republicanism, undergo a remarkable psychological and cultural turnabout and leave a profound mark on his times, impressed almost solely by dint of will and personality.

Even the carriage ride was a symbol of the racist and class-bound society into which the baby was being inducted. The conventions of conspicuous consumption demanded that a footman accompany the carriage, even though the functionary's service was at an end the moment he closed the door smartly behind the last boarding passenger. Convention also demanded that the coachman crack his whip and start the conveyance just as smartly at that very moment, leaving the footman to scramble aboard as best he could. Clark remembered how the lackey usually made it by climbing the revolving rear wheel; the entire effort was a fitting signification of the struggle of the working classes in the Gilded Age. The age was also mirrored in a site that is now a mélange of tacky shops but was then dominated by the Fifth Avenue mansion. Later generations would regard Cannon's as Neanderthal brownstone, a style featuring iron deer on the front lawn and bric-a-brac in the cluttered parlor.

After arrival at the mansion, the ceremonials continued with a buffet of the rich, heavy food that was a virtual staple of the culture. Also *de rigueur* were the long christening gown and the inevitable silver cup duly presented to the newborn by his godfather, H. Walden Webb, senior vice-president of the New York Central. Mr. Webb, himself an emblem of the successful businessman risen to social prominence, might well have given his godson a silver spoon to typify the newborn's endowment of privilege. Or perhaps not. Each age, it has been said, necessarily bears the seeds of its own undoing, and it has been noted that the Gilded Age, even at its meridian, carried the potential for a profound altering of the vulgarity, greed, and brutality that had become its hallmark.

In terms of race and class, 1882 was also the year in which the Supreme Court decided *Pace* v. *Alabama,* in which a speciously fair-minded opinion of Justice Stephen Field insisted that the visitation of heavier sanctions upon sexual misbehavior involving partners of two different races was consistent with the constitutional commandment of equal protection of the laws ("The punishment of each offending person, whether black or white, is the same"). It was in 1882 that Congress passed the Chinese Exclusion Act, the first exclusively racial immigration statute, whose interdiction of movement followed a steady stream of anti-Chinese discrimination. (Chinese were ineligible as witnesses, excluded from naturalization, and subjected to demeaning licensing and occupational requirements.)

Place and Prospect

That a child born in 1882 at 311 Fifth Avenue should grow up to play a significant part in constraining racism was not particularly unusual, but rather part of the inheritance of a grandson of an abolitionist ultra and admirer of John Brown. But what was unusual was the mode in which the new baby would ultimately aspire (at a most extraordinary moment) to be the instrument bringing the Chinese and American cultures into a nexus far more intimate than anyone could possibly have foreseen. Moreover, the baby was fated to be the herald and prophet of a new world order, in which power and property would be shared throughout the planet by all the inhabitants thereof, whatever their color or condition. That was a circumstance beyond the farthest horizon of Colonel Cannon's GOP fundamentalism. It was, however, hailed eight decades later on the dedication page of Edgar Snow's *Red Star over China:* "To Grenville Clark, Who Stood Taller Than His Time."

The philosopher Alfred North Whitehead has proclaimed the years 1880–1910 one of the happiest times in the history of mankind—not because nothing needed changing, but because needed changes had been foreseen and begun. The milieu, Whitehead said, was ideal for the middle class, for they didn't have too much money, there was much engrossing work to be done, and there was a sense of progress and purpose abroad in the world. But for the very rich, those years—especially the nineteenth century's last decade—were heaven.

Early Education

Fin de siècle New York resembled its twentieth-century descendant in that concerned parents considered the private school indispensable; the one young Grenville attended was under the tutelage of two spinsters and was located at Thirty-seventh Street and Lexington Avenue. The proprietresses were Miss Ketchum and Miss Cook, names their charges transmuted with great hilarity to "Ketchum and Cookum." Clark and an older brother (there were four siblings) walked the half mile from 311 Fifth Avenue as a matter of course.

There was no danger; that only came when the Clarks moved

from Fifth Avenue to 21 West Forty-seventh Street. (Interestingly, in terms of continuing intellectual domination and influence, the grandparent Cannons, in whose mansion the Clark family had previously lived, moved at the same time to the house next door, 19 West Forty-seventh). The move meant a change of schools, away from the maternal ambiance of Ketchum and Cookum to the spartan style of Cutler's School on Forty-seventh Street. Cutler's would set the tone for the rest of Clark's formal education. At Cutler's School, which had been founded by Theodore Roosevelt's tutor, the instructors were male and the emphasis athletic. The intellectual milieu provided an extended, subtly differentiated dimension to Le Grand Cannon's conservatism, and even though disciplined, purposeful, and elitist, still had a softening touch. The effect of the rigorous regimen came to be tested in the boys' brushes with the other New York, the Irish working classes from the dreary row tenements on Sixth and Seventh Avenues—hostile, aggressive "toughs" who regularly clashed with the Cutler boys in a kind of early *West Side Story*.

The battles, both en masse and by champion, were reminiscent of Henry Adams's recollections of the "battle of the Latin School against all comers" on the darkening plain of Boston Common. ("As the Latin School grew weak, the roughs and young blackguards grew strong. . . . As the night came on, the Latin School was steadily forced back to the Beacon Street Mall where they could retreat no further without disbanding and by that time only a small band was left, headed by two heroes, Savage and Marvin.") For Clark, impressment as an individual paladin produced only physical retribution: "they united in putting me forward," he once reminisced. "I hadn't any quarrel with this boy, of course, and it was all in absolute cold blood, so that I didn't have, I guess, very much spirit for the fight. At any rate, what happened was that this other boy, who was a wellpracticed fighter, very soon hit me with a tremendous upper cut and knocked me out cold. The next thing I knew, I was being carried upstairs and revived." The incident doubtless made welcome the modish pugilistic instruction afforded at the Racket and Tennis Club on West Forty-third Street.

The Racket and Tennis was part of the Four Hundred World, which included the Metropolitan Opera, on the verge of its Golden Age in its brand new "golden horseshoe." There were also the conventional dancing classes, as authentic and anthropological a ritual as anything in Papua or Patagonia, which recalcitrant young males protested by sticking pins strategically through their white gloves, in a mode guaranteed to draw a scream from an unwary female partner. Some release was necessary from the heavy social constraints, and the pinned gloves were essentially the same form of covert rebellion as the romping games of tag played in the corridors behind the boxes of the Met. There was also, on occasion, the escape of a baby alligator to Central Park, followed by the discovery years later of the four-foot saurian into which the escapee had presumably grown.

For all the spartan discipline of contact sports, the spirit of the age sanctioned—indeed encouraged—indulgence of the young. "Somehow or other," Grenville Clark recollected from the perspective of almost eight decades, "the psychology was in many cases that the fathers and grandfathers, having worked so hard and struggled so intensely, thought it was quite all right for the grandsons and sons to take it easy, and they didn't seem to mind their indulging in polo and steeple chasing and yachting and having four-in-hands."

Carousing was fine for some, perhaps, but certainly not for the young men of the family of Louis Crawford Clark. Or perhaps it would be more proper to say of LeGrand Bouton Cannon, that embodiment of the Calvinist ethos, in consequence of sustained residential proximity, if nothing else. One can easily visualize the picture: night after night, the colonel at the head of the table (even in his son-in-law's house), thumping it hard to varying responses of his audience. The nominal head of the house, Louis Crawford Clark ("not a very forceful character," a granddaughter recalled), heard the colonel out with the respect of a prince

consort of the Cannon family. But the bright, handsome Grenville listened intently to denunciations of the current low tone
of society and apostrophes to

> the theory of republican government, which assumes that every
> citizen shall be a politician and shall take an interest in public affairs
> . . . [and] the Republican party, whose cardinal principles are a
> protective policy designed to develop our resources, a stable cur-
> rency and a uniform standard of value.

The traditionalist-classical leavening continued with Grenville's matriculation at Pomfret School in the autumn of 1894.
The reason for choosing Pomfret was conventional enough—his
elder brother (the only one), Louis Crawford, Jr., the previous
year had attended St. Mark's in Connecticut, whose headmaster,
William E. Peck, after quarreling with the St. Mark's trustees,
had decamped to Pomfret Center, Connecticut, to establish his
own school there. Louis Crawford Clark, Sr., in one of the few
recorded decisions that affected his second son's future, supported
Peck by enrolling both Grenville and Louis, Jr., in the new
educational enterprise.

Generically, Pomfret was "prep," the English public school
transplanted to American soil—spartan in discipline, athletic in
emphasis, classical in intellectual thrust, with instruction provided
by a young Ivy League–trained faculty of scholar-athletes who
were expected to serve as role models to their charges. The
enterprise was also part of a new impulse in American education
—the exclusive, rural boarding school designed to insulate patrician children from the vulgar offspring of the newly rich indus-
trialists who were invading the private city day schools. As such,
the school was but one of the genre of which the Reverend
Endicott Peabody's Groton was the archetype. But Pomfret had
its own special differentiation from Groton, Andover, et al.
To provide a starting cadre of students, Mr. Peck brought a
group from St. Mark's. Facile transferability suggested they were

behavior problems whom St. Mark's was delighted to be rid of.

It was a pretty tough crowd, Clark recalled, and they made Pomfret no place for the insecure. The masters exerted a necessary counter-toughness. Mr. Peck had brought some fine teachers with him from St. Mark's, and they dispensed a superb education in which the public humiliation of laggard scholars was the standard teaching technique.

We can get a glimpse of the regimen from contemporary records—simplicity personified in dormitory commons and table settings, with frills such as heating and plumbing held at a bare minimum. Characteristic was the mixture of the freedom of the playing field and the strictness of the classroom, where absolute attention and prompt and accurate responses to the interrogation of a rapid-firing instructor were demanded. As one turn-of-the-century boarder put it, the philosophy was perfect freedom tempered by the threat of expulsion.

Among the exemplars of this philosophy was a young quarter-miler from Harvard named Hutchinson, who inspired his charges to attend secret early-morning practice in the hope of accumulating points. There was also a rowing enthusiast who similarly inspired Grenville Clark and a cousin to go to New York City, purchase a rowing shell, and return with it to Pomfret, in an excursion which included sitting up all night with their precious cargo in a freight car.

Pomfret afforded superb direction for a boy growing like a weed from five feet to six feet. More important, the athletic regimen was paralleled by an intellectual one where mastery of English grammar and syntax was the cachet of achievement. Half a century after Clark left Pomfret, Marion (Mrs. Felix) Frankfurter could provide the school's basic training with a high encomium of its style, which made script as natural as speech: "Grenny writes just as he talks."

The transition of an eleven-year-old boy from the *haute monde* of mid-Manhattan to the hardscrabble countryside of northeastern Connecticut could have been shattering, but for Clark there were ameliorating elements. Having a brother along helped, and coming to New England had a certain return-of-the-native quality to it, thanks to ancestor William Clarke the "inhabytante" of Northampton, Massachusetts.

Being a charter member of the Pomfret School, so to speak, made for a special sense of adventure and a deep instinct of proprietorship that more than compensated for the primitive buildings and rowdy student body. The young student Grenville Clark undertook faculty recruitment toward the close of the nineteenth century, just as liberated secondary students would in the trendiest days of the twentieth. The occasion was the quest for an English teacher. Sixth-former Grenville Clark was dispatched to Harvard, where he both interviewed and sold a promising young scholar named Samuel Drury, who did indeed come to Pomfret and who, after taking Anglican orders, became headmaster at St. Paul's in Concord, an academic career he attributed to the "fight talk about going to Pomfret" that the young student had delivered to him.

But the loom of the fates had a backward shuttle, too. As the nineteenth century passed into the twentieth, the hour came for Grenville Clark to be delivered, at the age of sixteen, to a major force of his life: Harvard University.

Fair Harvard

More than half a century after he left the Harvard Yard, Grenville Clark was asked to name the wise men who had influenced his life. Perhaps it was the distracting impact of the television lights and camera (for question and answer came on the NBC telecast "A Conversation with Grenville Clark" on April 26, 1959), but the name LeGrand Bouton Cannon was omitted, as were those of Theodore Roosevelt and Elihu Root. Instead, leading all the rest was Charles W. Eliot, president of Harvard from 1869 to 1909, who had "turned the university over like a flapjack," in the words of a contemporary town-and-gown idiom. And in expressing his estimate of Eliot, Clark necessarily disclosed his own ethos, in many ways holding a mirror up to his own face: "Great vigor of mind and great reliability of character, very insistent on speaking the truth under all the circumstances no matter how hard it was, great shrewdness in selecting men . . ."

Whatever other options were available, there was no doubt that Grenville Clark would attend Harvard. His father, a member of the banking house of Clark, Dodge and Company, had been a member of the Class of 1874. Moreover, Clarks had been associated with Harvard ever since "Lieut." William Clarke, the progenitor of the Clark clan, had contributed ten bushels of wheat (valued at one pound two shillings) as part of the Northampton subsidy to the college in 1672–73.

Thanks to the Eliot legacy, Harvard offered a superb educational experience, and fifty years after Clark's graduation the great names that had redeemed American culture from the tawdriness of the Gilded Age still lingered: "The names of the professors who stay in my mind include, in philosophy, George Herbert Palmer, William James, George Santayana, and Josiah Rice, all four famous men, a remarkable group . . . in economics, Frank W. Taussig, and T. N. Carver, a man I liked very much, but saw little of . . . in history, [Edward] Channing and Albert Bushnell Hart." There was a recollection of yet another professor, A. Lawrence Lowell: "an absolutely first-class lecturer" and future Harvard president, whose successor Grenville Clark would help to select.

The collegiate regime was almost monastic (Clark recalled attending only two dances in four years), but the ramrod intellectual discipline of Pomfret had admirably prepared the recipient for the intellectual smorgasbord of Harvard. There young Dr. Eliot, in turning the university over like a flapjack, had abolished the traditional liberal arts curriculum in favor of a broad system of electives. Just as rowing and fencing were bringing Clark's body to an optimum suppleness, so did the Harvard electives—

and at least half of what Clark chose to study were courses in English—broaden the mind beyond LeGrand Cannon's rigorism. The elective core did, however, emphasize the moral imperatives of truth, honor, and duty that were Cannon's credo.

There was a social as well as an intellectual and physical dimension. Clark lived in Claverly Hall with a Pomfret roommate and held membership in the Polo group and its rival, the fencing club ("slightly less disreputable, but not much so"). Significant, but unstressed in the television interview, was selection for the supersnobbish Porcellian Club, Harvard's inner social set of ultra-patricians, at a period when a "Grottie" named Franklin D. Roosevelt (who was one class his junior) was passed over for the honor.

Clark and FDR had known each other since boyhood—not intimately, to be sure, but in the kind of peripheral acquaintanceship to which the wellborn almost instinctively gravitate. More than that, there had been a familial business association: James Roosevelt, father of FDR, had succeeded LeGrand Cannon as president of the Lake Champlain Transportation Company, with melancholy results, duly noted in the corporate records ("the year 1896 does not show as favorably as the year 1895"). Nonetheless, the real beginning of a remarkable lifelong association between the two came at Sanborn's Billiard Parlor, where, Franklin Roosevelt recollected, "one could find most of the Groton, St. Mark's, St. Paul's, and Pomfret fellows." Yet even here an intellectual maverick strain emerged in Clark—the democracy of intellect transcending the sense of class and place. Particularly, it found expression in intellectual debates, thus producing the prophetic nickname "Wrangler" ("since others of my social group took no part in such things, and thought it very queer").

A singular episode occurred at Clark's halfway point, Commencement Day, 1901. The bravura commencement address had been given by Vice-President Theodore Roosevelt '80, and he and Clark may have met at the Porcellian Club, to which both belonged. (Roosevelt was already acquainted with Mr. and Mrs. Louis Crawford Clark.) Clark was not one to push himself forward, but Roosevelt was taken by the sophomore's manifest intelligence, charm, and good looks. The Vice-President invited Clark to the Roosevelt home at Oyster Bay, New York, where their shared masculine values produced an enduring sense of association and purpose. En route to Oyster Bay in response to the vice-presidential summons, and in danger of missing the New York train, young Clark had pulled out a would-be lady suicide who had jumped into the Charles, and then jumped back on the trolley just in time to make the train. A Boston paper duly reported the incident under the headline SAVED BY BACK BAY MAN, and commented on one of "the prettiest exhibitions of diving and rescue work . . ." The result was a medal, not the first Clark had received, but the second. At Pomfret, to the hilarity of his class-mates, he had received one for "general excellence." Now he got one from the Massachusetts Humane Society, continuing a sequence which would later comprehend the Distinguished Service Medal of the United States Army, as well as the golden medal of the American Bar Association. Personalized, rather than insti-tutional, honors would later include the Dag Hammarskjöld Award and the Theodore Roosevelt Medal, the latter foreshad-owed by a very special letter:

> The Vice President's Chamber
> Washington, D.C.
> Oyster Bay, N.Y.
> July 3, 1901

Mr. Grenville Clark
21 W. 47th St.
New York City

My Dear Clark,
   I have only just heard of what you did in rescuing that woman from drowning the night before you came to my house. It gave me

a thrill of pride as a Harvard man, and as a friend of your mother and father, when I learned of it. Will you give me just one or two rough details for my own pleasure?

Faithfully yours,
Theodore Roosevelt

2
The Path of the Law

. . . it gives you a sense of power that is
very pleasant to see people regulate their
conduct by what you say.

—Grenville Clark to Fanny Dwight, October 6, 1907

The Legal Threshold

In September 1903, Clark was back near the Harvard Yard, this
time at Austin Hall, then home of the Harvard Law School. He
met a heterogeneous collection of peers, whose backgrounds
attested the variety and richness of contemporary American life
and the magnetic power of the school itself. Two were New
Yorkers, coming from opposite ends of the state and its social
spectrum. One, Felix Frankfurter, was a five-foot Jew from
Manhattan's Lower East Side; the other, from Clinton, was the
son of the incumbent Secretary of War. Elihu Root, Jr., was
promptly nicknamed "Sec." Both became Clark's lifelong
friends.

Clark's matriculation was almost as much a mystery as the
acquisition of his first name. Why did he stay on for three years
of rigorous study, having so far had a lifetime of it? Possibly
because of the influence of one of his Harvard professors, A.
Lawrence Lowell, himself a lapsed lawyer. There was no tradition
of law in the Clark family, nor is there any record of someone
who might have sparked his interest. Rather, the family instincts
lay quite the other way, for banking had been the craft of both

father and paternal grandfather. Indeed, a seat was waiting for Grenville in the family firm of Clark, Dodge and Company.

The Harvard Law School was one of the many university institutions to undergo the transformations of the man who was to be Harvard's president for forty years. Here, the instrument of change, chosen by Eliot, was a relatively young New York lawyer, utterly without status or reputation, but with a flintlike conviction about what the teaching of law should be. His name was Christopher Columbus Langdell, and his conviction was that law was a science in which permanent principles were to be discerned and applied to the transient whirligig of life.

To that end, the deadening system of "read" lectures (and the discourses were precisely that, with the professor droning from a prepared text) was abolished, and substituted therefor was the "case system," which presented an actual legal controversy as the teaching vehicle and included a relentless interrogation from the professor, drawing out, Socratically, the lesson of the clash, much as a dissection might yield a ganglion. This iconoclastic system had become the established and conventional wisdom by the time Clark presented himself at the old Austin Hall as a first-year student. Notably, Langdell resigned upon Clark's arrival, but was appointed emeritus professor almost immediately. Nonetheless, his powerful influence was already at work on the impressionable mind of Grenville Clark, on several planes. The first was the case method of instruction, with its critical point—that there was a ruling general principle which, if steadfastly mastered and applied, could bring any conflict in human affairs to a happy resolution by sheer intellectual force. The second was the stellar faculty, which in a way was Langdell's true and enduring legacy to the Harvard Law School. "As to professors," recollected Clark many years later, paying Langdell tribute even without mentioning his name, "the oustanding personality for me, at least, was James Barr Ames, who was Dean of the School—remarkable personality, a wonderful teacher; and Samuel Williston; Joseph H. Beale; Edward Warren (usually called 'Bull' Warren); Eu-

gene Wambaugh, in property and constitutional law; John Chip-
man Gray, whom I revered . . ." Third was milieu. It is almost
impossible for a modern observer of the alienation and anomie
of the television program *The Paper Chase* to comprehend the
fraternal ambiance of Harvard Law School at the turn of the
century. As Felix Frankfurter put it:

> Austin Hall housed a family. A good many of the students knew
> each other, but in any event, they felt they were part of a common
> household. They at least saw each other, recognized each other, saw
> members of the faculty from day to day and lived under the same
> small roof, engaged in a common enterprise.

For Clark, all three years at the law school were passed residen-
tially at 52 Brattle Street and academically at Austin Hall, the law
school's second home, which by the twentieth century was beginning to show the ravages of time and increased student enrollments, but where, as Frankfurter noted, logistical pressures actually contributed to a sense of familial unity.

Perhaps this pressure took its toll on Clark, for his *cum laude*
degree from Harvard College was not replicated, nor was membership in the prestigious *Harvard Law Review* bestowed. A law
partner of Clark's, Emory Buckner, once gave a reason: "He
[Clark] could not operate on a three-hour basis," i.e., make the
high grades which were based solely on three-hour final examina-
tions and were the basis for election to the *Review*. Interestingly,
Clark unsuccessfully urged Buckner, a brilliant but impoverished
young Nebraskan in the class below, to aspire to the prestigious
journal. In the end, Buckner did not accept election to the *Review*,
being required by economic circumstances to work part-time.
Clark had no such excuse, but blamed the collegial method of
case study for his failure of membership: "I reviewed with Bob
Ewell—not a very good student or I might have done better."
He also belonged to the quasi-social, quasi-professional Pow
Wow Club and Phi Delta Phi. But his middling grades might

have had another source: "I got heavily involved in rowing again in the law school and worked out a lot with the varsity squad."

Clark also belonged to a lunch club, thereby reinforcing the perception of Felix Frankfurter and Emory Buckner—who hit it off on first meeting—that Clark and Root were really members of an unapproachable "Gold Coast crowd." Nonetheless, the dynamics of intellectual democracy exerted themselves against traditionalist class lines as the *Harvard Law Review,* under the spur of young Felix Frankfurter and the other editors, reflected a yeasty turbulence, with articles on antitrust, corporations, and stock transfers crowding the standard common law inquiries on the rule against perpetuities and medieval intestacy.

There were other shaping factors, far more permanent and productive. Langdell's case system stressed the critical importance of seizing the principle hidden beneath the transitory phenomena of appearance, and Felix Frankfurther summed up its effect on his friend in luxuriating reminiscence:

Grenville Clark, a great citizen, and I were in the same class. He was always a little behind the most active minds in the class. Joey Beale would get off those funny theories of his. Some of us who were more agile than Grenny—not deeper, but more agile, they're very different things—would give Joey Beale a run for his money. After a while everybody would know where everybody was, and we would quit. Beale one day got off a most preposterous theory, trying to reconcile the irreconcilable. After a while the hunt stopped, but Grenny Clark was still reflecting and said, "But, Mr. Beale, . . . the rule you've formulated is very difficult to apply."

Beale almost jumped across the table and beat him with one of his outrageous bits of casuistic repartee. "Mr. Clark, I haven't advertised this as a cinch course."

Cinch course or not, Beale wound up giving Clark a 74 (B) for his course in conflicts; the grade was on the high side of Clark's scholastic slope, whose peak was a surprising 79 (A) in torts from

"Bull" Warren. Otherwise, Clark's center of gravity was a middling 71 (B), as was his class standing—62nd of the 250 young
men who made up the Class of 1906.

First Steps

In the autumn of 1906, following graduation from Harvard Law
School in June, young Grenville Clark entered the offices of
Carter, Ledyard & Milburn at 54 Wall Street. New York law
practice was still a self-perpetuating caste system; Clark selected
that office because of friendship with a onetime roommate, classmate, and fellow Porcellian, Devereux Milburn. Another young
aristocrat, one of the six clerks at the firm, was Franklin Roosevelt, charming as ever, but restive, perhaps from the pressure
applied by his unhappy young wife, Eleanor, and his domineer-
ing mother, who lived next door to the pair at 243 East Thirty-
sixth Street.

Carter, Ledyard & Milburn was no halfway house, and FDR's
political ambition was soon given a fillip by a law office reprimand. The occasion was the routine service of some papers in
New Jersey by Clark and Roosevelt. Their dawdling return to
the law office on that summer's day involved a stopover at a
baseball park (probably the Polo Grounds) and the ingestion of
a quantity of beer by the President's cousin. Upon their return,
the middle partner, Louis Cass Ledyard ("a very powerful, high-
tempered, and able man," said Clark), demanded and received an
explanation, which he cut short with an explosively abrupt:
"Roosevelt, you're drunk!" The reprimand stung, but not because of its augury of FDR's future at Carter, Ledyard. "I remember him [FDR] saying with engaging frankness," Clark
once reminisced, "that he wasn't going to practice law forever,
that he intended to run for office at the first opportunity, and that
he wanted to be and thought he had a very real chance to be
president. I remember that he described very accurately the steps
which he thought could lead to that goal. They were: first, a seat

in the [New York] State General Assembly, then an appointment as Assistant Secretary of the Navy, and finally the governorship of New York. 'Anyone who is governor of New York has a good chance to be president, with any luck' are about his words that stick in my memory."

Clark's stipendary arrangement with the firm must have been the same as that made contemporaneously with Franklin Roosevelt: "That is to say, you will come to us the first year without salary, and after you have been with us for a year, we would expect to pay you a salary which, however, at the outset would necessarily be rather small." Indeed, any stipend was unusual, and the recipient of one ("Where's that *paid* law clerk?") was made to feel a distinct outcast.

Clark, however, had found his métier, and he wrote his future wife in Boston—perhaps too bleakly—of his monastic existence, in "one little rut, all of the time."

I get downtown by the elevated about 9:45, sit myself down at my desk and except for lunch and getting books from the shelf am anchored there till about 5:30. Then I usually dine at the Union Club and am home pretty early. So far, then, my observations have been confined to the Elevated, the Subway and Fifth Avenue between 42nd and 51st street.

But there was a reason for concentrated dedication:

The work here is most absorbing, even more so than I imagined. It is an utterly different proposition from studying just for the satisfaction of finding out and it gives you a sense of power that is very pleasant to see people regulate their conduct and change their business by what you say.

For Clark's classmate Felix Frankfurter, things were very different: "I went from office to office, and it was not a pleasant experience . . . I was made to feel as though I was some worm going around begging for a job." Perhaps the sharpest rebuffs came in the form of insinuations that the handsome recommendation from Dean Ames ("Yes, that's his signature") was a forgery, and in a well-meaning suggestion to change his name ("You know, there's nothing the matter with it, but it's odd, fun-making"). Then came what Frankfurter called a revelation. "There was one office, Hornblower, Byrne, Miller and Potter. . . . Lots of Harvard people were in there, I'd heard that they'd never taken a Jew and wouldn't take a Jew. I decided that was the office I wanted to get into . . ." Frankfurter did get in, but hardly stayed long enough to warm his chair before he left to accept Henry Stimson's appointment as assistant United States Attorney.

The Building of a Law Firm

In 1952, Louis Auchincloss, himself a Wall Street lawyer as well as a brilliant novelist of manners, wrote of "the modern corporate law firm, that bright and shining sword, [forged] . . . out of rusty materials lying about the old fashioned city lawyer's office of seventy years ago." Interestingly, the Auchincloss prototype of the founding father, Henry Fellows Everett, possessed many, but not all, of the qualities of Grenville Clark: "genial, available, democratic with . . . clerks and sympathetic with . . . clients, ready with a generality for every emergency and a funny story for every banquet."

Assembly of the rusty, nineteenth-century materials began in 1908 when Grenville Clark, now restive at Carter, Ledyard & Milburn, but not rebellious, suggested to Francis William Bird ("the most brilliant man of my generation," Clark later pronounced him), who was even more restive at Hornblower, Byrne, Miller & Potter, that the two of them strike out together in their own firm. Coincidentally, a like request to Bird was addressed by Elihu Root, Jr., Bird's co-worker and former room-mate at the Harvard Law School, who had persuaded his father,

Senator Root, that one year at the Hornblower firm was enough. "We hatched our partnership years ago in Cambridge," Emory Buckner later wrote of the firm's roots. The original members— Root, Clark, and Bird—were all members of the Harvard Law School Class of '06.

By August 1907, Clark had had enough of Carter, Ledyard, and he almost left on the lure of a handsome offer elsewhere. Nevertheless, he decided to stay one more year, a resolution that was as much ultimatum as stay-over. On January 1, 1909, the law firm of Root, Clark & Bird opened its doors on the tenth floor of 31 Nassau Street. Happily, it could draw on the psychological association of its name with that of Senator Root's firm, Root & Clarke (the latter unrelated to Grenville), in the same area. Still, it was a chancy time to start anything, for the fallout of the Panic of 1907 was still reverberating in Wall Street. The trio were $750 in the red by the time the first client arrived, and a war dance was performed when the first fee came in. Not that Grenville Clark was worried; his private portfolio was secure, and he had even prepared for independent practice by taking a trip abroad. Eventual fees and success were virtually assured, thanks to a felicitous combination of establishment connections, brains, and capability. Moreover, the advent of the famous Hand cousins, Learned and Augustus, acquaintances of the partners, to the federal bench (where they served with worldwide distinction) assured the firm a sequence of bankruptcy appointments, an instance where the old-boy network worked to public advantage. But in due course, and thanks to Senator Root, there arrived the proto-client whose patronage is indispensable to springing a fledgling law firm into the first rank. In this case it was the steel tycoon Andrew Carnegie, who, like most self-made men, fancied he knew as much as any attorney. Clark recollected that "Carnegie had the utmost contempt for all lawyers. The only lawyer he would pay any attention to was Elihu Root [Sr.]. When we set up our little firm, Carnegie was active in setting up the Carnegie Corporation to handle all his charities. And he was writing a new will. He told Senator Root to give the business to us. I drafted —I was a kid twenty-eight years old—the special act that is to this day the Charter of the Carnegie Corporation. And I drew his will." As Martin Mayer subsequently noted, in a characteristically brilliant aperçu, "Not that anybody drew Carnegie's will who wasn't named Andrew Carnegie—but the new firm got paid for trying to help."

Clark wrote to his wife of the legal dealings with "Andy" and "Mrs. Andy" and also received a salutary lesson in practicality and power from the client. After preparing a fresh draft of the Carnegie will, Clark was dumbfounded to get the executed instrument back replete with pen-and-ink deletions and interlineations. Aghast, he advised the client that the document would never pass muster, only to hear the tycoon burr: "Don't wurra, m'lad, just tell 'em it's Andrew Carnegie's." He was right; the document did pass muster, was duly admitted to probate, and doubtless reposes, flawed, yellowing, and undisturbed, in the Manhattan records to this day.

Of course, there was more to law business than getting clients, and two further elements filled in the interstices. One came on September 1, 1913, when the nascent firm of Emory Buckner and Silas Dent Howland moved from 32 Nassau Street to join Root, Clark at 31, and filled the void created by the departure of Francis Bird. (Bird had hoped to return to Massachusetts politics, but instead went home to die prematurely, at the age of thirty-two.) Emory Buckner was able, charming, energetic. The second personal element was the accession, as counsel, of Senator Elihu Root, when his legislative term expired at the beginning of 1915.

Around this structural mold of talent, the firm evolved a method of recruitment. Additional senior staff were not the survivors of an abrasive apprentice elimination but rather the end-product of a careful search that emphasized quality in three areas. The first was undergraduate education with a Phi Beta Kappa cachet; the second was professional training which was the functional equivalent of Harvard Law School's, along with a law review editorship; the third had to do with the intangibles of style and personality.

While the choice of raw, new graduates over seasoned veterans was probably not consciously intended to provide recruits especially malleable to the firm's ways of doing things, the result was precisely such a collegiality. These recruits benefited from a transmission mechanism that permitted Clark's style and personality to reach down and fire the newcomers. Emory Buckner subsequently elaborated on that *élan vital* which Clark called "absolute harmony and teamwork":

> We have here an association of a large number of lawyers who are practicing law together in a great joint endeavor. . . . No client is a "personal" client of any of us. He is a client of all of us. Frequently, the man who introduces a client to the office is not the best equipped man . . . to do the work.

In noting how Root, Clark (and thus was the firm invariably referred to) sought to replace the competitive Wall Street perception of a colleague in the office as "the fellow I have to beat" with one of seeing him as "the fellow I have to help," Buckner said that "Mr. Clark learned of a hurryup mass of mechanical work in a matter not under his charge and stayed all night to help a junior at it . . ."

Clark was able to demonstrate such liberality of spirit precisely because he was endowed with a liberality of mind unoccluded with legal minutiae and techniques. As Cloyd Laporte, a onetime firm member, later noted:

> Grenville Clark, as a practicing lawyer, can, I think, best be described as a "generalist." He took on a variety of cases and matters —corporation matters, litigation involving contracts, wills and estates and miscellaneous controversies. The fact that an area of practice was new to him did not deter him from taking on an assignment in an unfamiliar field. He always handled such matters with his

customary thoroughness and persistence, achieving the best results which were attainable under the circumstances of the case or matter.

His superb work was an exemplification of Clark himself, *suaviter in modo, fortiter in re,* who was in the habit of stretching his six-foot frame out on the floor while writing the first draft of a brief, sometimes with confusing appearances: "I see you're having the carpeting repaired . . . ?" "No, that's Mr. Clark . . . !" Nonetheless, not all was comfort. Every citation was double–checked, every reference verified. As Clark was wont to say later, a remembered reference was apt to be wrong by odds of fifty to one. And a partner summed it up: "He prepares like a scientist and hangs on like a leech."

There was something of a fault line in this massive aura of capacity. Clark's obsession with exactitude not only extended his working time almost interminably but left him utterly incapable of delegating tasks. Future Chief Judge Henry Friendly once recalled that assignment as Clark's in-house assistant had amounted to a *de facto* vacation, leaving Friendly with literally nothing to do, as the senior partner checked his own citations and polished his own drafts until satisfied ("convinced" is the better word) that the point of no return had been reached and well passed. Singularly, however, the quest for certainty never manifested itself in nervousness, insecurity, and pettiness, but contributed significantly to the air of well-being and courtliness that Clark invariably radiated.

The easy style went just so far, however. Once convinced of the merits of his case, Clark became like flint. "Grenny was an impossible man to settle with," recollected Judge Joseph M. Proskauer. "He was an indomitable hewer to the line." Often the merit of a partnership enterprise was proven, when the case would be transferred to Emory Buckner, equally the personal Puritan, but with a tolerant and worldly-wise attitude that made him a most amiable man to do business with. Once, when a client asserted that he would feel like a son of a bitch if he settled a matter, Buckner proposed the unanswerable: "Let me be your son of a bitch."

When it came to Clark, Buckner could eschew vulgarity and set down a view of his partner with almost poetic felicity; on one occasion the possibility arose that Clark might take his talents as a trainer of lawyers from the Wall Street firm to the larger forum of the Harvard Law School deanship. Clark was actually doing in the law office what he urged Frankfurter to do in the classroom —stimulating chosen men to find new solutions to problems. And Clark performed at the law school, too. "Subtle," wrote Frankfurter after a Clark visit to Cambridge, "was a very inaccurate way to describe your remarks the other night. Felicitous was the right word, for you put with firmness and tact the things that need to be emphasized in proper attitude of the whole school towards the task of legal education in our time." Buckner wrote a tribute that Martin Mayer later incorporated into his biography of Buckner:

[Clark] is an "abler" . . . man than anyone I have heard mentioned whom I personally knew. He is slow . . . I know, I know—but just calling attention to it. He is a good judge of men. A Dean doesn't have to pick a faculty out of a circus crowd during the 10 minutes he is on the flying trapeze. He is solid. He is open-minded upon everything and most zealous in a humble search for the right. When finally—and at long last—through, then he's through! His process of searching being long in time and wide in scope would be called by some "tact" and "diplomacy"—not the words—his final adherence after he gets through would be equally erroneously called "stubbornness" when it is conviction.

3
Lifelong Contract

*Was there anything ever so fortunate as you and I
being married and just once for good and all and ever
and ever. It was just meant, that's all.*

—Grenville Clark to Fanny Dwight Clark, January 26, 1911

They met at a dance, which should have been proof enough that
Providence was on their side. The muse Terpsichore had precious
little court at turn-of-the-century Harvard, at least in the spartan
milieu of Grenville Clark. ("As to girls and dances, I had nothing
to do with them, as I remember. I perhaps went twice in four
years to any dance.") In any event, contemporary canons of
behavior ensured decorum: "A gentleman," counseled *The Young
Ladies' Friend*, "never encircles the lady's waist until the dance
begins and drops his arm as soon as it ends."

One of those two dances was something very special. It was
held in Milton, not Cambridge, and it was necessary to rent a
hansom to get there. Appropriately, the name of the fellow
traveler in the hansom was Benjamin Joy of Philadelphia. And
even more appropriately, the day was Clark's twenty-first birthday, November 5, 1903. The anniversary was commemorated
with an introduction to Fanny Pickman Dwight.

She belonged to that rarest genre of American good looks, the
New England beauty, and her sequenced names attested an ancient New England lineage. The "Pickman" was straight out of
the codfish aristocracy of Salem, where the Crowninshield,

Choate, and White families inhabited the beautiful McIntyre houses against a harbor crammed with merchantmen bound from or returning to *divitatis ad ultimum sinum*—the farthest port of the rich East—as the town motto summed up its China trade. Even more significant was the "Dwight," a cachet of sturdy Yankee independence, once duly illustrated by old Timothy Dwight, Yale president, whose detestation of Thomas Jefferson was equaled only by his fear of the French Revolution and consequent forebodings of a Jefferson Reign of Terror.

Historically, however, the family had descended from John Dwight of Oxfordshire, who had settled at Dedham, Massachusetts, in 1636 and was decidedly unlike his descendant Timothy. John (so the town records attest) was "publicly useful and a great peace maker." An especially lustrous adornment of the family was Wilder Dwight, a beau ideal of a soldier who was killed at Antietam while serving with the 2nd Massachusetts Regiment and whose *Life and Letters* went through two editions.

In immediate genealogy, Fanny was the daughter of Daniel Appleton and Mary Silsbee Peele Dwight and had been born and lived her entire life at 12 Hereford Street in Boston. Blue blood did not guarantee opulence; the Dwight fortune had been lost a generation earlier, and Fanny had been raised in a regimen of scrimping, saving, and sewing. Still and all, she radiated a compelling gentleness and charm which overcame even Felix Frankfurter's lower-class defensiveness, so that years later the future Justice confessed to having been smitten with a "boulevard crush" on her.

But Grenville Clark was smitten with more than a boulevard crush. He was fortunate that the timing of their meeting—and the consequent trips between Hereford Street and the Harvard Yard—had come after his graduation from Harvard College, so as to permit the concentrated study required for an A.B. and a Phi Beta Kappa key as well.

Certainly there was no courting at Harvard, if the Parietal Board were obeyed: "No young lady or ladies should be received in a student's room. . . . It is desirable that ladies should not walk through the hall of dormitories unattended; and a student, when entertaining ladies, should see that they are escorted to and from his room either by himself or some other gentleman."

There were other obstacles in the quest for Fanny Dwight's hand. Foremost were the disabilities of being an alien in a town that took itself as seriously as Boston and where even a New Yorker born on Fifth Avenue was geographically handicapped in a quest for a daughter of Hereford Street. Moreover, even though Fanny's entire cultural heritage was programmed to the day she would be mistress of her own house, she was in no hurry whatever to get married for the sake of being married. Her Boston life was full and good, replete with interesting, accomplished people. Tutored by Amy Lowell, she knew both William and Henry James and had played charades with Mark Twain. She had learned to fly-cast on Canadian trips with her Hunnewell cousins from Wellesley. Dancing deserves a special mention, for Emily Post put it with an exclamation point: "Beautiful balls, Boston!" Dancing comprehended much—the august Assemblies, the Hunt Balls, the Waltz Evenings, and the Cotillions. When to these were added tea parties, sleighing parties, and skating parties, it was evident that even the rich, good-looking, and wellborn New Yorker had his work cut out for him.

There was a long waiting period in the tradition set by the courtship of Clark's father and mother, which bore the shadow of LeGrand Cannon. In responding to a written request for his Marion's hand, the Colonel had frostily replied to Louis Crawford Clark:

> Marie is especially dear to me. She is the only one left & I shall not consent to part with her unless I am *fully satisfied* that the man is entirely worthy of her.
>
> I shall not object to her receiving your attention but it must be with the distinct understanding that it does not involve an engagement.

After long maneuvering, Clark finally proposed—probably at Overlake, LeGrand Cannon's baronial estate literally overlooking Lake George—on August 15, 1909, and while the pair teased each other as to the conventions of their class and time, in practice they respected those conventions enormously. Fanny's trips to Overlake were always most *comme il faut* ("I'll get Mama or Mary to write you, so as to have it very formal"). The proposal came as something of a leap in the dark, for, while promising, the law firm was still marginal. Ever conscious of institutional obligations, Clark had a notice posted in the Porcellian Club and then had a long talk with his father:

> He was most kind and generous, more than I thought possible with all the will in the world. However, he told me that he wasn't going to do any more for us than would be convenient for him, and as I told you I have no objections to his helping us for a while, much as I should like to be independent. It would really make him really unhappy not to be allowed to do as he wants. He has written your father.

Even though Clark wanted a "small, small wedding," he got something else. A fifteen-year-old sister of Fanny left a record of the event—which took place November 27, 1909 (six years and three weeks after their first meeting)—as valuable as a social document as an item of romance:

> . . . we had a lovely day for it which is a boon at this season. Fanny was as calm and happy a bride-elect as I ever saw—she worked hard before the wedding to spare Momma everything she could—in fact she was quite wonderful for she did everything herself in regard to lists and clothes and arrangements generally and also wrote all her notes on time and was able to devote herself to Grenville when he came for Saturdays and Sundays. In the morning of the wedding day Louisa Hunnewell and I arranged some flowers and greenery (which she had brought in from Wellesley) in the parlour and library and hall of Mom's house. Mme. Santin, who has made the family hats

for years, came from N.Y. to put on Fanny's veil and wreath. She wore the wreaths (slightly changed) that both Momma and I wore. Her veil was of plain white satin, having in the front of the shirt and on the waist and forming the sleeves, some lace which Grandma Peele wore on her wedding dress. At her wrists she had frills of lace which belonged to Grandma Dwight; so there was much sentiment bound up on her costume generally. Grenville's wedding present to her was a diamond collar—the kind that is put on a velvet ribbon around the neck. For the wedding it was on white velvet, but she will of course wear it on black velvet in the future. Her father gave her a diamond chain which hung down on the front of her bodice and was lovely. Usually white is not as becoming to her as darker things but she happened to have very very pink cheeks on her wedding day and I think everyone felt she looked her very best and she has had many compliments. Greenville was the most absolutely absorbed bridegroom I ever saw and I don't think he knew whether he was on his head or his heels.

There was, of course, a reception ("not too crowded"), and the young couple left for a six-week wedding trip to California. They returned to an apartment at 500 Madison Avenue (leased well before the wedding and thriftily sublet until occupancy) and, three years later, went uptown, moving to a brand-new building at 1155 Park Avenue (remembered by one child for its fire escape, on which Grenville, Jr., was "aired" in his bassinet and from which a sister got revenge on another family by spitting on their youngest offspring below).

In some respects, Fanny Dwight's married years might have seemed incomparably privileged. In others, they included a hard life and a hard death. Fanny bore five children, three of whom survived. Eleanor Dwight was born in 1915 and died in 1922; Mary Dwight was born in 1916 and Grenville, Jr., in 1918; Dwight died at birth in 1923; and Louisa Hunnewell was born two years later. Undoubtedly, the lady herself would have regarded appraisal as both irrelevant and impertinent. To be sure, the children's deaths were desolations: Dwight had been born deformed, and Eleanor was lost to meningitis. Clark took the latter loss particularly hard; for a year he wore a mourning band on his arm, and over forty years later, he gave land at Oyster Bay to Harvard in her memory. (The incidence of epidemic morbidities among the rich is a striking commentary on the state of public health in that day. In addition to his children's deaths, Clark's sister Mary died in childbirth, and a brother, Julian, was a lifelong cripple from polio.) In Fanny's case, Manhattan apartment living at its best might still have discouraged a woman who loved growing things from the rarest flowers to the lowliest vegetables. A house near the railroad in what was then Old Westbury on Long Island was bought in 1920, first as a weekend retreat, but eventually displacing a town house at 216 East Seventy-second Street, between Second and Third Avenues, as a permanent home and refuge beyond the city. Summers were spent in the familiar country surroundings of the farm bought by Fanny's grandmother in New Hampshire.

Given her wealth and lineage, Fanny could have traveled in the *bon ton* of Manhattan society. She chose not to, and the reason, as well as being an insight into her style and personality, is illustrated in her engagement of domestic servants. Here Mrs. Clark was every inch the Salem matron, to whom home was the ultimate sanctuary. She ran it accordingly, with a staff which was scrupulously handpicked. ("No professional servants need apply" customarily closed her help-wanted ads.) Nor was there any first-name egalitarianism, all domestics being addressed as "Miss" or "Mrs.," followed by a family name. One mild domestic crisis occurred on the day Louis Crawford Clark's valet appeared with fifty-two of Grenville's suits. The incident was doubtless the inevitable consequence of a man who bought unconsciously, letting his wardrobe accumulate. The delivery of these soon after Grenville and Fanny had settled into their small first apartment was a challenge quickly overcome by the lady of the house.

In 1906, Clark began the habit of sending his wife violets on Christmas Eve (surely a touching counterweight to the diamond wedding collar and, some Decembers, perhaps almost as hard to come by). He did so for over half a century, even though on the first occasion the flowers were charged by the florist to Mr. Dwight, a gaffe kept secret for years to come.

The groundwork of an enduring, stable marriage had been set in the tone of the affectionate, respectful letters passing between Boston and New York during the long, pre-engagement separation, when Clark had written teasingly of the young ladies into whose company he had been thrown in Manhattan society, and Fanny had responded with cool Bostonian nonchalance. Grenville Clark shared the responsibilities of marriage, but was definitely a gentle and sometimes preoccupied partner. Fanny knew the workings of her house and, in later years, enjoyed cooking special dishes. The result was a bedrock oasis of serenity and security for a busy professional life, which in a way made success beyond the household inevitable, because there was success within. An observer summed up the relationship between Mr. and Mrs. Grenville Clark felicitously years later: "She may not have played his public role. But without her support he could not have either."

4
The Plattsburg Camps

Plattsburg was not just a military training camp;
it was, in a way, a secular retreat for a whole generation . . .

—John P. Finnegan, *Against the Spectre of the Dragon* (1967)

During the early years of Clark's marriage, the law office prospered and the accouterments of success proliferated. These included Clark's membership in the St. Andrew's Golf Club. At twenty-four, Clark's splendid body had passed the point of inflection from youth to maturity, and golf represented a minimum concession to physical well-being. It was Clark's special game, involving as it did studied self-mastery rather than the constantly shifting improvisation of, say, tennis, which he also played surpassingly well, on the grass courts of the Piping Rock Country Club. Indeed, given Clark's talent for intense mental concentration, with the slightest effort his golf playing could have been of tournament quality. The persisting Puritan ethic, however, drew a sharp distinction between work and play and made Clark's potential golfing career a companion casualty to the brilliant swath that he and Fanny could have cut at the balls, masques, and dinners of the New York social scene, had they chosen to participate. Nonetheless, the clubhouse of posh St. Andrew's was the backdrop to one of Clark's most important decisions. It came on Sunday, May 9, 1915, when Clark forewent a scheduled round with his law partner, Elihu Root, Jr., in favor of long and intense conversation over the sinking, just two days earlier, of the Cunard liner *Lusitania*.

Clark later asserted that the fate of the *Lusitania*'s 124 American passengers—sent to their death without warning and in violation of the traditional laws of war—left him "too angry and too horror-stricken" to play golf. While he was not an outwardly religious man, he was *pius* in the classic Latin sense—a person of intense natural virtue to whom mendacity, foul play, and sharp dealing were equally abhorrent. And that natural base was fortified by an enormous sense of economic, social, and physical security; "utterly without fear," a partner once said of him. The privilege of never having been threatened in any meaningful sense had left him particularly contemptuous of the type of bullying of which the *Lusitania* sinking was a heinous example. His conversation with Root left him with the feeling that "inaction was intolerable," and, Sunday notwithstanding, he went directly from the golf club to the law offices at 31 Nassau Street, where he met a young associate, J. Lloyd Derby. A second conversation ensued between these two intense young men on that lazy Sunday afternoon in the deserted canyons of lower Manhattan, with no particular purpose or goal save to call for "a new movement for greater unity and a firmer national policy."

It was early evening by the time Clark got home to 1155 Park Avenue. Later the same night he drafted a proposed telegram to President Wilson. Next morning, he presented the draft to a group of activists who had gathered in the law office:

The undersigned citizens of New York express their conviction that the national interest and honor imperatively require adequate measures both to secure reparations from past violations by Germany of American rights and secure guarantees against future violations. We further express the conviction that the considered judgment of the nation will firmly support the government in any measures, however serious, to secure full reparations and guarantees.

There were fifteen signers of the telegram, virtually all upper-class Harvard alumni. Significantly, the name of Theodore Roosevelt, Jr., led all the rest, for the wire certainly embodied that high sense of "national interest and honor" that the senior Roosevelt had been expounding both before and after the *Lusitania* tragedy. It was also significant because of the enormous germinal influence that the former President had exerted on Grenville Clark, beginning with the weekend at Sagamore Hill to which Clark had been invited during the Harvard commencement of 1901. Theodore Roosevelt was now out of office and serving as contributing editor to *The Outlook* in lower Manhattan. Clark had continued to feel a sense of affinity with the magnetic and infectiously exuberant "Teddy." "I really believe," he had written Fanny at the height of the Panic of 1907, "that the seat of government lately has been old J.P.'s library. But I'm still for the President [Roosevelt] after all."

Roosevelt had secretly opted for American intervention with the German invasion of Belgium. ("If I had been President, I should have acted on the 30th or 31st of July [1914], as the head of a signatory power of the Hague treaties, calling attention to the guaranty of Belgium's neutrality and saying I accepted the treaties as imposing a serious obligation which I expected not only the United States but all other neutral nations to join in enforcing.") Foreshadowing all his later interest in collective security, Clark had easily reached the bottom line of Roosevelt's opinion via the jump spark of instinct. He made up his mind early (one associate at Root, Clark recalled him as an "interventionist"), and, as he later observed, in the first years of World War I he had felt that sooner or later "we would be thrown into hostilities with Germany . . . and with far less chance of success than if we joined the powers who [were then] fighting her."

Hence, his sense of alarm rose as the initial German offensive rolled almost unresisted on the Western Front. His concern was doubtless fortified by memories of LeGrand Cannon's dinner-table reminiscences of the early days of the Civil War. Not unsurprisingly, Clark had written Roosevelt on November 19, 1914, well before the *Lusitania* sinking:

> I have had a little scheme in my head for the last month or two that I should very much like to have your opinion about . . .
>
> I have in mind to get organized a small military reserve corps composed of young businessmen, lawyers, etc., who would go through a very light sort of training to fit themselves to be of some use in case of any real national emergency.

> . . . I have in mind a corps of 150 or 200 men. I would like to make the age limits 25 to 35 on the theory that no one under 25 ought to be included because such men ought to be encouraged to go into the militia and no one over 35 because they would be a little too old if anything did come up. The men in the corps would be men of sufficient means to carry the expenses themselves, but I should think $100 to $150 each a year would carry it. I should have it arranged and understood that there would be no *legal* obligations on the part of *any* such organization to serve but also that there be no *moral* obligation to serve except in case of a real emergency.
>
> The plan would have in mind two general objects—first actually to give the men who would join the organization some sort of familiarity with military matters so that they would be some, though of course not of much use in any emergency, second to furnish an example by showing that some of us at least recognize the lack of preparedness of the country for any emergency and our willingness to take some positive step, however unimportant in itself, to remedy the situation.

Clark concluded by requesting an interview ("I could come see you in New York almost anytime you could spare me a few minutes"). He apparently got it, for there seems no record of any answering letter by Roosevelt in Clark's carefully preserved correspondence. Indeed, one can easily visualize Teddy's responding ebulliently to the younger man's proposal with characteristically explosive verve: "Bully! Great!!"

In any event, this reserve corps idea was already formed and galvanized in Clark's brain when the fifteen young signatories decided on their next move—calling at least fifty acquaintances of their temper and persuasion for a meeting at the Harvard Club on Forty-fourth Street in Manhattan. The meeting was held on May 11, 1915, in the Biddle Room of the Harvard Club, followed a few days later by a second and larger one, which produced a body of one hundred. This group later became the Military Training Camps Committee, Clark's administrative apparatus. The purposes were vague enough, as described by Clark to a classmate: "to get a crowd together so as to be in touch in case anything comes up and to educate ourselves, and the public, to the international issues and our duties with respect thereto."

The Harvard Club meeting drew in a man important in both the loom of history and the making of Grenville Clark. This was Leonard Wood, senior general of the American Army, who had been Chief of Staff from 1910 to 1914, and who was serving his second tour of duty as commander of the Department of the East. Given some plastic surgery around either nose, Grenville Clark and Leonard Wood could have passed for son and father. Beyond the sturdy athletic frames, however, lay an affinity of drive, spirit, and values. There was also a profound cleavage of purpose, which at times would manifest its flash-point differences.

In one sense, the encampment that Clark eventually brought to pass was the lineal descendant of a college student training movement, a development produced by Wood during his tour of duty as Chief of Staff. It had come largely in response to Assistant Navy Secretary Franklin Roosevelt's summer cruises for college students. Truly a charter member of what Dwight Eisenhower later called the trade union of generals, Wood had long chafed under the traditional constraints of American military policy, which featured the smallest of professional cadres and assumed that the bulk of wartime fighting forces would be supplied by the state militias. Wood's hankering for a large, efficient force on the German model (and one that would be the logical counterpart to the widely respected American Navy) necessarily went against the grain of the dominant public opinion and Federalist-Whig tradition. In the student training program, Wood believed he had found what he called a "most subtle engine," which, by operating on the best and the brightest, could produce the revolution in military policy he was seeking.

Clark, on the other hand, was seeking, not a mechanism of propaganda, but a source of combat officers for a war he believed to be at hand. But he did share Wood's doctrinal views. As a bright and impressionable child, he had doubtless heard his grandfather Cannon indict the shortcomings of the militia system during the Civil War. That the onslaught of the seemingly unresistible German Army during the first years of World War I paralleled the success of the Army of Northern Virginia could only have accentuated Clark's inherited reactions and insights. It must have spurred Clark's November letter to Theodore Roosevelt, which forecast in remarkable degree the development of the Plattsburg training movement. Interestingly, the student training program, which he must have recollected after the Belgian invasion, produced a sense of vision in him as it had in Wood. Clark's unique idea was simply to extend the student movement to an older age group, to those in their late twenties and early thirties. After recalling the announcement of the student program in the press and consulting with some youthful coadjutors, Clark made the first of many pilgrimages to Wood's headquarters on Governor's Island and secured the senior general's enthusiastic approval for the idea. He got it, and Wood went so far as to promise Clark that if at least one hundred business and professional men volunteered for the training program, he would provide the officers and equipment.

Clark came up with three times that many, and pursuant to War Department General Order 23, Clark's envisioned businessmen's camp convened at Plattsburg, New York, on August 8, 1915, twenty-four hours after the student cadres had quitted the post. In terms of publicity and exposure, the experiment was a resounding success. Bernard Baruch could not join, but contributed $100,000. The would-be soldiers were most news-worthy: Richard Harding Davis; Frank Crowninshield, editor of *Vanity Fair;* John Mitchell, future mayor of New York and incumbent collector of its port; along with former Ambassador Robert Bacon and assorted Ivy League and socialite types.

Despite an ambiance of élan and camaraderie—thanks to the wholly voluntary nature of the enterprise—the regime was deadly serious. Most sobering was the decision to cram five weeks of training into four. Consequently, every minute of the working, waking day was filled with purposeful activity.

The bugles sounded at 5:45 A.M. and heralded a forenoon devoted to close-order drill and calisthenics. The afternoon was given over to field maneuvers and weapons instruction. But even then the day was not ended. Evenings were the most important of all, for that time was devoted to lectures on military doctrine and national policy, where Clark's and Wood's views fused into a single oriented objective. At a distance of six decades, elder statesman John J. McCloy still remembered the charisma investing Clark's remarks around the Plattsburg campfires.

The campfire lectures were the most significant ideological component of the entire Plattsburg effort. From a technical standpoint, the close-order drill was worthless in preparing the officer candidates for the barbed wire and poison gas of the trench warfare of the Western Front. Here, however, techniques were insignificant, for conditioning the mind was everything. At this critical point, the Plattsburg effort to teach the managerial and professional elite to think of themselves as officers and soldiers succeeded admirably even down to latrine cleaning and kitchen police duty.

Clark was present for the first Plattsburg camp. With his self-effacing nature, he would have preferred drilling in the rear rank, but things did not quite work out that way. He spoke at the campfire sessions and, after hours, laid plans to mold the summer soldiers into a continuing civilian organization. There were other incidents of conspicuousness. "As I was walking down another company street today," Clark wrote Fanny, "someone set up a yell—'the man who started it all.' A number of people set up a yell, but I have endeavored to keep absolutely in the background which is no trouble, everybody being too busy to bother about anything except their work."

Things went smoothly enough in terms of military training and logistics. An unforeseen complication arose in late August, when ex-President Roosevelt not only paid a visit but delivered a fire-eating criticism of what he saw as Woodrow Wilson's pusillanimity. Given Wilson's touchiness and antipathy to Roosevelt, the Rooseveltian blast almost aborted the entire training camp experiment, but matters eventually smoothed themselves over; unquestionably, the incident was a contributing element to the resignation of the Secretary of War, Lindley Garrison, in February of the following year.

The Secretary's resignation illustrated the role of contingency in human affairs. Up to this point, Clark's progress had been a fairly predictable consequence of industry and talent. Now the forward path was facilitated by what can only be described as an immense stroke of good fortune. Lindley Garrison was, in Felix Frankfurter's perception, "a first-class mediocrity"—bright, able, but incapable of being galvanized by Clark's vision because he was incapable of sharing it. His resignation came at a particularly critical juncture, for it fell athwart plans to formalize and regularize the Plattsburg agenda for the current year. Then, out of the Midwest came Newton D. Baker, mayor of Cleveland, to take Garrison's seat. His background and experience, as his postwar writings proved, had left him not only sensitive to Clark's point of view but in a position to vindicate it.

The matter of the 1916 agenda was serious enough to take Clark on the first of many trips to Washington in early March. To his extraordinary surprise, he found the new Secretary of War cooperation itself in terms of regularizing and funding the Plattsburg experiment. (Possibly the new secretary had been predisposed to Clark through a selling job by young Felix Frankfurter, who had been a War Department functionary since 1911.) In fact, Baker actually permitted Clark to draft a War Department letter to the Military Training Camps Committee for his (Baker's) signature:

> I heartily approve and endorse the valuable and patriotic service that is being rendered to the country by the army training camps for civilians.
>
> I believe in the work of these camps, not only from the military point of view but as a value to the national [sic] educationally in promoting discipline, order, and good citizenship. The camps are exactly in line with the sound policy of reliance upon a citizenry trained to arms as our main safeguard of defense. . . .
>
> These camps were originated by the War Department in 1915 for the training of students, and have since been extended for the benefit of other citizens with gratifying results.
>
> . . . you will have the continued cooperation and support of the War Department.

It was, of course, complete victory, and Clark hurried back to New York to break the good news to General Wood. Wood, still sulking over fancied slights from the administration, even though inwardly overjoyed, responded with a barracks dressing-down. Clark proved he had come of age when he responded to the senior general in kind. Clark later replied to a historian, permitting use of both his account and his name: "the fact is that the incident shows the general at his worst and at his best at the same time."

Plattsburg and its summer soldiers could be fairly said to have been of critical historic importance by providing the mechanism for procurement of an officer corps with a sense of being precisely that. Without officers, beyond the trickle from West Point, the recruits of 1917–18 would have been merely riflemen replacements rather than an organically effective, unitary force. As John P. Finnegan, in his prize-winning historical work, appraised it:

Plattsburg was not just a military training camp, it was, in a way, a secular retreat for a whole generation. There, amid simple, material surroundings, the upper-class elite underwent a conversion experience of patriotism, individual responsibility and collective action . . . the most striking action of Plattsburg was the moral change it produced.

Clark later said that the most valuable lesson learned was that of American military incompetence. Finnegan concluded that the most important fact about the camps was that they were the entering wedge for a system of universal military training. "Some of the most influential men of the country were learning first hand the complexities of soldiering, the efficiency of West Pointers, and the failure of American military policy."

Plattsburg was also part of the national gravitation which moved the Wilson administration to abandon conspicuous neutrality in favor of visible preparedness, a development which spawned an outpouring of enormous Preparedness Parades. In New York City on May 13, 1916, 500,000 people streamed down Fifth Avenue. Up front were a top-hatted Woodrow Wilson, military brass (including Leonard Wood, on foot but with riding crop), and Cabinet luminaries. Grenville Clark, the man who had done the most to bring the day to pass, was not up front. Chances are that he was in a rear rank or on the sidewalk. Or perhaps he was back at 31 Nassau Street, working on more organizational detail.

5
Wall Street Lawyer: One

It was not much of a war for Clark, who spent it on Wyoming Avenue in Washington (Admiral Perry lived across the street), while on duty at the General Staff. He had volunteered immediately after the congressional declaration in April 1917, along with his partner, Elihu Root, Jr. He wished to go overseas. Training needs at home, however, took priority, and while Root joined the American Expeditionary Force, Clark was immediately commissioned a major and assigned to administration of officer instruction camps. Before the armistice was signed, Clark was promoted to lieutenant colonel. Subsequently, the Army made amends for its niggardly commission and promotion policy (surely a general's star and flag were warranted) by bestowing on Clark its highest noncombat award, the Distinguished Service Medal, for work in the administration of the newly hatched and rapidly expanding officer training camps, truly the seedbed of the new American Army.

Mustered out hard on the heels of the armistice, Clark made a brief detour to Cambridge and then appeared at 31 Nassau Street along with the other returning veterans, ready to start what Martin Mayer called the *annus mirabilis* of Root, Clark. The firm's docket reflected the turbulence of an America vainly attempting to regain the pastoral simplicity of prewar times. Senator Root had been retained to demand instant return of the railroads from wartime government control to regular peacetime ownership. Something of a parallel might be seen in his retainer to contest the constitutionality of the nationwide prohibition of alcoholic drink, as imposed by the Volstead Act and the Eighteenth Amendment to the Constitution. A datum on the turbulence of change might also be glimpsed in *The Masses* proceeding; this featured the ultra-radical magazine's effort to undo the New York postmaster's action to bar it from the mails. Actually, *The Masses'* involvement was atypical; it had come into the office in the first place thanks to Emory Buckner's widely assorted circle of friends, which included some far-out Greenwich Village types. (Possibly Clark's longtime friendship with Zechariah Chafee, Jr., a proper Bostonian liberal, might have been a factor as well.) A development of a totally different stripe came with the passings of Andrew Carnegie and Marshall Field, and the instant transformation of clientele from strong-minded testators, faintly contemptuous of all lawyers, to timidly insecure and unsophisticated administrators, eager for guidance through the intricacies of estate and inheritance law.

Meanwhile, the combination of establishment entrée and quality work produced a remarkable expansion in the firm's work load and size. There were six lawyers in attendance at the beginning of 1919 and twenty-four by year's end. By 1922 a staff of thirty-nine lawyers made Root, Clark one of the largest firms in town.

Change also showed itself in the "shingle" or formal firm name. The initial 1909 legend of Root, Clark & Bird lasted until arrivals and a departure made it Root, Clark, Buckner & Howland in 1913. This remained the firm name until March 1925, when Buckner was appointed United States Attorney for the Southern District of New York, an event requiring his withdrawal and excision of his name from that of the firm. At the same time, the name of Arthur A. Ballantine, a law school classmate of Buckner and Howland, was added, to make the firm name Root, Clark, Howland & Ballantine.

It is significant that Ballantine's name was not included in that of the firm until 1925, even though he had been a partner since 1919 and by that time had attained professional pre-eminence as a lawyer in Boston and as Solicitor of Internal Revenue in Washington. (There were a number of further changes in the Root, Clark name in later years, as will be apparent in subsequent chapters, but they were made only in circumstances compatible with the principle of firm name stability.)

Along with that stability went versatility. "We have between us," Clark reported in 1928, on the silver anniversary of his graduation from Harvard, "taken a shot at almost every branch of the law." And the partners were virtuosi. Clark's forte was railroads and bankruptcy; he had served the latter specialty as chairman of the special bankruptcy committee of the Association of the Bar of the City of New York. Bankruptcy also occasioned his first (and only) appearance in the *Harvard Law Review,* where he predicted the content of the Bankruptcy Reform Act of 1978. His ancestral interest in railroads made him *the* Wall Street expert in railroad reorganization.

Not all reorganization involved railroads—a typical instance of the firm's work came in the Paramount Pictures insolvency proceeding, from 1932 to 1935, in which Root, Clark's work was so extensive that the court allowed the firm total fees of $450,000 (a very large sum in those days) after reducing by a quarter million dollars the amount the firm originally requested.

In addition to railroad reorganization work, Clark especially enjoyed taking on apparently hopeless commercial cases and getting 15 percent for a client where everyone else saw nothing. Buckner was the trial advocate par excellence; Root handled estates and appeals. Ballantine was the head of the important tax department and, together with Howland, did most of the corporate work.

The firm was atypical in one respect other than size and

versatility: it included a number of Jewish lawyers, to whom the doors of some prestigious law firms remained resolutely closed. Most of the excluders denied anti-Semitism, but insisted their employment posture was dictated by client attitudes. "Our roster demonstrates what we think about *that* proposition," wrote Emory Buckner.

But *that* proposition was an ugly and dismaying fact of life, and it prompted a protest from young Professor Felix Frankfurter, now at the Harvard Law School, who himself had followed a bitter trail of job-hunting in Lower Manhattan: "I wonder whether this school shouldn't tell Jewish students that they go through at their own risk of [n]ever having the opportunity of entering the best law offices."

Following Louis Brandeis's counsel—that the way to deal with irresistible forces is to resist them—Root, Clark met the challenge head on. The occasion was the rise of Leo Gottlieb, Yale (Sheffield) 1915, U.S. Army 1917–18, and Harvard Law School 1920, where he had been honor man of his class. Gottlieb combined a steel-trap mind with compelling personal charm, and he had been apprenticed initially to Buckner, where his scholar's bent was alien to the cut and slash of the courtroom ("I hated litigation, but I liked Buckner"). His ultimate elevation to the policy-making councils of the firm raised sharp issues of contact and visibility, for this was not a matter of some faceless clerk looking up cases in the library, but a senior participant dealing with major clients face to face and making the major and unpopular decisions implicit in legal controversy. Nonetheless, in November 1925, Leo Gottlieb was made a full partner in Root, Clark, an event that was a milestone in communal relations in America and the history of the American bar. Judge Henry Friendly, Harvard Law School honor man, went on from Root, Clark to a career that culminated as Chief Judge on America's second-highest court: "Why did I start at Root, Clark? It was the only place in New York that a Jew could get a job." ("Not true," Leo Gottlieb said later, "but almost true.")

The Root, Clark firm was blessed with a special rapport within the senior personnel and the lower decks as well. Physical size, patrician birth, and inherited fortune had endowed Clark with a sense of detachment and security that left him in a particularly good position to take his own counsel: "You don't have many options in life, but one option we do have is that we can decide who it is we wish to give us ulcers." The counsel was especially suitable for the bright and ambitious cubs at Root, Clark. Remarkably, in one rare instance, Clark himself suffered not an ulcer but a nervous breakdown. A major cause was his own work load; other reasons surely included a delayed response to the deaths of two of his children, as well as the growing commitment of the entire enterprise (Clark would write sympathetically years later of Ballantine's "hard summer with the whole office on his shoulders"). The unremitting insistence on excellence of the firm's work product and the painstaking care with which personal and professional efforts were invested all took their toll in a culmination of exhaustion and depression which necessitated a year's sabbatical at Kerhonkson, New York, in 1926. Nonetheless, it was characteristic that Clark could turn adversity to account. His Kerhonkson physician, Dr. Andrew M. Ford, became a valued personal friend, and Hartford lawyer and fellow patient Edward M. Day was also admitted to that status.

Nowhere was Clark's outgoing humanity better exemplified than in his treatment of the office juniors. Harold Bennett Kline, Root, Clark apprentice and future top executive of Texas Gulf Sulphur, vividly recalled Clark's solicitude when he had begun to show signs of strain from the unremitting demands on energy and intelligence. Possibly remembering his own faltering, Clark was kindness itself in unconsciously revealing his own sense of religion: "Harold, have you tried the church?" Concern for the young lawyers lay at the heart of Root, Clark's élan, which differentiated the firm from most Wall Street law factories. The sense of community was especially sensitized via an office publication founded as *The Bulletin* and irreverently abbreviated to *The Bull* in short order.

The Bull had several functions. One was social—a gossipy potpourri of comings, goings, engagements, weddings, and other vital statistics, which gave a familial dimension to professional association. *The Bull* also carried professional news—the major cases engrossing the office—which made the younger men feel that these were their cases, too. A major staple was notes on the nuts and bolts of practice, touching things never taught at Harvard, such as recent high court decisions elucidating obscure statutes. Characteristic and typical was a note from Clark that insisted on the necessity of exacting line-by-line analysis of any document prior to submission to a client and stressed the irreparable psychological damage occasioned by client-witnessed manuscript correction on belated discovery of error. Institutional cohesion was fortified by two other customs. One was the annual bonus, by which a percentage of the firm's earnings was prorated to all hands promptly after the closing of the books for the year. A second was the January office party, usually held at a posh Manhattan club, which came close to combining a Roman bacchanal with a medieval court of fools, as the wassail flowed freely against a montage of spoof speeches and irreverent blank verse.

As the twenties approached their close, the office parties seemed to take on a note of *après nous le déluge,* with *The Bull* faithfully reporting the symptoms of the malaise of American capitalism. For, contrary to popular supposition, the system did not fall unexpectedly with a resounding crash in 1929. Rather, to the alert and keen-eared, the sounds of cracking ice had been apparent for years, and perhaps nowhere as clearly as in the moribund railroad industry.

Clark was the office expert on railroads, both by experience and by genetics, as the grandson of a railroad builder and operator. Moreover, his personal fortune included a cluster of railroad securities, and such was his expertise that he was frequently retained by security holders to deal with the problems and legal controversies which burgeoned during the twenties, as jerry-built capital structures and crazy-quilt operational networks were formed, reflecting the anguish caused by the diminished revenues of the almost invisible agricultural depression. "It must be hard for young lawyers today to comprehend an era," wrote Judge Henry Friendly of *temps perdu,* "when the ICC was spoken of as 'The Commission' and an argument before that body was treated as seriously as one before the Supreme Court. I doubt that anyone, Brandeis included, ever made a better argument before 'The Commission' than Grenville Clark did in these cases. What was impressive, beyond his command of the facts, was his moral force; Commissioners might disagree with him, and did, but they could not fail to be impressed by his complete sincerity."

Clark had to argue hard, for each week *The Bull* revealed another failing sign in the American railroad system, all the way from the Chicago, Milwaukee & St. Paul in the heartland to the New York, New Haven & Hartford, whose tracks might be seen from the windows at 31 Nassau Street.

It was, as Charles Dickens said, both the best of times and the worst of times. By 1932, as the Depression deepened, broadened, and sunk iron into the American soil, Root, Clark flourished. A third and fourth floor had been taken over at 31 Nassau Street, lawyer recruitment had been expanded to the Midwest, and seventy-four lawyers constituted the corpus of the firm.

Curiously, Clark had a sense of physical detachment from the law office expansion, for he had moved from a city which was never truly home to him, notwithstanding his pride in being the ninth generation of his family born on the island of Manhattan. Indeed, in many ways he was almost the quintessential, unflappable Manhattanite—when a sudden slamming town-house door had left him locked out, in a nightshirt, in midtown, it was but the work of an instant to hail a cab and go to the Knickerbocker Club, borrowing cab fare from the startled doorman on arrival.

Grenville and Fanny had quitted their Seventy-second Street

town house in the early twenties for a permanent situs in the fresh
air and open spaces of Albertson, Long Island. Mrs. Clark adjusted immediately to a milieu of gardens and flowers, but to the
husband befell the commuter's lot, complete with personally
flagging down the Long Island train as a prelude to the long and
boring ride to town. Clark made every good-faith effort to adjust
and put down roots. His "naturalization" efforts were typified by
his resignation from the Association of the Bar of the City of
New York and joining that of Nassau County, which later
became a forum for his landmark speeches. It was probably this
sense of place which led to Clark's representation of wealthy
Long Island landowners in opposing the building of the parkways
through their property. As Judge Friendly later noted, "The
result was not successful and the cause not a particularly worthy
one."

The parkways dispute caused the paths of Franklin Roosevelt
and Clark to cross once again. Clark probably voted for FDR
for governor of New York in 1928. In any event, his Harvard
association with the newly elected governor and his Long Island
residence were significant in causing Clark to be retained to
protect the residential grounds and stately homes of Otto Kahn,
Henry Stimson, and the like. Clark was perhaps ahead of his time
in opposing what later generations saw as environmental destruction. In connection with this, nothing could have excited his
contempt more than the suggestion that he should decline his
clients' cause just because they were rich and successful.

The parkways builder was Robert Moses, a career bureaucrat
who resembled Clark in his force of personality and strength of
will but, in contrast with him, was a man of homeric anger and
consuming hatreds. Greek met Greek as Clark and Moses faced
each other at FDR's desk in Albany, and the confrontation was
transferred south when the polio-crippled governor took therapy
at Warm Springs, Georgia. Roosevelt must have felt like a rat
caught between two mastiffs as the champions squared off.

Moses eventually got his parkways, but with modifications,

and after knowing he had been in a fight. Clark knew he had been in a fight, too, and so did his family. During an enormous thunderstorm, which aptly symbolized the battle, Clark's eldest daughter inquired, after a crash of lightning and a peal of thunder: "Did Bob Moses do that?"

6
Wall Street Lawyer: Two

The Complete Lawyer

Personality is one key to success in the law, and Clark was providentially endowed. His athlete's frame and inherited status gave him a unique sense of courtliness and courage. His mind was massive rather than quick, powerful rather than clever. It was of the "onion ring" variety, capable of fitting all his talent and will into a single focus to the exclusion of a variety of simultaneously competing items. For all its intellectual massiveness and power, Clark's mind was still capable of responding with intuitive sensitivity.

A mosaic of items is required to illustrate these facets of Grenville Clark as the complete man of law. The centerpiece of the mosaic was what Justice Holmes called the will in focus. It appeared even in recreational pursuits: in the duck blind, where, in the words of John Dickey, he and Clark practiced conservation through conversation, and Clark would say, "We missed that one, didn't we? We didn't focus. You should focus on things"; on the golf course, where, his daughter recalled, "one thing that was intolerable to him was if you putt and it was short. If it was short, he uttered one syllable and it went to the bottom of your soul . . . 'short.' " The focus accounted for an instinct of dispatch, utterly at variance with the all too characteristic dilly and dally of the lawyer's craft. "Lots of good men say, 'When [my] desk is cleared I will turn to that larger job.' Clark's procedure has always been the opposite," a friend, Henry James, wrote to *Fortune* magazine.

One case illustrative of Clark's powerful will involved Mr. and Mrs. Joseph B. Hoadley, whose flamboyant, credit-based life-style included a blend of calculation and insolence right out of Jane Austen. The husband, so labor law veteran and Root, Clark alumnus Henry Mayer recollected, was a transit securities speculator who had made and lost a number of fortunes. Probably none of his reverses, however, had quite the effect as the adverse legal judgment which brought him into the toils of Root, Clark.

The law of the matter was simple enough. After a judgment is entered, pursuant to a trial on the merits, the court will issue a writ to a sheriff or bailiff, directing seizure and sale of the loser's property in sufficient quantity to compensate the victor. In the event that sufficient property cannot be located, the law further provides that the defendant be summoned back to court and interrogated under oath as to the nature and location of his assets.

The Hoadleys, however, ignored the summons, and Mr. Mayer, armed with a warrant for their arrest and accompanied by a deputy sheriff to effect it, cornered his quarry in the early hours of the morning at the Sherry-Netherlands Hotel, where the Hoadleys maintained a suite in addition to their two town houses (one of which had an escape tunnel to a yacht on the East River). The scene could have been straight out of *Fledermaus*—Mrs. Hoadley was wearing a white opera cloak and Mr. Hoadley was ordering rounds of drinks for all hands. Attempting a psychological bluff, Hoadley summoned the head of the United States Secret Service, William Flynn, a friend, and Bainbridge Colby, future Secretary of State, his lawyer. The flustered deputy, who technically had the pair under arrest, sent for his office's counsel. Henry Mayer sent for Grenville Clark.

Clark entered, seated himself, opened a newspaper, and announced that the Hoadleys had one hour to raise $10,000 or go to jail. Colby threatened to get a judge to void the summons; Clark genially told Colby to proceed and "be damned." The inebriated Hoadley ultimately acquiesced, sending his banker out at 3 A.M. to raise the cash. When he returned, money in hand, Clark took it over. After counsel for the sheriff insisted (correctly) that the cash was to be paid into court, Clark excused himself and stepped into the corridor with Mayer. Continuing the variance from the nonprofane suggested in his rejoinder to Colby (Clark's customary expletive under stress, so his daughter recollected, was "Oh dear, oh dear, oh *dear* me"), his orders to Henry Mayer were vulgar, laconic, and unmistakable: "Run like hell, Henry."

Mayer did just that, and slept with the money under his pillow that night.

Old Brushface

The meteoric rise of Root, Clark over the next few years can be exemplified by another thread pulled from the Grenville Clark tapestry. This was the matter of the Root, Clark client All America Cables, Inc., which differed from *l'affaire* Hoadley almost as night differs from day.

At issue was rivalry in the cable field between two monopolies —All America, which maintained the Buenos Aires connection via the west coast of South America, and the British Western Telegraph Co., Inc., which had their wire down the east coast. Thanks to a deft alliance of the British enterprise with Western Union, the eastern network had been extended from Buenos Aires to the environs of Miami, thereby outflanking All America's position. Miami was the critical pressure point, for American policy had forbidden United States land sites to cable companies whose foreign deployments effectively excluded American cables.

The Wilson administration had repulsed the British company from a Miami base, but a federal district court had ruled that the exclusion exceeded presidential authority. The issue had then been appealed to the Supreme Court, and an eleventh-hour effort had secured congressional action, vindicating presidential authority and thereby mooting the issue. However, the Court's judgment seemed aborted by a subsequent State Department action which permitted the Miami linkup upon informal assurances by the Argentine government of abandonment of the east coast monopoly. Informal assurances fell considerably short of ironclad guarantees, and Clark cornered Secretary of State Charles Evans Hughes aboard the SS *Pan America* as he was about to sail on a state visit to Brazil.

The case was Elihu Root, Jr.'s, but no matter, for such was the Root, Clark élan and camaraderie that the case was also Grenville Clark's, and he took over when Root was detained at Clinton, New York. Nor was Clark's taking over the case a matter of obligation. "What fun things were when the office was beginning," Root later wrote Clark, in what was almost a firm motto.

Clark forcefully stated his client's case. Hughes responded that the assurances would be effectuated and dismissed the forty-two-year-old lawyer: "Now you must leave this ship at once." Clark stood his ground: "I am sorry, then, but I am obliged to charge a breach of faith by the Department of State." The Olympian, bearded secretary responded with Jove-like wrath: "How dare you?" Clark, unshaken, repeated his charge. It was Hughes who retreated: "Now, Clark, we have both raised our voices and become emotional. Let's take a fresh start. Sit down here quietly and we will cool off and talk it over, and I want you to take your time about it." Although it held the ship's departure for an hour, the confrontation provided re-examination of the issue and an eventual Root, Clark victory.

Clark came out of the controversy with a "lasting admiration" for the man he called in private "Old Brushface." Almost four decades later, Clark's comment on a miscarriage of justice within the United States Supreme Court was compressed in an irreverent one-liner: "Old man Hughes would never let them get away with this." With characteristic felicity, Clark summed it all up after Hughes's death, when he wrote the former Secretary of State's son:

> I did not know your father very well, I suppose, but I knew him for quite a while soon after I went to Carter, Ledyard & Milburn's in 1906 until last I saw him which was when I went to see him in Washington in 1941. And in that 35 years I had four or five experiences with him, all of which left a tremendous impression on me. He showed me several times a personal kindness, which I have never forgotten, besides impressing me with his wonderful all-around character. In truth he has long been one of my heroes in the older generation along with Charles W. Eliot, Mr. [Senator Elihu] Root, and General Pershing—not bad company, even for your father.

If the Hoadley incident had combined Jane Austen with Damon Runyon, and the international cable controversy had invoked the shadow of E. Phillips Oppenheim, the Pope affair constituted one item in Clark's legal career which could have been written by none other than F. Scott Fitzgerald.

John W. Pope was a poor but extremely bright boy out of Starkville, Mississippi, who came to Manhattan to make his fortune after educational stints at Washington and Lee, the University of Alabama, and the Harvard Business School. He made it. Starting at near bottom as a Dillon, Read statistician, he worked his way up in that company, and on the financial ladder generally, to his own associate membership in the New York Stock Exchange and full membership on the Curb. As sensitive to market movements as some people are to the weather, he formed and merged his own investment companies. Working the short end of a falling market, he coined money. Then disaster struck: in the spring of 1930 he was called before the Exchange's Governing Committee and charged with circulating rumors calculated to undermine the price of a listed security. Specifically,

Pope had sold Fox Film Company stock short, and then sent the following telegram to friends:

> At the risk of being considered a pessimist I wish to warn customers against long commitments in another dangerous issue. The Fox Film Company in reporting earnings for the first six months of seven dollars available for its common shares has apparently grossly overstated income for these earnings were derived at the expense of a reduction in contingency reserve amounting to almost six million dollars. Thus Fox actually earned only a few cents on its outstanding common stock.
> If I had any Fox I would dispose of it.

The Chase National Bank, heavily invested in the stock, complained directly to the White House. The harassed President Hoover virtually demanded that the Exchange expel Pope summarily. Pope sought the assistance of Grenville Clark, who dug in, indicating that he would file suit, complaining of unwarranted federal interference in the affairs of the New York Stock Exchange. (Indeed, in his memoirs, President Hoover asserted that the health of the Exchange was primarily the concern of New York Governor Franklin D. Roosevelt.) Clark had little sympathy for the financial chicanery of Roaring Twenties Wall Street, but the sheer arbitrariness of the presidential demand had offended his sense of fair play; he demanded and secured a delay and a full-scale hearing, at which Pope was completely vindicated, only to die the following year at the age of thirty-two.

The Fiduciary Trust Company

Willard Hurst, dean of American legal historians, once raised the question as to how Clark's intellectual stature and moral sensitivity permitted him to practice law with apparent equanimity in the noisome Wall Street of the twenties. The short answer is: they did not.

That the Street was noisome there can be no doubt, and Justice Douglas was unquestionably right in proclaiming its cleansing as his most distinguished achievement as SEC chairman. One of the most squalid aspects was the almost incestuous union obtaining between sellers and buyers of investment securities. The nexus was in the interlocking whereby the great investment houses placed their own men strategically in the management structures of institutional investors such as banks and trust companies. The linkage effectively destroyed the critical scrutiny which should attend the placement of other people's money; after the Great Crash, a high priority of the New Deal became the divorce of commercial from investment banking, a procrustean separation embodied in the Banking Act of 1933, alias the Glass-Steagall Act.

Here Clark anticipated his Harvard schoolmate Franklin Roosevelt by a number of years. In 1930, he was instrumental in founding the Fiduciary Trust Company. The name spoke for itself, for the institution was one organization where the depositary and lending business was strictly subordinated to trust activities. Clark's unwritten prohibition—later the keystone of both federal and state statutes—was that no officer, director, or employee of a securities house could simultaneously hold a like position with the trust company. A similar constraint inhibited counterpart service with the trust company by personnel of "portfolio companies" in whose securities trust company funds had been invested.

The fiduciary effort deserves stress if only to underscore that Clark's view of the fiduciary function was not that of a cowering stakeholder. On the contrary, Clark entrusted his own personal fortune to the Fiduciary Trust Company, thereby exemplifying the canon that a trustee should at least give his beneficiaries' money the same care that he gives his own.

And what was that standard of care? A Fiduciary officer, Edward P. Stuhr, has left a picture of the conferences at which Clark examined his own stewardship and, necessarily, that of his company:

The first order of business was a wide-ranging discussion of the economic background and outlook and other factors which might affect stock prices . . .

Stocks were listed by industry groups and each industry was reviewed from the standpoint as to whether the total fund invested in it was too high or too low in relation to its prospects. Each individual company was then examined and accorded a buy, sell, or hold rating.

The officer also remembered Clark's characteristic courage in adversity, itself a testimonial to a system of price and choice: "Buy when the blood is running in the gutter."

The National Economy League

I've got to start with a rigid economy program.

—Franklin D. Roosevelt to Grenville Clark, January 1933

The parkways controversy was one of the relatively few contacts between Clark and FDR as the latter progressed on the path to the presidency, along the line he had foretold to his fellow law clerks at Carter, Ledyard. It is safe to assume that Clark assisted in the attainment of the goal by voting for FDR for President in 1932, as the victor won not only the national election but also the straw poll at Root, Clark, duly reported in *The Bull*.

Both before and after the election, a temporary association between the two men emerged in their joint concern for the integrity of the national fiscal process in the Great Depression. Perversely enough, Clark's effort for national economizing was fueled by law office prosperity, and the growth of his shrewdly invested personal fortune afforded an opportunity for public service, untrammeled by the meshes of occupational commitment. His joining the widespread concern over the state of the national budget came as almost second nature. The budget, skewed on the income side by falling revenue and on outgo by demands for federal assistance, was in disarray.

Clark responded with the organization of a National Economy League in mid-1932. Its formation was announced in *The*

New York Times, and its structure was a public relations tour-de-force. Hero-explorer Admiral Richard Byrd was the honorary national chairman; Archibald Roosevelt, Teddy's son and Clark's up-front surrogate, was secretary. Ex-President Coolidge chaired the advisory committee, while President Hoover and Presidential candidate Franklin Roosevelt sent messages of support. Built largely on the same infrastructure as the Plattsburg organization and itself composed of veterans, the group naturally enough singled out what it saw as the abuse of nonservice-connected veterans' pensions.

Typical of the League's efforts was its petition to the harassed Herbert Hoover, compressed into an eye-catching headline: CUT IN VETERANS' AID OF $450,000,000 ASKED TO ABOLISH "RACKETS." Hand in hand with the effort to arouse Congress were other tactics. One was a *Reader's Digest* article, instigated by the League, which presented the tales of abuses ("less than one per cent of the people of the United States receive 25 per cent of the entire federal revenue"). In another, Al Smith took to the radio waves with an adenoidal denunciation of ex-soldiers whose sole World War I experience had consisted of having teeth straightened and flat feet fixed sharing the pension rolls with the heroes of the Argonne.

It was a miserable struggle. The pensioners were unemployable middle-aged men whose government pittances were their sole resource against utter destitution. Clark manifestly took no pleasure in the task, but addressed it nonetheless with characteristic drive and dedication. Indeed, after World War II had brought home to him the difference between soldier and civilian, he announced that "I would never again oppose anything in reason that the veterans want."

The League, however, caught the attention of FDR, who was in mid-campaign, denouncing Herbert Hoover as a profligate spendthrift. Raymond Moley, inner-circle adviser of FDR, invited Clark to cast the candidate's ideas on economy in the form of a statute radically constraining federal outgo. Clark summed up the effort in a letter to his onetime law office associate, shortly after Roosevelt fulfilled his own prophecy by becoming President-elect: "If you expect to govern you have got to take hold of federal finances."

Clark had an appointment with FDR to go over his statutory draft on the day of a New York Harvard Club dinner honoring the President-elect, a club member. The logistical pressure of FDR's appointment calendar transferred the meeting from the Roosevelt Manhattan town house to the dinner itself, where Clark was seated five or six seats away from the guest of honor. After Thomas Lamont, Morgan partner and past club president, had given FDR, in Clark's characteristic colloquial remembrance, "a terrible ear ache," the President-elect pointedly inquired why he was not seated next to Grenville Clark and demanded that Clark be moved alongside him: "[Lamont] has been telling me how to run the country. I think I know as much about it as he does. Please sit down. We've already wasted half an hour." Clark sat down, and the pair conversed for an hour, Roosevelt concluding, "I agree with you a hundred percent and you don't have to argue it to me. I've got to start with a rigid economy program."

Clark worked with a group of conservative Democrats, including Clifford Woodrum and Lewis Douglas, to get the Economy Act of 1933, as it was called, written into law within days of FDR's inauguration; the act slashed overhead and curtailed outgo, and it had some curious and dysfunctional results. One came in the judicial area, for Clark's statute did not concern only veterans; judicial retirement allowances were also affected, particularly those for Supreme Court service, where Justices "resigned" rather than "retired" and were hence without constitutional guarantee against reduced salaries. The aged Oliver Wendell Holmes saw his pension cut in half overnight, a development which inspired the aging, crotchety, and conservative incumbents to cling tenaciously to their posts.

FDR tried hard—government salaries were pared by 15 percent, pensions were cut almost in half, and nonservice-connected gratuities were abolished. However, the impact of the Economy Act on the deflation-riddled economy could only be compared to the debridement scrubbing which contemporary medical wisdom prescribed for massive burns: infection was forestalled, but shock usually killed the patient. Analogously on the economic side, diminution of government spending, the one dynamic force in the flagging economy, only tightened the Depression vise, thereby tilting the New Deal leftward to deficit spending and the prescription of John Maynard Keynes. Overzealous administration also provided a political backlash. In the rush to economize, some truly battle-disabled veterans were inadvertently dropped from the pension rolls. Duly publicized, these cases provided a rallying point for the restorational effort mounted by the veterans' organizations.

The counterattack was launched in early 1934 with the Independent Offices Appropriation Bill, which included the allocation for the Veterans Administration, so that about half of the cuts of the previous year were restored. The measure passed both houses, and FDR found the bill on his desk the day that Clark dropped into the Oval Office. Roosevelt prepared a weak veto message—"one of the worst things I ever did," he told Clark after a *viva voce* reading. Nonetheless, the President was confident that his solid Democratic support, with just a few Republican votes, could sustain his veto, and he prepared to depart on a long-anticipated vacation. Clark was apprehensive over the consequence of presidential absence in the hard cloakroom politicking that lay ahead: "Please stick around until after the vote." FDR demurred: "I can't. I'm exhausted, and the doctor says I have got to leave for a real rest."

Clark's apprehension was justified, for the Democrats defected in droves while only two Republicans stood by the President. Clark tersely summed up the consequences: "His veto was overridden. It was his first big defeat."

It was Clark's defeat, too, but he learned to live with it. Probably it was too much to ask that he formally surrender his inherited commitment to stable values and sound money; certainly it persisted into December 1934, when he wrote an article for *The Atlantic Monthly* which acutely put a finger on the Achilles' heel of the welfare state by questioning whether "federal expenses could be met without an excessive rise in prices— 'inflation'—on one hand or taxation beyond bearable limits on the other."

By the end of 1937, Clark had adjusted to a new order in which a balanced budget would be the exception rather than the rule, as the National Economy League vanished into the mists of history and the cuts of 1933 were restored with a vengeance. The payment of the veterans' bonus in 1938 over FDR's veto completed the rout of the economizers. However, some lessons, useful for the future, were learned. Clark had organized affiliated state organizations in forty-odd states, and the experience in grass-roots mobilization was to stand him in good stead. Moreover, he had learned to live with the new order of things. He tersely summed up his hard-bitten realism in 1937: "The general level of federal expenditures cannot be much reduced. FDR is right on this. Morgenthau's talk about reducing expenditures 700 million in the next fiscal year is all nonsense . . ."

8
Harvard Fellow

"I have retained a lively interest in Harvard affairs," Clark reported to the 1928 *Harvard Alumni Directory* on the twenty-fifth anniversary of his graduation. ". . . I have served on several visiting committees, and have already run, unsuccessfully, three times for Overseer. Now I am up again for a fourth time—one more than W. J. Bryan. Someone must think I would make an adequate Overseer, but 'so fur' not the voters."

Clark's steel-vise tenacity, perhaps with an establishmentarian assist—"And let us resolve," interpolated the *Directory*'s editor, "that insofar as it lies in our power, he shall be elected an Overseer of Harvard next June"—paid off, as he did win that year.

The Overseer effort proved but a threshold to accession to the real locus of power: in 1931, Clark was selected to be a Fellow of the Harvard Corporation. This was an honor of no small proportion, particularly in New England. "When I was a boy and for many years afterward," recollected Theophilus Parsons of nineteenth-century Massachusetts, " 'the Corporation,' in common conversation, always meant the [Harvard] Corporation." Clark was not insensible to the same instinct. "At Harvard," he asserted in a television interview, "there is an absolutely unique American institution, a body of men, legally entitled the President and Fellows of Harvard College—seven men. They are the President, the Treasurer, and five Fellows. They operate under a statute of 1650 of the General Court of Massachusetts that has never been changed by a comma, an archaic old statute. They serve for life or during good behavior. Nobody can impeach them. I have often said that the Supreme Court of the United States can be impeached, but not the Harvard Corporation."

Unlike the cumbersome electoral procedure of the Overseers, accession to the power-centered, self-perpetuating Corporation was simplicity itself. An artless telephone inquiry from Thomas Nelson Perkins, incumbent Fellow and Beacon Hill aristocrat, as to Clark's interests and available time, preceded the summary vote by which the Fellows added Clark to their number. It was an exciting time to come aboard. President Abbott Lawrence Lowell was reaching the end of his term, and the responsibility for the succession and, with it, the institutional future of America's oldest university, would soon devolve upon the small power-centered group. More than that, the malaise of the Great Depression was slowly enveloping the national scene, producing, along with its tincture of despair, a sense of rebellion and impatience with what had hitherto been deemed eternal verities.

Interestingly, the format of change was already apparent in Clark himself, and accession to the Harvard Corporation was providing another catalyst by which he would move beyond his ancestral Calvinism. Indeed, by the spring of 1932 he had moved from heading up a committee to ensure that railroad rates were sufficient to provide institutional investors their bargained rate of return on railroad securities to excitedly corresponding with Professor Felix Frankfurter on the legalized and orderly repudiation of corporate financial structures:

You seem to be doing precisely what I had in mind—taking picked men and stimulating them. . . . If out of a graduating class there can be turned out ten men who instinctively seek for a solution cutting through all the underbrush and traditions, that would be a greet contribution to our civilization, and perhaps even more so if out of the ten, two men of very extraordinary resource and imagination are produced. . . . One other thought which you are doubtless applying is that these men should be encouraged . . . to take subjects having to do with current problems. Heaven knows there are enough current problems requiring original thought. I cited one possibility the other night which might be shaped into a subject like this: What ought to be done in this period, when scaling of corporate obligations is imminent on a great scale, to facilitate corporate reorganizations and bring in new management with the least delay and red tape? . . . Or the thing you spoke of about the Reconstruction Finance Corporation and the I.C.C. A few months ago, when this problem became imminent, an original mind might have made a great contribution by writing on some subject such as this: "Assuming that some Federal agency should be created to prevent bank failures and railroad receiverships, what should be the exact terms of the statute?" Or again, "Should Governmental machinery be created for the study of the railroad problems, and, if so, what?"

Already the loom of the fates was busily at work, and Clark's questions, which thought the unthinkable and spoke the unspeakable in terms of anticipating deposit insurance and railroad reorganization, were destined to surface in a concrete quandary, an interface of Harvard responsibilities, Frankfurter's infuriating busybodyism, and the burgeoning of the first New Deal. All in all, Clark would undergo a searching test of heart and mind, straining both institutional and personal loyalty and calling especially upon all his qualities of common sense, perception, and analysis.

The particular catalyst to this quandary was the first election of Franklin D. Roosevelt to the presidency on November 10, 1932, which imposed an unforeseen crisis on many Harvard relationships. One stress was laid on Dean Roscoe Pound at the Law School, where the usual scholastic tensions became sharpened by Depression-born faculty "moonlighting." By mid-November the intramural malaise had penetrated the presidential offices of Abbott Lawrence Lowell and prompted an inquiry to the dean of the Law School on the importance of observing academic schedules. After talking to the law faculty, Pound conceded that lectures were being postponed, that the hit-or-miss procedure persisted, and that the elitist-reformist American Law Institute was a *de facto* competitor:

It is not easy to find a remedy. The American Law Institute pays very large sums to a number of our teachers, and the pressure to prefer the work of the Institute, while it may be unconscious, is very strong. Other members of our teaching force, seeing their colleagues making large sums of money through the Institute, solicit outside legal employment, or continue connections with firms in which they were formerly employed, and soon find themselves tied up in business in such a way as to interfere with their teaching schedules. Moreover, one member of the Faculty is absolutely incorrigible about such matters and no rules which could possibly be made would affect his conduct in the least.

The "incorrigible" one was obviously Felix Frankfurter, who thereby became the object of an extraordinary arrangement in which Dean Pound passed the responsibility of discipline to President Lowell. The resulting academic formula provided that faculty absences would be undertaken only after written application to the university president.

Dean Pound did not know when he was well off, for with the Roosevelt inaugural, the situation worsened. The prime cause was the keystone of FDR's Hundred Days' legislation, the Securities Act of 1933. Nominally authored by Representative Sam Rayburn of Texas with Senator Joseph Robinson, the measure was intended to forestall future stock market crashes. Its importance can hardly be overstated; even though based on a flawed model, the proposed act "stood at the center of the President's program to place the vagaries of speculation in Wall Street and the power of corporate finance under some measure of public regulation."

The act became something of a *de facto* subsidy from the Harvard law students to the New Deal. It was more symbol than substance, embodying the neo-Populist suspicion that the stock market collapse had "caused" the Great Depression, and was based on the British Companies Act, which required disclosure before the sale of securities. The Harvard law faculty was called on to serve as the medium to bring the Companies Act to America. Resulting faculty absences strained Frankfurter's relationship with Dean Pound to the breaking point, and called upon Grenville Clark to show his best qualities in judgment and sensitivity.

Usually, the members of the Harvard Corporation have little to do with the faculty. But the case of Felix Frankfurter was something else again. Lowell actually wrote the members of the Board of Fellows and laid the Frankfurter controversy in their laps. Clark warily conceded both the importance of the matter of his friend's absences and the cavalier behavior of the accused professors. He then passed to the defense:

> With regard to Frankfurter, I recognize his defects but I do think that he has demonstrated two very important things: first, a real devotion to teaching in general and to the Law School in particular; and second, a capacity to interest and stimulate his students. . . .
>
> I have an idea in Frankfurter's case that the Administration has been asking him a good deal in recent months for advice and that it has been put up to him pretty hard to help out. I do not mean to say that this sort of thing could go on indefinitely or to an extent that over a long period would seriously interfere with his duties at the school, but I do think that if this be correct (as I surmise and have some evidence of), it should be taken into account in view of the difficult times and the fact that the President undoubtedly values his judgment and help on some subjects.
>
> I wonder if a talk by you with these men in which you yourself could go into all the facts and circumstances would not clear the question up.

No species of warfare quite compares with the infighting of academe, where the stiletto is the basic weapon, ambush the doctrinal tactic, and the half-truth the *lingua franca*. Lowell opened his attack, perhaps to oust the Byrne Professor, perhaps only to vindicate his own presidential authority, at the meeting of the Harvard Corporation on May 10, 1933. As fate would have it, Clark was a few minutes late for the meeting. The tardiness was uncharacteristic, for the Harvard Corporation came as close to a sacred trust as any responsibility Clark ever assumed, surpassing even the other trusteeships he had already undertaken for the New York Orthopedic Hospital and Pomfret and Green Vale Schools.

L'affaire Frankfurter was already under discussion when Clark arrived, Lowell obviously having made it the first order of business. Perhaps the seemingly precipitate action was calculated, for Lowell was beyond question aware that Clark, who was one of the accused's judges, was also the accused's good friend. Undoubtedly, Clark amplified the sentiments of his letter, defending Frankfurter with special vigor. While Clark had successfully beat off Lowell's attack within the Board, the Harvard president still had one weapon left—Frankfurter himself. And perhaps Clark realized that his own good-faith suggestion to Lowell, that the latter "have a talk with these men," could lose the war. For the "talk" might provide just the occasion for a skillful inquisitor to bait the prickly, defensive, intellectually arrogant Frankfurter into an unfortunate statement or action.

Accordingly, Clark moved to save Frankfurter from himself: immediately after the meeting, he phoned him to suggest that the pair of them have lunch alone at Gomates in Harvard Square. Characteristically, Frankfurter wrote a literal scenario of the event. Clark began by disclosing the accusation, to which Frankfurter replied:

FF: Would you like to know what the facts are, Grenny?
GC: No, I don't care to know the facts (with a wave of impatience), no, I don't want to know the facts. I am telling you all this—

I suppose it's a little irregular, but it's all right between us—because I was a little afraid if this were jumped on you suddenly by Lowell, you might get so damned mad that you might tell him to go to hell. And it would be the most natural thing in the world for you to do. I know I would—I'd be mad as hell and resent it, and probably tell him to go to hell. You have more patience and calmer temper than I have. But even you might do it, and I didn't want you to do that and I thought I would prepare you. If Lowell were on the job another year, it might be worthwhile having a real fight, but the old man is going to be on the job only two more months, so what's the use.

FF: Of course, I am not staying here because of Lowell or Pound, and I would not leave on their account, of course; it's an indignity.

The moral reinforcement and psychological counseling did not come a moment too soon, for the very next day Frankfurter received a portentously decorous call to the presidential carpet, much in the nature of a summons or subpoena.

Frankfurter also left a self-serving scenario of the Lowell interview, in which he put on a superb defense of his undeniable derelictions. Insisting that he had missed classes only to comply with "the President's wishes—the President of the United States" (the latter phrase doubtlessly suitably intoned), he added that he had wired his dean in suitable time to arrange a substitute or order a return to Cambridge. However, the damning telegram—still preserved in the Harvard archives—had not been delivered until after classes had started. Nonetheless, his explanation carried the day and Frankfurter was not disciplined. That the professor was aware of the stimulus for his uncharacteristically submissive and deferential response to Lowell's velvet hectoring was disclosed in an equally untypical thank-you note to Clark: "It was very sweet of you—but characteristic—to talk to me as you did the other day." Clark, in turn, acknowledged the report of the "highly interesting conversation with Mr. Lowell," and added disarmingly, "The incident came out just about as I expected; and probably it would have been just the same as if we had not had our little talk."

The magnitude and morbidity of the Frankfurter ego was disclosed concurrently in his kibitzing and commentary on the selection of Lowell's successor to the Harvard presidency. It was an exciting contest between an urbane dean of humanities, Kenneth Ballard Murdock, clearly the winter-book favorite, and a dark horse, James Bryant Conant, outspoken and maverick professor of chemistry. Frankfurter plied his stiletto with subtlety and skill ("From all I have seen of Conant . . . he seems to me to have an essentially unperceptive mind, however distinguished in its speciality") and thrust his condemnation hard ("We need a man and a mind of distinction. A distinguished chemist is not enough"). With evident relish, Frankfurter also relayed astronomer Harlow Shapley's appraisal of Conant as, of all the candidates, "the only one who really will not do."

Perhaps the thrust overcarried, reminding Clark of another chemist, Dr. Charles Eliot, who had headed Harvard with great distinction for many years. ("For years I followed President Charles Eliot's reports and addresses, and am conscious that his personality, his individualism, and his religious attitude have been strong influences in my life"). But the idea of the chemist as president was lent special point by a contemporary jape: "Ah! But you see Eliot wasn't a particularly good chemist and this boy is."

There was a touch of irony here, for of all the possibilities for the Harvard presidency, Clark most closely resembled the Eliot mold. He would have made a superb head of the university, but forwent his own claims (indeed, by agreement, all members of the Corporation took themselves out of consideration for the office) in favor of his personal candidate for the Harvard presidency—his law partner "Sec" Root—but finally cast the deciding vote to make Conant head of Harvard ("I meant to make it clear in my last letter that Conant will have my support"). Graciousness was not the new Harvard president's long suit, but he did write Clark with courtliness and polish: "Whatever people may say about the wisdom of this action [of the Fellows], they cannot question its courage, and perhaps mine."

There was indeed a question of courage here. Conant was but the second scientist to head Harvard in 294 years. He was not the overwhelming favorite for the job, and some aspects of Clark's correspondence with "Brother" George Agassiz, a university establishmentarian, might suggest to suspicious minds that corporate selection was merely the legalistic validation of a backstairs Porcellian choice. Nonetheless, the Conant selection had a critically important dimension in restoring Harvard's scientific leadership, which had waned under Lowell. In fact, over a decade later, Conant's contribution to American development of the atom bomb would be remarked on by Clark: "Congratulations on the bomb." Appended was a sobering afterthought, all too often forgotten: "How fortunate [that] we and the British were the first to work it up."

Conant's early days as president passed routinely, but the 1934 commencement was replete with controversy. The occasion was what Clark saw as the most boring part of his Harvard duties: conferring honorary degrees. Under Harvard's bicameral procedure, the process began with the Fellows and then passed to the superintending Board of Overseers for final approval.

The proposed 1934 honorees included the venerable Supreme Court Justice Louis Brandeis, the Harvard Law School's most distinguished son. Here Harvard's LL.D. was already painfully overdue. Two decades earlier, his accession to the Court had been the subject of major controversy, which included a remonstrance of his unfitness signed by Harvard president Abbott Lawrence Lowell. Given the capacity of the New England mind for unforgiving resentment, two decades had not been enough to cool the controversy engendered by Brandeis's early crusades against the financial establishment. On April 25, 1934, in a standoff vote of eleven to eleven, the Overseers declined to approve the degree for Brandeis. Clark, ever sensitive to the ugly nuances of contemporary American life, was dumbfounded: "I don't know what to think. There is evidently a revival of the old prejudices and possibly the recent wave of antisemitism has something to do with it."

Clark had every reason to savor accomplishment, however, at the 1936 Harvard Tercentenary, where Conant restated with eloquence Eliot's 1869 encomium to the free university ("a university . . . must be rich, but above all, it must be free"). Clark's contribution to the event was the editorship of an anthology, *The Future of the Common Law,* whose title might forecast his concern "to seek law's constant improvement for the ordering of a better world . . ." Another memorable item of the day was a photograph of Clark and President Franklin Roosevelt: two remarkably unlike men captured in a pictorial representation whose lights and shadows suggested a classic daguerreotype, reuniting, after a third of a century, on the spot where they had been students together, men who had burst the bonds of culture and class to walk very different paths in leaving their mark on their times.

9
Court Packing

*A small army that believes in principles can beat
a bunch of mercenaries.*

—Burton K. Wheeler, *Yankee from the West*

The President's Proposal

The collapse of the economy drive and the leftward drift of the
New Deal probably caused a subconscious estrangement between
Clark and FDR. Nonetheless, Clark voted for the President's
re-election in November 1936. Deep doubt was suggested by a
private memo to files—"Notes on the Election" ("I have decided
to vote for Mr. Roosevelt, but the Republican ticket otherwise")
—and also by a congratulatory wire to the winner ("Best congratulations. I voted for you because I have complete confidence
in your sense of balance and your resolve to be President of all
the people . . .").

So Clark must have been startled when he opened his *New
York Times* on the morning of February 6, 1937:

ROOSEVELT ASKS POWER TO REFORM COURTS,
INCREASING SUPREME BENCH TO 15 JUSTICES.
CONGRESS STARTLED BUT EXPECTED TO APPROVE.
SEES NEED OF "NEW BLOOD."

As a lawyer, Clark naturally had closely watched the growing
tension between the Supreme Court and the President. His insight

brought the realization that the presidential plea to add one new Justice to the Supreme Court for every incumbent over seventy-five years of age (subject to a maximum of six appointments) was not due to the Justices' alleged age and enfeeblement but rather to Court decisions that the President had disliked. It came to be known as FDR's "Court-packing" plan.

Clark's Response

What to do? Clark was wealthy, successful, but essentially powerless. He did, however, have special respect for the unique American nexus between law and politics, which was being threatened by the President's manifest effort to violate the constitutional principle of separation of powers. Clark's response, following the example of Plattsburg and the economy drive, was to create a National Committee for Independent Courts. Typically, Clark took a rear-rank job, and gave top honorary billing to the respected C. C. Burlingham of the New York Bar. A recruiting letter sent to leading lawyers of each state made a virtue of Clark's re-election vote for FDR:

> If you voted for the President at the last election and if you are opposed to this [Court] proposal, we should like very much to have you as a member of this committee.

With the dispatch of the letter, Clark went into virtual exile in Washington at the Carlton Hotel, to act behind the scenes as field marshal of the seemingly sparse forces of opposition to the President's plan. ("I have been unable to get in touch with you for nearly two months," complained a cousin.)

It could be fairly said that there was *no* opposition, for already Senator Arthur Vandenberg of Michigan had decided that overt Republican hostility could only catalyze Democratic unity, and he had imposed a virtual gag on his GOP minority in the Senate. Hence, it fell to Clark, with the aid of a few young lawyers, to organize a mini-legislative reference service during the fortnight the Court-packing bill was before the Senate Judiciary Committee. Each evening, the transcript of supportive administration testimony was combed for errors, misstatements, and non sequiturs, and a devastating sequence of rebuttal and cross-examination was prepared for opposition senators to use on the morrow. Clark did not testify, but sent the nominal head of his committee, C. C. Burlingham, who persuasively stated the opposition thesis: ". . . this bill is designed to do a thing which, in my opinion, should be done by constitutional amendment . . ."

Another critical contribution was made via personal contact at a dinner Clark gave for a number of anti-packing senators. Senator Burton K. Wheeler, a liberal Democrat from Montana, showed up "in a blue funk," one of Clark's young assistants recalled. The senator's depression was understandable, for opposing FDR at the height of his power was no small matter. Nonetheless, such was the contagiousness of Clark's optimism and vitality that Wheeler stiffened his spine, assumed Senate floor leadership of the opposing senators, and, ironically, received the laurels of history for preserving the balance of American government.

By March 24, 1937, the Senate committee had finished its appointed two-week hearing, and what had been planned as a triumphal overture to an easy presidential victory had turned into something of a bloody ambuscade. Senator Ashhurst of Arizona, chairman of the committee, got a telephone call from the man identified as "Eff Dee," accusing him (correctly) of sabotaging the bill's progress by procrastination and delay. The petulant telephone call signaled the sad plight of the administration; its message was seconded when FDR attempted to have his measure reported without recommendation. The committee, however, reported it unfavorably, and the battle was transferred from the committee room to the larger arena of the Senate floor.

At this point, Clark assembled a new executive group of the National Committee for Independent Courts at Washington's

Mayflower Hotel. Douglas Arant, a young Alabaman, was named chairman, and William Marbury, of Baltimore, secretary. Clark took the no. 3 job of treasurer. The group adopted a threefold plan of battle:

(1) opposing the President's proposal as embodied in the pending bill or any substitute which will impair the independence of the Supreme Court; (2) endeavoring, to the best of our ability, to impress on all citizens, the vital importance of maintaining the independence of the judiciary under our system of government, and (3) studying suggestions with respect to constitutional amendments.

These points were set out in a circular report letter issued *ex post* to prospective recruits and members on grimly professional stationery, with the letterhead:

National Committee for Independent Courts
1223 Shoreham Building
Fifteenth and H Streets NW
Washington, D.C.

A bracketed phrase beneath the title showed the masterstroke of Clark's strategy: "A Committee of Citizens, All of Whom Favored the President's Election in 1936, and All of Whom Are Opposed to the President's Supreme Court Proposal."

Clark probably forged his most effective tactic by insisting on restraint and rationality in place of the apoplectic rhetoric of the anti-FDR forces generally. Such denunciations had proven worthless in the preceding election, particularly in the web of small towns throughout the South that formed the power base of the Southern oligarchs who ruled the Senate, now the critical battle ground for the Court-packing bill.

Clark had not consciously plotted a Southern strategy, but his letter-writing campaign had covered the area well. He had divided the country's lawyers by Federal judicial circuits, and it happened that the Fifth—truly the heartland of the Democratic

Solid South—received special care. Alabama was organized town by town—Montgomery, Brewton, Eufaula, Mobile, Wetumpka —from Gadsden to the Gulf and from Mississippi to the Georgia line. Florida was also well covered. Georgia was encased in a network that included Quitman, Brunswick, Swainsboro, Valdosta, Augusta, Rome, Cairo, and Moultrie as well as Savannah and Atlanta. In Louisiana, a viceroy rather than small-town coalitions did the job. Explaining the absence of rural coalitions, a regional activist wrote Clark: "The situation in this state has been admirably handled by Mr. Monte M. Lemann of New Orleans, and as a consequence of his work, we have no record of invitations [to join the committee] in this office." Mississippi was similarly captured by volunteers in Oxford, Woodville, Natchez, Vicksburg, Jackson, Collins, Gulfport, Hattiesburg, and Meridian. Across Texas, from Fort Worth to El Paso, a special effort was made to get men who could call Senators Connally and Sheppard by their first names. The end result was the enlisting of the bar's elite from forty-one states.

The far-flung apparatus of resistance slowly triumphed, as senators previously counted in the administration fold deserted it with differing degrees of visibility. Typical was the defection of John Bankhead, Democrat stalwart, undertaken at a monster meeting of the Alabama Bar Association. As July began, the presidential battle line wavered, with a proposal for "compromise" whereby the six new faces on the Supreme Court would be added at the rate of one per year.

As historian William Leuchtenberg later wrote, the second proposal presented the greater damage of institutionalizing judicial subordination to the presidency. Clark only increased his opposition. "The Supreme Court proposal is *not dead*. A careful study shows the fate of such a compromise is hanging in the balance," Clark wrote Wheeler. "The substitute is in no sense a compromise." While declining to use the word, he proposed a Senate filibuster to kill the bill: "The public will support you in extending debate until the opposition has had the opportunity to develop."

The battle plan for the filibuster was drawn soon thereafter. Clark sent a cadre of his young activist lawyers to a Sunday-morning session at the Mayflower Hotel, where they received an unforgettable lesson in dillydally and stall from a past master, Senator Josiah Bailey of North Carolina. Paragraph after paragraph of the "compromise" was rewritten, each with minuscule changes, each draft programmed for extensive consideration by the Senate and a vote thereon after full-dress and time-consuming debate. Young Mr. Douglas Arant of Alabama never forgot the lesson in Fabian tactics he received from Bailey on that lazy Sunday morning at the Mayflower Hotel:

> . . . taking a copy of [Roosevelt's] court bill, he [Bailey] asked one of the young men to prepare for dictation. Turning to the section limiting the enlargement of the Court to fifteen, he began:
>
> Strike out the word "fifteen" and insert in lieu thereof "fourteen." Take another. Strike out the word "fifteen" and insert in lieu thereof "thirteen." Take another. Strike out the word "fifteen" and insert in lieu thereof "twelve."
>
> And so it went. The possibilities of the word "fifteen" were soon exhausted, but there were plenty of other things about the bill from its enacting clause to its last sentence which Senator Bailey desired to see amended. Under the popping eyes of his visitors, he rattled off one hundred twenty-five in less than two hours.

The immediate result was a bundle of one hundred twenty-five filled-in amendment blanks, but this magnificent armory was to become superfluous. Although twenty senators had been mustered into the filibuster team—a number roughly equal to those committed to the President to the very end—the issue was finally decided, not by either extreme, but by the vast majority in the center, normally neutral but especially sensitive to Clark's grass-roots pressure. As the humid Washington summer dragged on, the Senate made a long filibuster unnecessary by voting (on July 1, 1937) to recommit the bill to committee, ostensibly to give the President a second chance, but in fact burying the measure beyond recall. The measure of Clark's victory emerged in the recommittal vote: only twelve of the supposed twenty stood with the President, his perceived majority vanishing like chaff in the wind.

How doomed the measure was became apparent on Bastille Day 1937, when Senator Joseph Robinson dropped dead of a heart attack brought on by the Washington heat and his unavailing efforts to break Clark's "extended debate." Thereafter, there was no possibility of resurrection of the Court-packing proposal and Clark, on vacation in northern European waters, savored his triumph by reading a cable from one of his young lions in Washington:

COURT BILL DEAD FOR THIS SESSION. FINISH TRIP.

The bill was dead not only for the session; the prospect of future attempts to pack the Court had been scotched permanently, as the first frustrated assault had only served to fortify the principles of the Constitution. The historic epigraph to Clark's accomplishment in defending the balance awaited the dedication page of Louis Lusky's *By What Authority* (1937): "To Grenville Clark, Private Citizen, Defender of the Court and the Constitution."

The Frankfurter Agony

Professor Felix Frankfurter did not have to read about the President's Court plan in *The New York Times*. In a characteristically feline way, the President had forewarned him. A month before the plan was unveiled, FDR had written: "very confidentially, I may give you an awful shock in the next two weeks." Interestingly, the President sought not approval but only a chance to be heard: "Even if you do not agree, suspend final judgment and I will tell you the story."

Frankfurter's quick, brilliant mind and formidable memory told him what was coming. Only two years before, the day after the Supreme Court had unanimously invalidated three major New Deal measures, FDR had sent for Frankfurter, excoriated the Court's action, and threatened to end the judicial veto over-hanging the New Deal by crippling the Court itself. The President had mentioned two methods, neither of which would re-quire a constitutional amendment but could be accomplished by congressional action. One was enlarging the membership of the Court to give the administration the validating majority it needed; the other was limiting the Court's jurisdiction, so as to withhold cases from it where its judgment might be adverse.

The passage of time obviously tipped the President's choice toward enlarging membership. But reflection after receipt of the President's letter must have awakened another Frankfurter mem-ory—of an incident four years earlier, when FDR had half promised Frankfurter a seat on the Supreme Court (of which Frankfurter had been both student and critic during his years at the Harvard Law School).

Doubtless Frankfurter saw immediately the dilemma with which he was faced—on one side, aborting his chance at the half-promised Supreme Court appointment and, worse, deserting a beloved friend; and, on the other, collaborating in the deep subversion of the constitutional principle of separation of powers. The tension provided an apt context for the exchange of letters between President and professor. In an uncharacteristic "Dear Frank" letter, Frankfurter first noted that the Court proposal came as something of a volcanic eruption. His closing lines took almost an hour to compose, and they were the most heartfelt Frankfurter ever wrote: "It was clear that some major operation was necessary [and] I have . . . deep faith in your instinct to make the wise choice."

FDR never forced Frankfurter to declare himself, but Grenville Clark (who had introduced Roosevelt to Frankfurter when all three were young lawyers in Manhattan) tried to do so, even though at the time he was immersed in tactical direction of the Senate fight. Clark was confident that if he could just force Frankfurter to break his silence, the resulting statement would support the anti-packing position. He fired off a letter to Harvard:

March 4, 1937

Dear Felix,
   It really bothers me that you do not publicly express your views about the Supreme Court, whatever they are. Whatever one's opinions are, it cannot be denied that the question that has been raised is of fundamental importance. Accordingly, on such question it is no more than normal and natural that people should expect those who are competent to speak on the subject to express their ideas. This is, of course, preeminently applicable to yourself because you have written and talked about the Court for many years with the obvious and necessary result that thousands of people assume that you must have views on the subject that would be interesting and valuable....
   If I am wrong, show me. But the more I think of it, the more it seems clear to me that no complications or subtleties ought to be allowed to cloud what normal common sense seems to lead to. Incidentally, you would, I think, by making a statement, strengthen your influence in the future and this wholly irrespective of what your expressed views were. The thing that is really not understandable to the average man is why, at a time like this when everyone is seeking light, you of all others should remain silent.

Yours as always,
G. Clark

The reply came on March 6:

Dear Grenny:
   Candor about delicate themes is one of the essential attributes of friendship, and yet how rarely it is exercised. And so I value very

deeply the plain speech of your letter of the fourth as one more manifestation of a friendship that is very precious to me.

Frankfurter, in an extended but not entirely convincing exposition, insisted that as a teacher he did not comment on public issues, and then came to the heart of his position:

And why have I not spoken out? Fundamentally, because through circumstances, in the making of which I have had no share, I have become a myth, a symbol and promoter not of reason but of passion. I am the symbol of the Jew, the "red," the "alien." In that murky and passionate atmosphere anything that I say becomes enveloped. I would be heard and interpreted by what you call the average man —the reader of the Hearst papers, the Chicago *Tribune,* the Legion, the D.A.R.'s, the Chambers of Commerce, I am sorry to say the "leading" members of the bar all over the place, the readers of *Time,* the *Saturday Evening Post,* etc., etc., etc.—not as the man who by virtue of his long years of service in the government and his special attention to problems of constitutional law and the work of the Court spoke with the authority of scholarship, but as the Jew, the "red," and the "alien." Instead of bringing light and calm and reason, what I would be compelled to say about the work of the Court— and it is the only subject in this debate on which I can speak with a scholar's authority—would only fan the flames of ignorance, of misrepresentation, and of passion.

Frankfurter protested, perhaps too much, against being catapulted into the political arena, and pointed out that for years he had undeviatingly kept out of politics. Explicitly asserting the opposite of Grenville Clark's assertion of a duty to speak out, the Harvard professor noted that he had been importuned by anti-FDR forces *not* to speak out, at least now. He then disclosed his wound at being thought deficient in moral courage, but persisted in his determination to stay silent.

Frankfurter's enormous ego was almost shattered by the opposing pressures of his two friends, Clark and Roosevelt. To be sure, he had played the innocent bystander par excellence, but his silence surely was not simply the consequence of a four-year-old hint of a seat on the Supreme Court. Rather, as he himself had written Roosevelt, he had a deep faith in the President's ability to make a hard choice from a mélange of unacceptable alternatives. Running with the hare and hunting with the hounds imposed its costs. Never once did Frankfurter break his self-imposed silence and say a word on the subject, but privately, by nuance, hint, and innuendo, he implicitly assured the President of his backing, especially in forceful condemnation of opponents. No one knows what he wrote of Grenville Clark, but his pukka sahib excoriation of New York's governor, Herbert Lehman (who came out against the plan), surely was not atypical: "I was—and am—hot all over regarding Herbert Lehman's letter. Some things just aren't done—they violate the decencies."

Only one group came close to smoking Frankfurter out. Caspar Weinberger, future Defense Secretary, then a brash young editor of the Harvard *Crimson,* called him on the telephone and flatly put the question as to how he stood on the Court plan. Frankfurter liked students docile, submissive, and respectful, and he virtually exploded in response to the impertinent question. The *Crimson* duly printed the story of the professor's apoplectic expostulations: PRESIDENT'S SUPREME COURT MESSAGE LEAVES FACULTY MEMBERS SPEECHLESS. Reportedly, Frankfurter sought to have the brash student reporter disciplined. However, he surely did not seek to use his friend on the Board of Fellows in the effort.

The Roosevelt Response

Midway during the hundred and ten days of FDR's plan to pack the Supreme Court, his effort was frustrated by a fiscal complication: the receipts from the (then) March 15 income tax exaction had failed by far to measure up to budgeted estimates.

Apparently, someone in the administration must have had a brilliant inspiration to which FDR was especially receptive.

What if one stroke might resolve two difficulties? More specifically, what if scapegoats were found for the fiscal shortfall, and the very act of discovery also unmasked the evil geniuses stalemating the Court plan?

Only one difficulty seemed to impede the *deus ex machina* solution. From its very Civil War beginnings, the income tax law had sternly forbidden revealing, in any manner not provided by law, the affairs that a taxpayer had disclosed in confidence to his own government. The statute penalized such revelation by a $1,000 fine and up to one year's imprisonment, and, additionally, the Constitution implicitly made it grounds for impeachment.

The specific issue brought to the presidential attention concerned, not disclosure of outright wrongdoing, but the exhibition of sophistication to minimize taxes or to avoid them altogether. While the line between tax avoidance, which was simple prudence, and tax evasion, which was simple fraud, was about as fundamental as one could get in the law, the President did not see matters that way. He said so in a meeting with Secretary Ickes held on his return from an ill-timed Caribbean fishing trip, which he had taken at a critical stage in the Court fight. Ickes noted in his diary that the President asserted a personal acquaintance with most of the alleged miscreants. Presumably, the aside involved a baleful view of Grenville Clark. For thanks to the tale-bearing, espionage and surveillance which made FDR's White House the equal of any Enlightenment court, the President knew who really ran the Committee for Independent Courts, and a long acquaintance made no difference on the tax evasion accusation.

The issue was fought out in an upper-echelon Treasury conference the day after FDR's meeting with Ickes; Secretary Morgenthau overrode the reservations of his senior aides about whether the alleged tax evaders should be publicly exposed. In particular, Under Secretary Roswell Magill was disturbed not only at the patent illegality of disclosure but over the fact that there was nothing to disclose—the supposed evaders had "not invented any new devices for avoidance but were only employing old methods more widely." Morgenthau, however, quickly put the issue in focus with the double observations that "everyone in tax trouble is against Mr. Roosevelt" and that "these men who are fighting the President on the court plan are the real issue." The Secretary followed up with a ringing peroration:

> The question is whether we are going to have a fascist government of the people, whether rich men are to defy the government and refuse to bear their burdens. The rich are getting richer in this country and the poor poorer. Let us give the President what he wants without quibbling as to whether this or that is legal.

On May 17, 1937, Morgenthau was at the White House for an even higher-level meeting. The participants reviewed staff qualms over the legality of disclosure, and then discussed the possibility of adding twenty-five names to the list. FDR left no doubt that the foundering Court-packing fight was the true focus of the effort:

> The time has come when we have to fight back, and the only way to fight back is to begin to name names of those very wealthy individuals who have found ways of avoiding taxes both at home and abroad.

The President was adamant: "I want to name names. I'm going on the air and tell this story. Bring up the tax bill in May rather than November." During the meeting, the President read Magill's report in a singsong, monotone voice. Halfway through, he sharply asked the aging Attorney General, Homer Cummings (who, as the government's chief law enforcement officer, was present but not immediately involved) why there had been no prosecutions, and then, after reading the details of one case presented in Magill's bland prose, glanced at Cummings and inquired, "Why don't you call him a son-of-a-bitch?"

There was to be no Fireside Chat on the matter, although a

press conference did produce some darkening hints and nothing more. But by late May, FDR was still persisting in his view of a *cause célèbre*. A May 27 note to C. C. Burlingham suggested with feline syntax the deviousness of the presidential ploy. In writing the patriarch of the American Bar, FDR was probably sending a message to Clark, and the latter was as clearly the target of the gambit as if his name had been entered in uppercase and underlined in the presidential missive, whose bantering tone suggested FDR's disbelief in the addressee's substantive leadership of the opposition:

> Under your hat—within a few weeks quite a storm is going to break over the heads of individuals who have been cheating their own government. Watch and see how many lawyers condemn them and how many lawyers condone them.

By May 29, Secretary Morgenthau's report had been signed and was ready to go to Capitol Hill. It listed essentially six tax avoidance devices, ranging from foreign personal holding companies to family partnerships, which in the light of later complexities were almost two-dimensionally simplistic. FDR's covering message to Congress professed shock at the tax avoiders' "boldness and . . . ingenuity," quoted Justice Holmes on taxes being the price of civilization, and added the barb that too many individuals wished this civilization "at a discount." The President conceded, as he had to, that some of the instances had "the letter of legality." Nonetheless, he insisted, all were definitely contrary to "the spirit of the law," and represented a determined effort "to dodge the payment of taxes which Congress based on an ability to pay" and shifted the tax load to the "shoulders of others less able to pay . . . mulcting the Treasury of the Government's just due."

Legislative reception suggested that the message was less than a bombshell; in fact, it barely interrupted the humdrum of legislative routine. Presidential clout, however, was sufficient to secure the establishment of an impressively staffed Joint Committee on Tax Evasion and Avoidance, which turned to the job at hand. The joint committee was studded with the names of leading legislators. The first hearing, held toward the close of June, provoked little interest and scarcely offset the lumbering attack on the whole tax gambit undertaken by Congressmen Hamilton Fish before the Orange County, New York, Republican Committee, which had suggested that the committee investigate FDR's own farm losses and depreciation taken on Hyde Park and his Georgia plantation; the charitable contributions of Mrs. Roosevelt and her radio and newspaper honoraria; the tax status of Roosevelt; and even (a final barb) the affairs of the President's aged mother. (The last was actually exacerbated by a disclaimer: "Personally I am unwilling to believe that there is substantial foundation for the persistent rumors that Mrs. James Roosevelt receives any rental from the Federal Government or claims depreciation on the Hyde Park estate . . .")

Despite Fish's thunder, FDR had moved to the attack as June opened:

ROOSEVELT ASKS CONGRESS TO CURB BIG TAX EVADERS,
EIGHT TRICKS CITED

The second joint committee hearing was held July 1, 1937, as the Court fight was reaching its crescendo.

Morgenthau Report on How It Is Done Sent with Message

AMAZING, SAYS PRESIDENT. SENATE VOTES FOR INQUIRY

House Is Not So Swift—Names of Tax Dodgers
Likely to Be Brought Out at Hearing

Made in early July, the Joint Committee disclosures produced wrath—but not of the kind FDR anticipated. The *Times* put the story on page 22, under a headline that reflected not scandalous tax evasion but rather bipartisan congressional ire over laggard Internal Revenue reporting of tax law deficiencies ("INQUIRY

BACKFIRES ON REVENUE CHIEFS"). Nonetheless, Clark's capitalized name led the roll call of seven accused tax evaders:

> GRENVILLE CLARK, member of the New York law firm Root, Clark, Buckner and Ballantine. Credited by the Treasury official with sixteen trusts, arranged jointly with his wife for members of the family, the proceeds of some of which could be used to pay the insurance premiums and through all of which Mr. Clark was credited with a tax savings of $90,000 in one year.

Anticipating the worst, Clark almost lost his nerve, and dictated an explanatory, detail-filled, eight-page letter to Douglas Arant, the formal chairman of the Executive Committee of his National Committee for Independent Courts:

> This is a very confidential letter about something that came up yesterday and that I think I ought to inform you about fully as bearing on the National Committee for Independent Courts and my connection therewith.
> . . . I think it will be very likely that I will be required to appear before the proposed joint committee of Congress that will soon be constituted to investigate all these matters, and the thought insistently occurs to me that the mere fact of my being involved in the matter, might lessen my usefulness to the Committee.

There could be no question that being "required to appear before a committee" was, as Clark realized in a flash of insight, the stiletto point of FDR's thrust. Senator Hugo Black had already demonstrated the enormous propaganda potential of the hearing room, where the hapless witness, much as a bear in a pit or a bull in a Spanish *corrida,* was driven from pillar to post by simple inquiries which required long and complex answers. All questions, of course, were framed by an inquisitor who drew them with an eye to the most damaging nuances and inferences. Needless to say, the entire spectacle received complete press coverage, both photographic and reportorial. Clark had actually represented clients who had appeared before Senator Hugo Black's committee, so he knew whereof he spoke.

Obviously moving to a concluding paragraph of resignation —or of leaving the decision in Mr. Arant's hands—Clark broke off his dictation abruptly and never finished the letter. What he did dispatch was a brief communication which reflected his determination to tough the matter out and his obvious relief at having done so:

> I enclose a memo about the tax matter I mentioned to you on the phone. I also enclose the President's message and have marked the sentence in Morgenthau's letter that apparently (I think quite certainly) was intended to apply to me.

He was right.

The hearings opened with the Internal Revenue staff at work on the scenario. Tensions had developed over the issue within the Bureau of Internal Revenue and the top two lawyers there quit. Chief Counsel Morrison Shaforth, member of a prominent Colorado Democratic family, issued a stiff press statement:

> Assistant Chief Counsel Russell J. Ryan and myself were unable to convince ourselves that it was proper to use the Bureau of Internal Revenue as planned in the tax avoidance and evasion investigation. Being given the choice of participating in the presentation of names or of resigning we tendered our resignations as of the 29th of June.

The defection bent but did not break the administration ranks. "Lights burned late in a feverish and unprepared Treasury Department," recalled New Dealer Randolph Paul, "which assembled an outside group including Thurman Arnold, Abe Fortas and me to work on an inside committee." Both Democrats and Republicans became nervous, in a Washington summer session that came to naught because of the stalemate on Court packing.

Both parties rebuked the Treasury for having failed to direct congressional attention to the so-called loopholes when the Internal Revenue Code had been up for comprehensive revision in 1932 and in 1936. Moreover, most of the "devices" disclosed had been reportedly displayed in Under Secretary Magill's 1937 edition of *Montgomery's Federal Taxes on Estates, Trusts and Gifts.*

However, the President received a face-saving palliative in the form of the so-called Revenue Act of 1937, which tightened the fiscal screws on personal holding companies and applied some cosmetic provisions to family trusts. But, like the Court plan itself, FDR's Machiavellian ploy was too clever by half and badly miscarried. A headline from *The New York Times* of July 2, 1937, told the epitaph: SENATE CHIEFS SHELVE COURT BILL; SUBSTITUTE READY.

Other internecine difficulties unforeseen by FDR cropped up as a result of his foiled scheme. For one thing, the First Lady of the Republic became the subject of a tax problem. An innocent ambiguity had resulted from the shibboleth of liberalism, the progressive income tax, which could be used to make the ubiquitous activities of Mrs. Roosevelt look like a net tax liability of herself and her husband, notwithstanding the wife's gift of her newspaper and radio earnings to charity. The applicable tax law permitted such charitable contributions to be deducted from gross income, *but* only up to 15 percent after including the contributions which the taxpayer sought to deduct. Given the nature and sources of the income of the presidential family, a serious question existed whether the total of Mrs. Roosevelt's radio and newspaper income lay outside the allowable percentage, and in any event, the failure to declare it (before deducting) was probably a violation of law—even by 1937 standards.

If a joint return was involved, as was probably the case, the President was implicated, too, and therefore in a poor position to insist on scrupulous exactitude in others' tax dealings with the government. One can only visualize the flurry of apprehensive telephone calls between Capitol Hill and the White House as to how the vindictive gambit had backfired so badly, leaving the President facing a possible problem of explanation.

The administration committed another gaffe in auditing the income tax return of Senator Burton K. Wheeler, whose outraged inquiry to Secretary Morgenthau ("Are you checking up on the income tax of any other member of the Senate?") was capable of summoning the upper house into a mutual defense phalanx.

The *Times* of July 16 told the whole story. Several pages away from the report of President Roosevelt's sending a misleading letter to Senator Barkley, the new majority leader, asserting that the Court-packing effort would continue, was a seemingly unrelated Washington-datelined dispatch that said something else. The use of Quotation marks carried a comment: "EVADERS" OF TAXES NOT TO BE CALLED. It signaled that the game was up, under a lead sentence to the effect that the joint committee had decided that no individuals mentioned as tax avoiders would be called to testify. The spokesman, North Carolina's tobacco-farming Robert ("Muley Bob") Doughton, Chairman of the Joint Committee, was not a man given to subtlety or irony, but his words carried both. Of the accused evaders, he said none would be forced to testify. In an ironic understatement, Chairman Doughton added that none had volunteered.

IO
The Making of a Liberal

*. . . there is only one sound attitude for conservatives
consistent with a real understanding of the essence of American life,
namely, an attitude of firm and impartial defense of the rights
of the citizen under the Bill of Rights in every case where
those rights are threatened and irrespective of whether we approve
or disapprove of the sentiments and policies of the persons affected.*

—Grenville Clark, July 11, 1938

Two Speeches

Where political sequence stops it is a tricky business to pinpoint,
but it can be said truthfully that Franklin Roosevelt's Court-
packing plan had as one fortuitous consequence the growth of a
liberal viewpoint in Grenville Clark. It helped turn a rich, wellborn conservative into a paladin of civil liberties. It gave Clark
a sensitivity toward all constitutional guarantees, quite apart from
any personal disagreement he might have had with the persons
whose rights were being threatened.

Prior to his confrontation with the President, Clark had given
little thought to the specific subject of Bill of Rights guarantees,
aside from some collaboration with Conant of Harvard in opposing teachers' oaths. Two personal circumstances guaranteed that
the Court episode would have permanent and mutational effect.

Just as an abrasive brings a fine sheen to metal, Felix Frankfurter's waspish kibitzing and mordant dislikes had given luster
to Clark's responsive views. Even as Professor Frankfurter was
professing to "read with delight" some lectures on the Constitution Clark had committed himself to give at New York City's

New School for Social Research, he reproached the lecturer to the effect that the latter's "view of the Supreme Court as the great safeguard of those democratic institutions, which you and I so passionately care about, is much too romantic and too simplified." Clark's powerful mind always rose to the challenge of grappling with an idea, reducing it to complete psychological possession in order to follow it implacably to logical conclusions. Then his publicist's instinct ensured that the idea would be turned inside out before his conclusions were exhibited in a public forum.

Hence, tactical defense of the Supreme Court led necessarily in Clark's mind to a defense of the Constitution in general terms and constitutional guarantees in particular. An immediate consequence was Clark's glowing defense of the Court in the *Yale Review* and in the New School lectures. Frankfurter replied covertly, in the form of a letter to a mutual friend with a carbon copy to Clark, who was probably the real addressee:

The fact of the matter is that the Justices who resist the social obligations of property and apply Herbert Spencer's "Social Statics" instead of the Constitution are also the Justices who have no respect for civil liberties, *i.e.,* for the protection of ideas they regard as dangerous. To think of Butler & Co. as safe-guards against fascism is really funny. But in any event, while I have no respect for them as constitutional interpreters, I have respect for them as men because they respect their own convictions.

Yet Frankfurter could also be on the side of the liberal angels, for in the course of their correspondence he subsequently admonished Clark:

At the height of the "red" hysteria after the war, Senator Beveridge addressed the ABA and said that "he was for the *whole* Constitution —for the Bill of Rights on behalf of freedom of speech as well as for the rest."

Unquestionably, the *Yale Review* and New School polemics led to an even more highly visible declaration of Clark's ideological turnabout, which came in April 1938, when he was invited to address the annual convention of the American Newspaper Publishers Association. In a sense, to accept was to enter the lion's den, for the American press of the day was overwhelmingly anti-Roosevelt (indeed, the President himself said that the editorial offices were ruled from the countinghouse) and, in consequence, had taken an extremist conservative position, which included a lukewarm concern for the protection of civil liberties, the very shield of their own existence.

Clark did accept, and if the assembled newspaper publishers thought that their speaker's anti–Court-packing credentials guaranteed them a slam-bang exercise in conservatism, they were fated to be disappointed. Indeed, after all allowances were made, Clark came out on the same bottom line as, say, the socialist leader Norman Thomas. But his route to the bottom was entirely different:

> I agree with the view that we are facing a period in which governmental regulation will continue to grow. I believe that further experimentation with governmental controls will go on. But I, for one, refuse to adopt the defeatist attitude that even a considerable increase in regulation needs to be inconsistent with the maintenance of the basic rights that are our heritage. On the contrary I believe that if we could hold our sense of values and use our intelligence the reconciliation can be achieved. Nevertheless the danger is great and the problem urgent. We cannot do better than take counsel on its solution, since the press will play a great and perhaps determining role and upon the firmness and intelligence of our publishers the ultimate result will depend.

Having thus made his meliorist accommodation with the status quo, Clark went on to give his definition of civil liberty: "American liberty, as I conceive it, should be used to express the same concepts as the phrase 'the liberties of the subject' in England whence our basic rights historically derive. Now it is true, in England as with us, that one aspect or meaning of liberties of the citizen is the restriction within bounds of reasonable necessity of the kind and degree of interference with the personal life of the individual." Clark had reached a spiritual homecoming, so to speak, for this premise moved him ineluctably to the ethos which would dominate and overshadow the remainder of his life—faith in the rule of law. Clark insisted that there were other components in the liberty of the subject. He went on to enunciate that because in democratic self-government a majority of the people "really and not nominally" make the laws under which they live, they must agree to accept the "reign of law"—not just the few specific rights mentioned in the Constitution, but a larger penumbra—"the absence of arbitrary action by the government in every field and the general existence of a decent spirit of fair play which will compel the government to refuse the recurring opportunities to abuse through harassment or intimidation of the individual."

Clark posed the question of what the press might do "to ... support the great principle of fair play which I call the 'reign of law.' " He responded with two desiderata—to stand up for freedom of discussion and to resist abuse of official power, whatever the source or direction from whence this might come. Obviously intending the popular President as his target, he twisted the knife by quoting Roosevelt's praise of "the free exchange of views."

He also insisted that freedom of expression was not a monopoloid privilege of the press alone. Radio, he suggested with his lawyer's realism, must be even freer. Far ahead of his time, he then urged clarification of the existing regulatory statute and, beyond that—noting that 80,000,000 Americans per week attended the movies—insisted that censorship of newsreels could not be a matter of indifference to newspaper publishers. He especially urged perpetual vigilance against governmental intrusion in "every other medium of expression whatsoever." Then, getting down to particulars, he cited contemporary abuses of power, exemplifying from current events the pathology which he had previously described only in theory—"a flagrant instance was the cancellation virtually overnight of the air mail contracts in 1934." And, more recently, "the notorious and unconstitutional inspection of private telegrams" by the Black senatorial committee in 1936. He summed up by calling on his hearers to recognize warnings when they appeared, to find lessons in history, and to accept "a stimulating challenge, not only to the spirit but to the informed intelligence of your great profession."

And that was that. *The New York Times,* which had reprinted the address in full, also applauded it in an editorial entitled "Liberty and Tolerance," endorsing not only Clark's general content but specifically the phrase, and his definition of, "the reign of law." From the other flank, Professor Felix Frankfurter, in a characteristically fussy and pedantic note, fired out a defense of Hugo Black's investigatory activities, including an interpolated volume-and-page citation of the *Congressional Record.*

Just as ripples spread outward in a pond, the ANPA speech led to yet another speaking invitation, this one from the Nassau County Bar Association. Clark was glad enough to take it, for he and his wife already had moved their permanent residence to Albertson, Long Island, and as part of the change he had resigned from the Association of the Bar of the City of New York, affiliating in lieu thereof with the Bar Association of the county of which he was a resident—far from what he was to call the "modern Babylon" of New York City and where his wife might have her gardens and flowers.

The speech was delivered July 11, 1938, at the Nassau association's annual dinner, held in Garden City, Long Island. The *New York Times* headline writer admirably caught the message:

BAR URGED TO FIGHT FOR CIVIL LIBERTIES

Grenville Clark, Corporation Lawyer,
Says Conservatives Are Lagging in Duty

Groups Should Be Named to Battle Against Bigotry

Clark opened by emphatically asserting his conservative predilection, deploring the fact that the active defense of civil liberties had been "allowed to drift very largely" into the hands of the left-wingers. Reproachfully, he implied that American conservatives were more interested in defending the vested rights of property than "the great rights guaranteed by the First Amendment, including freedom of speech, of assembly, and of petition." He hammered home his major premise of reproach:

> I wish to make the point that American conservatives cannot for a moment afford to discriminate in their defense of civil liberty. They cannot have it both ways. They cannot expect to have their own rights safeguarded in the future when in particular communities or in the country as a whole they may conceivably be an unpopular minority if when they are in the ascendant they show the slightest degree of intolerance or lack of zeal in the defense of minority groups.

Warming to his theme, he reprimanded those of his own class and interest who had shown, especially in patriotic clubs, little disposition to a modicum of tolerance of elements they regarded as undesirable:

> But I suggest to you that a little intolerance is as dangerous to the body as a little potassium cyanide in the human body, that it is nothing to be played with and that the sole security for the civil liberties of *any* of us is dependent on the firm defense of the civil liberties of *all* of us.

Then followed a bill of particulars applying this indictment of reproach chapter and verse to the DAR-sponsored teachers' oath, enacted in twenty-two states, and to a current proposal for barring New York's public offices to members of the Communist

Party. He then firmly enunciated what was emerging as his personal credo:

> I venture to say, therefore, that there is only one sound attitude for conservatives consistent with a real understanding of the essence of American life, namely, an attitude of firm and impartial defense of the rights of the citizen under the Bill of Rights in every case where these rights are threatened and irrespective of whether we approve or disapprove of the sentiments and policies of the persons affected.

He could well have stopped there, but he went on to add a coda which would have a profound effect on his own life and career. The Bar Associations, he told the 250 diners, were in a unique position to take a leading part in the fight for civil liberties. He suggested that Bar Associations form committees to be exclusively concerned with watching for violations of civil liberties and taking a formal position. Zeal was not enough, he concluded. What was necessary was a full understanding of the subject, and "beyond that, there must be organized vigilance and preparation for considered and prompt answer."

In his speech to the newspaper publishers, Clark had borne down heavily on his key theme:

> . . . what I want to emphasize is that this great question cannot be handled piecemeal. In the long run we will not have some of our great media of expression free, as the press now is, and others subject to censorship. We will have freedom to meet in halls, but no freedom to meet in open squares . . .

The reference to "open squares" was neither abstruse nor theoretical, but almost literally on his doorstep, for only a few miles from where Clark spoke the precise condition to which he referred existed, under the aegis of a man about as unlike Grenville Clark as he could be. Francis (Frank) Hague, the mayor of Jersey

City, New Jersey, was not only plebeian and vulgar but was plagued with an instinct for malaprop utterance (he once announced with braggadocio that *he* was the law in Jersey City, with the calm air of stating a fact). This trait especially contrasted with Clark's instinctive flair for public relations. Ruling Jersey City much as a *condottiere* might run a fief, Hague had imposed his version of morality on the squalid town, outlawing prostitutes and Communists with equal fervor. Labor organizers were frequently assimilated under the Red ban by Hague's police and, as the "boss" told *The New York Times:* "We in Jersey City are God-loving, law-abiding, peace-desiring Americans, and there is no place in our community for Communists or the things they stand for." Nonetheless, both the organizing efforts and the responsive opposition continued and came into confrontation over the right of organizers and would-be CIO members to use the parks of Jersey City to assemble and discuss their problems.

Hague's anti-union stance was not ideological but opportunistic, born of the wish that incoming employers would keep Jersey City a mecca of employment opportunity in a sea of national unemployment (JERSEY CITY HAS EVERYTHING FOR INDUSTRY was his motto). Hague's particular tactic was rigid enforcement of ordinances regulating the distribution of circulars and requiring an official permit to be issued for public meetings.

Clark knew New Jersey well. On one occasion, in pre-World War I Trenton, a number of horse-drawn drays had blocked the path of the trolley he was riding to the federal courthouse there. A fracas ensued in which Clark joined. The dray-riding brawlers were soon put to flight, although Clark was still engaged in an exchange of fisticuffs when the conductor's bell summoned him back aboard the trolley and presented him with the predicament of whether to finish (and win) his fight or get to court—"a most perplexing situation," he recalled with typical understatement. Characteristically, Clark dispatched the job at hand, stepping up the speed and snap of his punches, and then caught the trolley with a sprinting effort worthy of his quarter-miling days at Pomfret.

Physical prowess was also involved in a second New Jersey experience, which took place in the waning days of Woodrow Wilson's governorship. The occasion was an intramural corporate struggle involving the machinations of a defaulting corporate treasurer and a struggle for the company records. The episode was something of a replay of the Hoadley *opéra bouffe*. A Sunday-morning standoff occurred between the treasurer and some henchmen on one side and some Root, Clarkers with detectives, led by their eminent partner, on the other. Clark, who had dragged a local judge from his bed, took an iron bar and burst the clasps securing the repository of the critical records. He then stood his ground and preserved the status quo with his iron bar rampant.

Hence, there was a note of reprise when Clark mentioned the Hague-CIO controversy in his Association speech, which denounced "the callous disregard of the Constitution by Mayor Hague," and excoriated the conservative silence on the subject. With that reference, Clark threw down the gauntlet, joining Republican stalwart and past Presidential nominee Alfred Landon, and ABA president Arthur Vanderbilt in defense of the civil liberties of the embattled CIO.

The loom of the fates was already in motion. Clark's Nassau Bar address was widely noted, eventually being reprinted in the widely read *Journal of the American Bar Association*. But it was probably through the agency of Arthur Vanderbilt that Clark's clarion call to the conservative conscience was relayed to Vanderbilt's successor in the ABA presidency, Washington establishmentarian Frank Hogan.

Thanks to Hogan's suave, sympathetic support, the 1938 ABA convention created a special committee on the Defense of Liberties Vouchsafed by the Bill of Rights. The group was authorized, after Association approval, to take such steps as it might deem proper in defense of such rights. Hogan named the nine-man committee, selecting Clark as chairman and (undoubtedly, with Clark's discreet assistance) appointing nine individual members whose ideological cachet ran a spectrum from the Alabama conservatism of young Douglas Arant (who had been Clark's coadjutor in the Court fight) to the trade union progressivism of Joseph Padway, onetime general counsel of the AFL. They were all good men, and their caliber encouraged Clark to rely on their talents because, between the affairs of the law firm and the business of Harvard, he was busy enough. Nonetheless, he graciously yielded to the psychological estoppel: "I guess the appointment was caused or anyhow stimulated by a speech I made at a meeting of the Nassau County Bar Association," he wrote Felix Frankfurter. "I was a bit reluctant to take this on but having agitated the subject I would not feel in a very good moral position to decline."

Clark put his full vigor into the committee's first task. This was the defense of the CIO before the federal courts in New Jersey, to which the labor group had turned after being denied relief by the state tribunals. A federal district judge, William Clark (no relative), had issued an injunction forbidding interference with the CIO organizers, and appeal of this decree to the Third Circuit Court of Appeals afforded Clark's committee the opportunity to enter the litigation by throwing its weight behind the respondent labor union. The decision to enter the fray was not reached without a sharp struggle with the ABA standpatters.

To say Clark's impress was on every line of the ABA's resulting brief would be an exaggeration, for he purposely orchestrated the efforts of the group to allow each member the opportunity of authentic input. Nonetheless, as chairman, he had to choose the parameters carefully, for on the law of the matter, the CIO had an uphill fight. As Judge John J. Gibbons noted later, because of constricting Supreme Court precedent, "the legal problems seemed insurmountable." Gibbons further recollected: "Most people thought the [Federal Civil Rights] Act would never be applied to conduct of the Jersey City Police Department." Judge Gibbons' comments were apparently based on the formidable precedent of *Davis* v. *Massachusetts* where the Supreme Court, speaking through the great Oliver Wendell Holmes, Jr., had upheld a Boston ordinance similar to that of Jersey City.

Clark first checked with Felix Frankfurter: "Do you think it would be a good idea for this ABA Committee on the Bill of Rights of which I am chairman to apply for leave to file a brief in one of these New Jersey litigations?" (Another proceeding had been commenced by Norman Thomas and Arthur Vanderbilt.) Frankfurter was supportive: "Most assuredly your Committee should intervene." However, he offered no help on the law: "I know of no explicit repudiation by Holmes of his opinion in the *Davis* case."

Fortified, Clark struck for the jugular, utilizing his talent to hit the nail squarely, overcoming by force majeure what he could and minimizing or distinguishing what he could not. His argument ran along four principal lines—first, that freedom of assembly was an *essential* part of the American democratic system; second, that protection of this freedom by federal courts comported with the "modern" doctrine of the Supreme Court (this not only enabled Clark to exorcise disabling precedents but to invoke both the name and the teachings of Chief Justice Charles Evans Hughes, before whom the question would eventually come); third, that mere apprehension of disorder was not a valid excuse for denial of permits to use Jersey City's parks ("Public order and the protection of property are precious, but freedom of expression is precious too. The answer is enough policemen on hand to quell apprehended disturbances . . ."); and fourth, that a city cannot constitutionally close both its streets and its parks to public meetings, but must make both available at reasonable times and places. Clark won the case when he hit *Davis* v. *Massachusettes* head on, for, Holmes notwithstanding, Clark felt that *Davis* "evaded the real point":

> *Davis* v. *Massachusetts* relied on by defendants is distinguishable in respect to its facts and the issue involved . . . A city does not

control its parks like a private owner of property, but holds them for public purposes including meetings.

The brief supplied the decisive element in the case, for, thanks to the double cachet of Grenville Clark and the American Bar Association, on December 23, 1938, the sturdily conservative *New York Herald Tribune* found in it "a cause of good cheer," while the rival *New York Times* concurrently asserted that the document should "stand as a landmark in American legal history . . . It ought to be on file in every police station. It ought to be in every public library, in every school library, and certainly in the home of every voter in Jersey City." From Cambridge, Professor Frankfurter wrote: "How funny, with the whole country acclaiming your brief, that there ever should have been any question about the wisdom of this intervention."

The real endorsement came on January 26, 1939, when the Third Circuit Court of Appeals upheld the brief—and the lower court's injunction—in virtually all particulars, especially the federal right of assembly and the irrelevance of *Davis* v. *Massachusetts.* That opinion, however, was something of an entr'acte, for, as everyone had anticipated, the Supreme Court decided to take the case.

By special leave, Clark's brief was filed there and the truly final opinion was had at the end of the 1938 term. The seven Justices who participated wrote five opinions, but the most decisive was that in which Justice Owen Roberts, joined by the newly appointed Justice Hugo Black, wrote officially for the Court and asserted of *Davis,* following Clark's lead:

. . . we cannot agree that it rules the instant case. Wherever the title of streets and parks may rest, they have immemorially been held in trust for the use of the public, and, time out of mind, have been used for the purposes of assembly, communicating thoughts between citizens, and discussion of public questions.

All in all, the effort fully justified Judge Gibbons' subsequent encomium of it as "a stunning triumph of advocacy." The case was the spark of a major constitutional revolution in federalizing the provisions of the Bill of Rights against constraining state action, and, in addition, it marked the beginnings of a revived activism of the American Bar.

Keeping his enthusiasm at peak pitch, particularly after his presence was withdrawn, was out of the question, and years later, on his NBC telecast, Clark was inclined to deprecate the ABA committee he had founded:

> . . . a very interesting and powerful committee, influential for a few years. I regret to say it then became nothing, became futile, and even worse, and I consider it one of my real failures in life . . .

He should not have been so pessimistic. After *Hague,* neither the ABA nor the Constitution would ever be the same again.

And neither would Grenville Clark.

II
Pledges and Allegiance

Liberty and justice for all.
—Pledge of Allegiance

Grenville Clark's most vigorous defense of Bill of Rights guarantees came at a time when he was also heading an effort for national rearmament to prepare for a war which he foresaw as inevitable. He saw no paradox, and characterized as a fallacy the proposition that America could not organize for defense without permanent loss or great impairment of democratic liberties. Clark's germinal effort doubtless forestalled a repetition of the excesses of World War I, and also exemplified his earlier credo denying the incompatibility of rearmament and constitutional guaranties. And as a matter of history, Clark helped to make it so.

In early 1940 at Harvard, Bertrand Russell was fast becoming a matter of concern. He had been appointed to give the William James Lectures on "Logic and Fact" ("whatever that means," Clark impertinently observed). Word of Russell's disorderly sexual and civic behavior in Britain had already sufficed to abort his appointment as professor of philosophy at CCNY, at the behest of a lawsuit filed by a Mrs. Kay of Brooklyn. The court had ousted Russell on three counts—first, that an alien could not teach in a New York public college; second, that the appointment was subject to a competitive civil service examination; and third, that as a legally adjudicated adulterer, Russell was incapacitated to teach, since the public subsidization of immorality was manifestly *ultra vires* under the applicable New York statute. When La Guardia's corporation counsel had refused to act, Clark had enlisted his partners Buckner and Harlan to attempt to overturn the judgment *pro bono,* but the effort to get to the New York Court of Appeals—"where there might be a pretty good show of getting a well-considered decision"—had miscarried.

The third count cited by the court especially disturbed Clark, as he wrote James Landis, now dean of the Harvard Law School:

> . . . I am quite concerned about Harvard's position in connection with the Bertrand Russell appointment . . . Thomas Dorgan, the politician who . . . appears to have it in for Harvard, has written J. B. Conant demanding a revocation of the appointment, stating that failing a satisfactory answer, he will bring suit to test the legality of the appointment . . . He invokes a statute of Massachusetts of 1789 which you will find quoted on page 7 of the H.U. Catalogue. The matter isn't so easy. The alternative seems to me to back up and revoke the appointment on the ground that the public discussion of his views, especially about sexual morals, has destroyed his usefulness, or submit to a lawsuit and see what the law is by getting a decision of the Supreme Judicial Court. My first impression, as I told Conant, was that we ought to stand on the appointment, and undertake to cooperate in getting a legal decision, if desired. However, I am not clear about the matter.

As in the Court-packing struggle, Clark's decision was to tough the matter out, and his boldness paid off. Russell, quite aware that his presence was an embarrassment, duly gave the James Lectures, pocketed his fee, and departed.

The Russell contretemps was not as remote from Clark's new preoccupations with U.S. security as its superficialities—such as Russell's resistance to serving his own country—might indicate. Clark's sensitivities to the delicate linkage between law and liberty were apparent from the pages of his *Bill of Rights Review,* which began publication in the summer of 1940.

Within a year, the pressure of events forced Clark's relinquishment of the *Review*'s editorship, but only after securing a distinguished legal scholar, John Mulder, as a successor. In a joint appearance at the Association of the Bar of the City of New York, the two insisted that U.S. rearmament and civil liberties were compatible (CIVIL LIBERTIES HELD NO BAR TO ARMING):

We utterly deny the validity of such alternatives. We affirm the practicality of organizing the manpower, the industrial power and the moral power of our people in such a way to meet the threat of Hitler and Japan over as long a time as necessary to overcome that threat without any essential or permanent sacrifice of our constitutional liberties. A denial of this is not only a counsel of despair; it is untrue as a judgment from the lessons of history.

This declaration of faith—for such it was—was the appropriate overture to that defense of the rights of conscience of a nation in arms which was to constitute Clark's most distinguished constitutional effort. The precise focus was that commonplace of village patriotism—the flag salute and pledge of allegiance by schoolchildren.

One Justice said he approached the salute and pledge issue the way a skittish horse came alongside a brass band, and the nervousness was logical enough. Three times before, the Supreme Court had held that the "liberty" guaranteed by the Fourteenth Amendment did not include insulation from state action calculated to encourage patriotic sentiment. Experience, however, gave new insights into the constitutional guarantee. The case presented by the renewed controversy seemed real enough—the expulsion of two Jehovah's Witness children from public schools of Minersville, Pennsylvania, with the consequences of forfeiture of education by the children and possible prosecution of the parents for contributing to truancy and delinquency. As proselytes to the fundamentalist, aggressively evangelical Witnesses, the Gohitis family were virtually pariahs in the overwhelmingly Catholic, first-generation, blue-collar community, and the record implied that the flag salute confrontation had been both programmed and forced by the authorities, with an eye to the proscription of the detested nonconformists. The method was simplicity itself—requiring that the children render obedience to the national colors via the pledge of allegiance to the flag, which parental counsel and Sunday-school teaching had anathematized as a literal violation of the command in Genesis against homage to an idol.

The case brought another confrontation—Frankfurter against Clark. Not only did it almost cause the end of a friendship but it also marked the end of Frankfurter's leadership of the liberal bloc on the Supreme Court. The controversy came to the Court during the 1939 term.

Frankfurter had strong feelings about both the flag and the American public school. He fought for them in the conference of the Justices, where he ridiculed the idea of judicial oversight of ten thousand citizen-run school boards and upheld the necessity of venerating national symbols on the eve of a war that crept ever closer to the United States. Indeed, his eloquence was such that it won him the assignment to write the opinion in the case.

There was another view to be heard, for Grenville Clark had entered the lists and submitted an eloquent brief from his ABA committee on behalf of the Gohitis children. Years later, he re-examined his handiwork and grudgingly conceded its quality: "I must say it's not so bad." He also told how the brief came to be written:

> . . . Z. Chafee, Jr., and I wrote every word of it . . . He came down from Cambridge to our house on Long Island, and we shut ourselves up for a whole week with one secretary, divided the work, then went over every sentence together and turned it out in that one week of hard work, although of course we had two or three printed proofs

afterward, to see how it "stood the test of print." Then we circulated it to the rest of the Committee, all of whom accepted it without change . . .

Clark explained the importance of the issue he was trying to drive home in the knife-edge balance of right against right;

Perhaps the most important point we made was (p. 21) that the Court should affirm and make definite the proposition that there should be a more exacting judicial scrutiny in cases of alleged violation of First Amendment rights. As of the spring of 1940 when this brief was written, it seems that the Court had hardly done more than say "may be" that such a stricter standard should prevail . . .

One member of the Court was especially receptive to Clark's remonstrance. Associate (and future Chief) Justice Harlan Stone fundamentally shared Clark's liberal strain and was amenable to the suggestion that the Court forcefully restate the primacy of religious freedom. Stone must have liked what was presented, for, notwithstanding the Chafee participation, the brief was vintage Clark, and, characteristically, it presented an opening premise whereby the case was won or lost:

The Committee believes that the compulsory flag salute regulation . . . violates the constitutional provision against deprivation of liberty without due process of law, because without sufficient justification it requires the suppression of a sincerely held religious scruple; and also because, apart from any religious aspect, it transcends the limits of governmental power in attempting to compel a particular form of expression without sufficient reason for such compulsion.

Four hammerblow middle points backed up the preliminary statement. First, that whether a flag salute was a religious exercise was not determined by legislatures or courts but by the uncoerced, private judgment of the individual believers. Second, that while religious scruple might be overriden in particular circumstances, no such showing of essentiality was made in the confrontation between the school district and the recalcitrant children. Third, religious belief apart, and conceding broad state power to encourage loyalty, that the instant exercise violated the broader secular liberty of being left unmolested from ceremonials. Tucked away as a subsidiary and seemingly thrown in for good measure was the fourth, whether the right to attend state-supported schools was a mere privilege that the state might condition in any way it saw fit.

The brief then undertook to examine religious dissent in the context of supervening secular power—from observant Jews in Roman Palestine to the troubles of Quakers in seventeenth-century England, all of whom, it was duly noted, seemed as obdurate and idiosyncratic as the Witnesses in twentieth-century America. Conceding that Mormon polygamy crossed the line, the brief drew a sharp distinction between restraining certain expressions and *compelling* such expressions; this was especially true in school flag salutes, which had first made their appearance in Kansas in 1907.

Paramount, however, was the standard of judicial scrutiny which should be brought to bear. Artfully citing, by way of contrast, Justice Stone's protest against wholesale and generalized invalidation of legislation (in the famous footnote 4 of the *Carolene Products* case, which surrendered an economic veto for a political one), the appeal summoned Stone against Stone in pointing out a diminished presumption of legitimacy when a statute collided with a specific prohibition of the Constitution. Here the prohibition was "the great affirmative principle expressly declared by the First Amendment and embodied in national emotions since the landing of the Pilgrims." So strong is this policy "of safeguarding the basic individual liberties—including religious freedom," the Clark-Chafee thesis continued, "that the presumption should be against, rather than for, the validity of any statute abridging those liberties."

After summoning the Court to a more activist liberal role, the brief boldly left religious liberty and moved to its least defensible salient, the constraint of the compulsory salute on individual freedom, a concluding paragraph noting:

> For nearly five generations since 1789, the nation relied wholly on spontaneous and voluntary manifestations to preserve sentiments of loyalty. We have survived five wars during that period without resorting to compulsory salutes from the civil population.

Predictably, however, in a time of national unity against eastern threats, the compulsory flag salute was affirmed by an almost unanimous Supreme Court. The newly appointed New Dealers had been almost mesmerized by the strong-minded Felix Frankfurter. The lone holdout was senior Associate Justice Stone, like Clark a strong-minded Yankee liberal.

Eventually, Stone handed down a powerful dissent which essentially replicated the thesis Clark had urged:

> The guarantees of civil liberty are but guarantees of freedom of the human mind and spirit and opportunity to express them. They presuppose the right of the individual to hold such opinions as he will and give them reasonably free expression, and his freedom and that of the state as well, to teach and persuade others by the communication of ideas. The very essence of the liberty which they guarantee is freedom of the individual from compulsion to bear false witness to his religion.

Stone's clerk, Alison Dunham, later doubted whether any *amicus* brief—even Clark's—could have had such an effect on a member of the Supreme Court. On the other hand, grounds exist for a divergent estimate. Obviously, Clark and Stone knew each other from the milieu of the practicing Bar of New York, and, equally obviously, Clark's name on a brief was an incentive to a careful reading of the document. We can assume that Stone did

read it, and read it carefully, for his own experience as a member
of a World War I conscientious objector review board sensitized
him particularly to the Clark brief. For, as Stone had written
earlier: "It may well be questioned whether the state which
preserves its life by a settled policy of violating the conscience
of the individual will not in fact lose it by the process."

Assuredly, Felix Frankfurter read the brief, too, but he was not
persuaded. In fact, Frankfurter's views about those he called
"absolutists" were unchanged from World War I, when he had
recommended Leavenworth as the remedy for such nonconfor-
mance. Neither the passage of two decades nor the advocacy of
Grenville Clark changed anything, as the closing lines of his
majority opinion plainly showed:

> Judicial review, itself a limitation of popular government, is a
> fundamental part of our constitutional scheme. But to the legisla-
> tures no less than the courts is committed the guardianship of deeply
> cherished liberties.

Why did Frankfurter behave thus? Clark later ascribed the
position to "intangibles," and noted how the intangibles had
dragged virtually the whole Court along:

> F.F., who was then only one year on the Court, had a reputation
> for standing up for the underdog and minority rights (Sacco-
> Vanzetti, etc.); and when *he* went for the flag salute, other new
> judges (Black, Douglas and Rutledge?) went along almost as a
> matter of course.

Stone did not press for his view in conference (Frankfurter
did) and did not circulate his dissent beforehand to his colleagues.
Moreover, it took a major effort by his law clerk to persuade
Stone to read the dissent aloud rather than merely submit it in
writing. But the powerful sonority of the spoken word eventually won the day. When the flag salute issue returned to the Court

a few years later in *West Virginia School Board* v. *Barnette,* it was the proposition of the Clark brief which became the law. The Court reversed itself to so hold, and this time an embittered Felix Frankfurter stood quite alone.

Winning World War II

The Selective Training and Service Act

There is no question that Clark's sensitivity toward civil liberties increased with, and was increased by, his awareness of the hazards of Nazi totalitarianism. Indeed, even before the Nazi offensive during the so-called Phony War, Clark had been upset over the implications a Nazi-dominated world held for the United States, and, by his own later recollection, his concern for the state of American defense became acute "before the great attack on France by Germany."

Clark's sponsorship of the ABA *Bill of Rights Review* and his military preparedness experience caused him to observe the Nazi threat with special insight. One forced reflection on the barbarism of the totalitarian state; the other engendered doubt of America's ability to defend itself against that barbarism. A reinforcing perception came from a legacy of his Plattsburg days, the Military Training Camp Association (MTCA), which had been organized to parallel the Army's own structure by corps areas. A prophetic admonition in 1931 from Henry Stimson had been especially formative:

In May 1931 Henry L. Stimson, while Secretary of State, in a long talk with me made an amazingly accurate forecast of coming world events. He forecast that Germany and Japan would strike hands and there would be a second world war within ten years. He thought that this time Germany would run over France and all Europe and Japan would run over much but not all of China and that Germany would attack Russia. He foresaw a ten-year war in which the U.S. would wind up bearing the brunt *unless* there could be formed a coalition of Britain, the U.S., and Russia in which case the war could be ended in five years with much less suffering. He then asked me to undertake a five-year official mission with some suitable title devoted to preparing the way for such a coalition so that it could come into existence as soon as possible after the beginning of the coming war. My mission would not be made public but actually it would be to travel back and forth between China and Russia reporting back to Washington from time to time and sticking at it for at least five years. I did not undertake that mission but kept in touch with Stimson and his forecast actually made me think.

In the spring of 1940, after the conquest of Norway but before the fall of France, I concluded Stimson's forecast would come true.

Everything came together at an MTCA dinner on May 8, 1940, at New York's Harvard Club. The affair was held in the same Nicholas Biddle Room where Clark had launched his Plattsburg movement just a quarter of a century earlier, just after the *Lusitania* sinking. Yet it must have seemed to Clark that the more time passed, the less things changed. Once again a Germany in arms was rolling, almost without hindrance, toward the Atlantic moat which constituted a flaccid America's sole defense.

As in 1914, the U.S. Navy was inadequate, the Army appalling. Indeed, the Army seemed to be back at square one, still consisting of a small and creditable professional nucleus, backed up by a sprawling, inefficient National Guard, which still exhibited all the infirmities of the politics–ridden militia system. Aside from a trickle of officers supplied by West Point, supplemented with the collegiate ROTC and Clark's MTCA program, it was almost as if the experience of World War I had passed through America without pausing.

But if the structure of America's military apparatus was bad, the spirit within the structure was even worse, in at least three particulars. First came the moral differentiations between the commanders in chief. While Clark doubtless shared Theodore Roosevelt's perception of Woodrow Wilson as the pedant risen to power, Wilson nonetheless was possessed of a forthright intellectual acuity which suffused each action with a momentary, if maddening, righteousness. FDR Clark sometimes felt to be the artful dodger of American politics, for Roosevelt, notwithstanding a secret commitment to intervention on behalf of the Western allies, was fully prepared to outdo America's dominant mood of isolationism with even more isolationist rhetoric, in the interest of his own continuation in power. No hope for an adequate national defense could be found in that quarter.

Below the presidency, the dramatis personae deteriorated even more. During the Wilson administration, the successive heads of the War Department had been Lindley M. Garrison and Newton D. Baker, men of intellectual stature, personal presence, and executive capacity. In 1940, the Secretary and Assistant Secretary were Harry H. Woodring and Louis Johnson, whose appointments testified to the political power of the American Legion and National Guard and whose administrative stewardship reflected such origins and ambiance. Clark, with his aristocratic hauteur, could only shudder at what he saw in that quarter. No help was forthcoming there, either.

A similar but morally distinct disability beset the professional military cadre. An engrained antipathy toward political activity had caused the cream of the officer corps to lean over backwards to avoid any lead in matters of national policy and to eschew involvement therein.

An apprehension weighed heavily on Clark's mind at the Harvard Club dinner, and made the levity of badinage and reminiscence almost unbearable. Accordingly, he broke into the small talk and dominated the gathering with the bombshell announcement of what was really on his mind—"a peace-time conscription act so that the U.S. could do its share promptly when inevitably drawn into the big war."

Once the declaration was made, Clark swung into action in the mode that he had virtually patented, by shrewdly selecting a small nuclear group with an eye toward each member's capacity and vision. Once again, Clark remained inconspicuous in the background, perceiving his role as inspiring and directing others. A low profile, however, did not mean passivity.

The MTCA reunion on May 8 was followed by a smaller working meeting on May 22, also at the Harvard Club, thus following the classic Clark *modus operandi:* ". . . he would have a program, and a sensible one, one that something could be done with. A group of people would have met in some downtown or uptown club, each would emerge with a task assigned, and something would happen."

Despite the unpromising prospects for presidential support, Clark had moved quickly to involve FDR at this stage, manfully risking rebuff if the estrangement of the Court fight had not softened. Characteristically, he saluted the chief executive with utmost respect:

May 16, 1940

The President
The White House
Washington, D.C.

Dear Mr. President:

I am presiding at a private meeting of the old Plattsburg Camp Group on Wednesday evening, May 22, at the Harvard Club. (About fifty picked men will be there—DeLancey Jay, George McMurty, Judge Robert P. Patterson, Julius Ochs Adler, and men like that.)

We propose to debate the question of recommending and supporting compulsory military training of a sort suited to our conditions—on the idea that nothing less may suffice to safeguard the U.S. (This particular lot of men should be in a sound position to propose compulsory service, since all were in the previous war and many served with distinction.)

Assuming that we decide to support such a proposal, the question will arise whether, as a matter of timing, it is opportune to put it forward publicly at this time.

We will also discuss the public support of a concrete set of measures "short of war" to aid the Allies, that should be put in effect immediately.

Presumably, also, we will vote to support your immediate proposals for preparedness.

I inform you of this so that if you wish to send me any comment, you may do so.

With great respect, I am

Very truly yours,
Grenville Clark

Clark had interpolated in manuscript "private" in the first sentence, and had drawn a bar alongside the last paragraph to indicate the real nature of the message, and the presidential reply showed that FDR had gotten the point:

May 18, 1940

PRIVATE AND CONFIDENTIAL

Dear Grennie:

Thanks for yours of the sixteenth. I see no reason why the group you mention should not advocate military training . . . I am inclined to think there is very strong public opinion for universal service so that every able bodied man and woman would fit into his or her place. The difficulty of proposing a concrete set of measures "short of war" is largely a political one—what one can get from Congress.

I hope to see you soon.

As ever

The nuance indicating that the President was really on their side and the suggestion of a meeting sufficed to send Clark and Adler to Washington on the last day of May. The pair had emerged as a committee of two from the fifty-man assembly at the Harvard Club on May 22. Apparently, Clark felt the crisis to be too acute to take his usual back seat, and the Washington trip was made by air, an unusual enough occurrence in 1940. There were programmed stops at the White House, the War Department, and the Supreme Court.

The first two stops seemed only to exacerbate Clark's frustration. The President, apprehensive owing to memories of the Wilson administration's having led a divided nation into war, was evasive on the conscription issue, and General George Catlett Marshall, the new Chief of Staff, almost lost his temper, visibly flushing when Clark, with civilian brashness, sought Army support for immediate conscription.

The presidential inertia resulted from two reinforcing pressures. An inclination to drift with the tide, lagging behind rather than forming public opinion, and his distaste for summary discharge of subordinates made Roosevelt evasive. The core difficulty was Secretary Woodring, a Kansas isolationist with an ingrained ideological antipathy toward compulsory national service. As Clark later wrote, all efforts to mount a conscription effort were doomed "without a sympathetic secretary of war."

And it was doubtless to this effect that Clark spoke at length on his last appointment of the day. Seemingly the least promising, the event turned out to be the most significant. The particular meeting was lunch with Felix Frankfurter.

For almost a year and a half now Professor Frankfurter had been Mr. Justice Frankfurter. Clark had rejoiced at the appointment ("eminently right—a good thing for the Court and the country"). But nonetheless, he was nostalgic. ("Twenty-four years—active ones—are quite a long while. I shan't like it a bit when I go to the Law School and know that someone else is sitting in your room. And I will like it still less when I go up

Brattle Street and might have turned down your narrow path to your hospitable door. These are real regrets that are uppermost in my mind.") The new danger of American vincibility had provided whatever solvent was necessary to wash away the estrangement of the Court-packing fight, and Clark and Frankfurter's enthusiastic conversation must have carried them back to their first meeting in Austin Hall a generation before.

Such was the enthusiastic give-and-take of the conversational flow that neither remembered later who first suggested the key contribution to the conscription effort. This was the idea of the ouster of Harry Woodring (much easier said than done) and the suggestion of a successor. But who could serve? Almost providentially, both Clark and Frankfurter came up with the same name simultaneously: Henry Lewis Stimson, conservative Republican stalwart, old Plattsburger, old Rough Rider, former Secretary of State and of War. Stimson's massive integrity, selfless patriotism, and charismatic air of command made him almost heaven-sent. (Also heaven-sent was Clark's change of attitude, for, by his own word, he had awakened one morning in mid-May with the determination that the only way to obtain conscription was to obtain a new Secretary of War who would "push it through." Stimson had occurred as a possibility then, but Clark had dismissed the seventy-two-year-old elder statesman as "a very tired, decayed old man," doubtless pondering the negative effects of age and health.) Stimson would need an assistant. Almost as spontaneously as Stimson's, there emerged the name of the old Root, Clarker "Fighting Bob" Patterson, now a Federal District Judge, whose qualities, outlooks, and virtues matched Stimson's to a remarkable degree. And so the "ticket" was struck.

Frankfurter had unknowingly already done a little campaigning on behalf of the ticket. On May 3, he had arranged for a White House lunch for Stimson, after which he had written the President:

It was very sweet of you to have Harry Stimson for lunch. He is a fine old Roman—he is, you know, close to 73—and wants to feel he is still of use to the Republic. And he is—though his party for narrow, partisan reasons professes departure from its traditional foreign policy. You made Stimson feel he is of use—and gave him the fresh impulse to go on. Many thanks for taking me out of my marble palace.

Indeed only one random element of fate portended disturbance of the elaborate schema of Frankfurter and Clark. On June 10, Italy entered the war via a surprise attack on the southern border of France. Addressing the University of Virginia at commencement, President Roosevelt summed up the event by saying that "the hand which held the dagger has struck it into the back of its neighbor." While the rhetoric may have provided a release for anger, it also affronted many Italian-Americans, who were an important element in FDR's electoral coalition. The consequence was a movement to afford ethnic reparation via the appointment of Fiorello La Guardia as Secretary of War. Frankfurter later pronounced the sequence "an interesting illustration of Cleopatra's nose—the factor of contingency in history. If anyone were to tell me that it would have made no difference if FDR had appointed La Guardia as Secretary of War, as he strongly contemplated doing, he might equally tell me that 2 and 2 make 7." But the courtier-like Frankfurter wrote FDR, magistrally praising the speech: "the 'stab-in-the-back' speech was a grand tonic. We needed that kind of moral summons." However, Frankfurter used the same letter to assure the President of Stimson's and Patterson's availability ("I've assured myself that they both regard themselves as soldiers and you as their commander in chief"). As part of the assurance, Clark, in an extraordinarily uncharacteristic move, actually confronted Stimson's physician to obtain ("an extraordinary thing") a good report on Stimson's health.

One more providential development came in the resignation of Secretary of the Navy Charles Edison, and the President's offering the portfolio to Chicago's Frank Knox, a GOP newspaper publisher. Knox, while not declining, responded that he had no wish to be the only Republican in the Cabinet.

While the President might listen to his old acquaintances in Manhattan law practice, he still did things his own way. He called Stimson long-distance on June 19 to make his offer by telephone. Predictably, the old Roman accepted, subject to three half-explicit conditions, each of which actually enhanced his desirability—freedom from the expectation of his political support of the administration, freedom to support compulsory military service, and freedom to run the War Department, including naming the Assistant Secretary. Roosevelt had already covered the points in his opening commentary. "I was called up by the President who offered me the position of Secretary of War," Stimson noted in his diary. "He told me that Knox had already agreed to accept the position of Secretary of the Navy. The President said he was very anxious to have me accept because everybody was running around at loose ends in Washington, and he thought I would be a stabilizing factor in whom both the Army and the public would have confidence." Nettled that Clark and Frankfurter's elaborate ploy had been undertaken without his knowledge, Stimson immediately called Clark to tell him: "Your preposterous plan has succeeded."

Success, however, was for Clark not an end but a beginning. The key piece on the chessboard, the War Department secretaryship, had been captured, but a further envelopment was now required. Since late May, Clark had been at work on the bill which was to become the Selective Training and Service Act of 1940. Drawing heavily on James Anthony Froude, the English historian, and the sonorous drumroll of the Tudor defense statutes ("The Congress declares that in a free society the obligation and privilege of military service should be shared generally in accordance with a fair and just system of compulsory military training and service"), the draft bill contemplated universal registration of able-bodied males from eighteen to thirty-five, selection by lottery, service at $5 per month, and release from the military after a one-year term.

By one of the random factors which weave the fabric of history, a missed appointment by Senator Henry Cabot Lodge, the bill entered American history as the Burke-Wadsworth Act. The Senate sponsor of S 164, getting the assignment by default of Lodge, was Edward Burke, Nebraska's lame-duck anti-New Deal Democrat, who had proven himself a staunch ally of Clark during the Court fight of 1937. In the House, James W. Wadsworth, former senator from New York, put his name on the counterpart bill HR 10132. Republican Wadsworth, longtime proponent of an adequate defense, had stepped down to the House after long Senate service; he served singularly free of the anti-Roosevelt hatred which characterized most of his party's stalwarts and was popular on both sides of the aisle. "Why, Jim's just like a Democrat," once observed Missouri Democratic congressman John B. Sullivan (who was fated to lose his own seat in Congress for adherence to Wadsworth's proposal).

By the first of June, printed drafts of what was to become the Burke-Wadsworth Act had appeared, and from his headquarters in the Carlton Hotel, Clark was moving to organize and to deploy his forces for the legislative battle ahead. A June 28 conference at the White House showed no change in the apparent presidential neutrality, but already Stimson, now confirmed and aboard as Secretary of War, was explicit in his clarion call for selective service. Clark's tenacity was paying dividends in winning interviews which ran a gamut from Senator Morris Sheppard, chairman of the Senate Military Affairs Committee, to General of the Armies John J. Pershing, then an infirm octogenarian in Walter Reed Hospital.

Hearings opened before the Senate Military Affairs Committee on July 5. Among the first witnesses was James Wadsworth, who struck a note of déjà vu in reminding Senator Sheppard of previous efforts to pass a selective service act in 1920, which had been undertaken in that very room (Sheppard and Wadsworth being the only men present who had participated in the earlier effort). Clark also testified, as did Harvard president Conant and "Wild Bill" Donovan, Medal of Honor-winning colonel of the Fighting 69th. However, clearly the star of the show was General Pershing, who appeared by statement rather than in person (thanks to an advance Clark-Sheppard arrangement). He had written it himself, rebuffing Clark's offers to provide a ghost writer ("I compose my own statements"). The statement included an arresting point, that with selective service in 1914, World War I "could have ended earlier."

Clark's testimony reflected a man every inch the self-possessed and unselfconscious man of affairs:

> My name is Grenville Clark. I live in New York and New Hampshire. I came originally from Vermont—at least much of my youth was spent there, and I like to say I am a Vermonter.
>
> I am and for over 30 years have been a practicing lawyer in New York with the firm of Root, Clark, Buckner & Ballantine.
>
> In 1914 a group of men got together—most certainly not to advocate war, for they were not warlike men, but men who believed that without any choice on our part we might be driven into it and wanted to prepare themselves to participate effectively.

This hearing gave the conscription campaign a momentum it never lost. However, with the introduction of formal legislation, the struggle shifted from the halls of Congress to the wider arena of public opinion. This was a development for which Clark's leadership against Court-packing had prepared him superbly, and in many respects the two struggles were similar.

There were differences, however. This time the Roosevelt administration, while not actively opposed, was benignly neutral. Even worse, General George C. Marshall, the new Chief of Staff with whom Clark had already tangled, obdurately felt that public opinion would not support a draft and prepared his own plan for a volunteer army. It made for an interesting contrast, with Marshall, the cloistered soldier, setting his views on the point against Grenville Clark, the seasoned man of affairs. Nonetheless, Clark, who did quail against setting his face against the commander in chief, was not about to back down before a mere general.

At a New York rally to drum up support for the Burke-Wadsworth Bill, Clark, preparing to introduce Governor Lehman, was summoned to the telephone to receive an important call from the Secretary of War. A recollection of William Marbury completes the story:

> Mr. Stimson said that General Marshall had developed a plan for recruiting an army by a call for volunteers and had submitted it to the President for his approval. The President had consulted Mr. Stimson and asked for his opinion. Mr. Stimson told Mr. Clark that he did not see how he could oppose the recommendation of the Chief of Staff. Mr. Clark replied that if the President approved the Marshall plan, selective service was dead. When Mr. Stimson undertook to argue the point, Mr. Clark, who felt rather pressed for time, said very bluntly that he thought the point was so clear that he felt confident that if Mr. Stimson would simply think about the matter for a while, he could not come to any other conclusion. Congress would certainly not pass a Selective Service Act until the volunteer plan had received a thorough trial. He said that he was rather abrupt and that Mr. Stimson was annoyed and said to him: "Clark, you are being very difficult about this."
>
> About three hours later, Mr. Stimson called him up and said: "Of course, you are quite right in what you said. When I thought the matter over, I saw this and I have discussed the matter with the President and he agrees entirely. He will not approve General Marshall's plan."

Doubtless a score of incidents like this helped shape the Burke-Wadsworth Bill into law during the long, hot summer of 1940. A powerful assist was given by the Nazi air assault on faltering Britain, the only remaining Atlantic bulwark of the United States.

There were necessary changes and parliamentary snags. Marshall did overcome the Plattsburg patricians' naïve belief that $5-per-month pocket money would suffice for the conscripts and substituted the usual $21 Army stipend. The final flurry of legislative approvals came in September, with the approved bill ricocheting between the two chambers. Final House passage came on September 8, by a vote of 266–145, and final Senate approval followed a week later, by 58–31. General George Marshall, who had badly misgauged congressional sentiment, hailed the congressional action as miraculous. Clark deprecated the compliment: "nothing miraculous about it, but rather the consequence of extremely careful preparation."

On September 16 came the formal presidential signing in the Oval Office, and, with FDR's approval, the Burke-Wadsworth Bill became the Selective Training and Service Act of 1940. The usual news photograph was taken of the President, Secretary Stimson, General Marshall, and the congressional military committees' chairmen, Representative Andrew May and Senator Morris Sheppard. As with the Preparedness Parade, the man most responsible for it all was not in the picture. But Clark did provide an appropriate epigraph for the photograph some five years later when he wrote Stimson:

> I don't imagine that on June 19 or 20 when FDR called you up that you had any idea that your tour of duty would be as much as five years, two months, and eleven days as I figure it was. But it was a great thing for the country and I never did as good a day's work in my life as that day I went down to see Felix Frankfurter and we jointly worked up the Stimson-Patterson ticket.

The Extension Act

Clark himself was soon personally enmeshed in the extension effort, though not quite as a volunteer. "After the appointment of Stimson," Clark later wrote, "he said that because I had got him into the job I must help him." Clark thus became part of the superb civilian staff—Robert Patterson (whom Clark had virtually inducted), lawyer John J. McCloy, banker Robert A. Lovett, and himself. Clark, with his obsessive sense of privacy, resolutely resisted appointment as assistant secretary and even spurned the dollar a year which was Washington's counterpart of the King's shilling. The rejection caused a storm in the professional bureaucracy of the War Department, raising questions as to whether Clark was truly a constituent of the effort and therefore privileged to see top-secret documents. Stimson later pronounced the group "the best team of associates he ever had in any office."

Clark was not only part of that team; in fact, he had had a hand in constructing it. In a memorandum of October 25, 1960, which was styled "Note on the activities of G. Clark" and which was about as close as he ever got to writing a memoir, Clark modestly compressed the tumultuous years of World War II into half a paragraph:

> From October 1940–June 1944 I acted at Secretary Stimson's request and with President Roosevelt's approval, as Mr. Stimson's confidential assistant and advisor on many hard problems, e.g. on the selection of two Assistant Secretaries (J. J. McCloy and Robert Lovett) when Judge Patterson became Under Secretary . . .

The draft bill had passed, but the triumph soon seemed ephemeral. The European War, with the Continent a Nazi *Festung Europa,* settled into something of a stalemate, and as 1941 dragged along, the one-year training period set by the 1940 legislation loomed like a deadfall for the newly assembled American Army. It was necessary to fight the 1940 fight all over again, but this time in an effort to keep the newly conscripted army together longer than the one year's training provided by the original act. The opponents dug in with the defense that no *new* danger had emerged. A second statute, an Extension Act, became a priority for Clark, certainly as important as the original legislation had been, and perhaps even more difficult to pass. Judge Henry J. Friendly has provided a picture of the pre-Pearl Harbor summers of 1940 and 1941:

> I happened to be in Washington both summers when Grenny was working on the Selective Service Act and its renewal. I stayed at the Statler and he at the Carlton, where he had an apartment; the room would be in a delightful state of litter, and he would be writing out again on those yellow pads those messages to Senator this and Congressman that, how we would do now. One thing would be sure, he would have a program. One can almost see him with his coattails flying, going down to Washington and saying, "Get out, get out, all of you. We've really had enough."

Peacetime conscription was a triumph; so was the Extension Act—passed by one vote—which ensured that the newly fortified American Army would not disintegrate at the moment a faltering Britain might receive a death-thrust from Nazi Germany.

"The Officer Problem"

Not all events were triumphs, nor did all programs emerge the way Clark wished. In his biographical memorandum, he tersely compressed one of his defeats under the rubric "The officer problem." This was a reference to losing a round to George Catlett Marshall, which he did with grace and good humor.

Passage of conscription had assured the soldiers for the Army, but finding the officers to lead the troops was another question again. As Stimson's authorized biographer has noted: "Grenville Clark, and many others who studied the problem, strongly urged that in addition to promotion from the ranks, the War Department should go straight to the civilian world, organizing training camps for civilian volunteers on the lines which Stimson himself had so much admired in 1916–1917." However, the Chief of Staff thought differently, feeling that the officers should come from the ranks.

Who was right? Both men had had experience with the problem, Marshall as a junior officer in a satellite Plattsburg at the very time when Clark was a mover and shaper of national policy. But the intervening years had profoundly changed American views and values. The consequence was an open question, at least, whether the most broadly based service could be commanded by officers drawn from a frankly elitist apparatus composed of the professional and managerial classes. Indeed, the Navy and Air Force successfully did so. Nonetheless, Marshall won and Clark lost, as the Officer Candidate Schools became the main source of the leaders of the new Army; the new officers were to be drawn from the ranks, initially inducted without commitment as to command. Plattsburg became embalmed in history.

Malaise and Its End

The successful extension of selective service and preservation of the Army failed to bring a sense of élan to the administration, but rather became merely a holding action in an unsatisfactory status quo. Stimson, alarmed at the deterioration in the British position, pressed Roosevelt to provide cobelligerency against the U-boat menace in joint operations by the Royal Navy and the U.S. Atlantic Fleet. In a letter to Frankfurter, Clark echoed Stimson's despondency over presidential inertia and the general Washington atmosphere:

> It looks, does it not, as if we were at last getting to the decisive point where the position will be irretrievable and Hitler will win a vast victory—unless we become a belligerent. Of course, this has been the trend all along; but now it is simply that the development of events that could have been anticipated (and which I have anticipated) makes the diagnosis clearer.
>
> I have had long talks with Conant since his return and with two

or three other people who have recently been in England; and the "estimate of the situation" that England cannot last indefinitely or perhaps even very long unless we go in with our naval and air forces, is the only sensible conclusion on the reported facts. (Conant said that Averell Harriman, who has seen a lot of Churchill, took the gravest view of the situation.) On the other hand, it seems pretty clear too that we could turn the scale, although naturally with more difficulty and over a longer period than if we had intervened earlier.

What then can be done to prevent Hitler's winning by default, so to speak? FDR seems unwilling to act *effectively* unless he gets a clearer mandate . . .

A measure of both Clark's malaise and that of the nation can be seen in a letter to Stimson, which was doubtless prompted by a speech by Clark's old ally, Senator Burton Wheeler, now an isolationist stalwart, who had accused the administration of planning to plow under every fourth American boy:

> I have worked up a memorandum of what I consider pretty clear violations of the Espionage Act by Senator Wheeler and General Robert E. Wood, and probably by several others whose identity I don't know. I have written a memorandum of fact and law to Acting Attorney General Biddle suggesting a careful investigation . . .

The uncharacteristic action was a measure of how Clark's sense of alarm overwhelmed his concern with civil liberties. Also significant was his failure to mention the Japanese-American incarcerations in the *Bill of Rights Review* (which expired in the summer of 1942) or among the "hard problems" of his biographical memo.

The end of the malaise came in time, however, and from a most unlikely source: "the Japanese attack on Pearl Harbor which ended the months of indecision . . . and restored to America the freedom of action she had lost by many cunning bonds of her own citizens' contriving. The self-imprisoned giant was set free."

There is a nice historical footnote here. Clark actually drafted the document by which the self-imprisoned giant was freed: "When the Japanese struck Pearl Harbor [Clark was in Washington that Sunday], Stimson phoned me to come immediately to his office, and asked me to draft a declaration of war." This, one suspects, was the way things frequently went. Several problems attended the declaration. Formally, it had to be retroactive. Substantively, there was a brief controversy during the drafting process as to whether the declaration should encompass all the Axis powers or (as was finally effected) limit the declaration to Japan. The overt Nazi and Italian belligerencies completed the transition from uncertain peace to overt war, a war that was also to afford Clark his most important and least publicized forum for the public service of a private man.

The Hidden Service

Presidential Cabinets are a superb mirror of Presidents. Henry Stimson, who served under five of them, pronounced William Howard Taft the most accomplished administrator of them all. Presidential greatness Stimson reserved for a man named Roosevelt, but he was unwilling to specify either Franklin or Theodore. Clark, known to both Roosevelts as "Grenny," did have an opinion on the greater: "Oh, I guess FDR. He was a more flexible man than TR and more capable, I think, of grasping the big issue." Clark developed a deep respect for FDR's wartime performance. As he wrote the President in late 1944:

> About this date every year for several years I've felt like sending you a line of best wishes and heartfelt prayer for your health and strength. May you be given these in the New Year with all your vitality and powers.

Taft's Cabinet meetings were an administrative joy—a carefully selected agenda which moved briskly from topic to topic, with points of view expressed sequentially and fairly. Each item was resolved or reserved for ultimate presidential decision.

Franklin Roosevelt's Cabinet meetings were almost a mirror-image opposite, the chaos being the inevitable product of the mélange of ideologues and self-seeking second-raters included among the wartime secretaries. Little wonder that Stimson refrained from discussing grand strategy in such a group and one Friday may have actually dozed off when Francis Biddle or Harold Ickes held forth at excruciating length, expounding liberal pieties. *Time* reported the alleged incident in its lead section on "National Affairs":

> Now no cocktail party passes in the District without a new anecdote about the secretary's dozing off in some important conference, of his inability to work more than a few hours a day, of his valiant but losing struggle to keep abreast of the demands of war in 1941.

Stimson's "lust for combat briefly stirred him to thoughts of a libel suit." Instead of suing, Stimson sought out Grenville Clark, who, in a letter, subsequently told of the request and the reaction:

> You may have forgotten it, but you once asked me (I think in the summer of '42) to give you a tip if I ever thought you were weakening at all and that it was time to get out. I took that perfectly seriously and thought about it at various times, but I never saw any occasion to take you at your word. Quite on the contrary, it seemed to me that you were going strong and that no one else could have done as well.

Clark, in fact, protested too much. Exemplifying the phenomenon of transference, his constant surveillance and the radiating ebullience of his own spirit did vastly sustain the septuagenarian Secretary, but at the price of Clark's own reserves, as the latter wrote Frankfurter in early 1942:

I was intending to be back in Washington two weeks or more ago but was held up and now shan't be there for a while. The reason is that I had a periodical physical checkup lately, and the doctor was very definite and severe that I must "lay off" entirely for a while —too much blood pressure and some aftermath from the flus and bronchitis I had last autumn, which was apparently more severe than I knew at the time.

Clark concluded with Calvinist resignation that "there was nothing to do but conform and possess my soul in patience, so as to avoid being knocked out for a long time."

Manpower

Enforced retirement was a big disappointment, but a larger one was in store. He concluded his letter to Frankfurter: "Recently I have been chiefly interested in trying to get a really comprehensive plan put in effect for the mobilization of manpower, since, if this is not done, I think our whole effort is likely to fail."

Actually, Clark had been working on a comprehensive manpower blueprint for some time, and, in view of the officer problem precedent, he was not sanguine as to results. For, as he had written Frankfurter exactly four months before Pearl Harbor: "Last winter, our Memorandum . . . went to the White House and was turned over to one of the administrative assistants who sent it on to the War Department with a memorandum about like this: 'This is such a clear, logical, and effective plan that I am sure it will be unanimously disapproved by the General Staff.' "

As has been well noted, manpower was the last of the shortages to emerge in the political economy of wartime America, but Clark's piercing foresight went beyond the bonanza of humankind, both employed and unemployed, which seemingly constituted an inexhaustible resource, and almost as soon as he had settled in at the War Department, he made universal, compulsory national service legislation a special priority. Stimson's official biographer noted that "national service legislation was urged by such men as Grenville Clark."

The Washington milieu provided the strongest incentive for action. Alone of the major nations in arms, the United States had no legislation providing overall structural direction for the mobilization of labor in total war, and the Roosevelt administration drifted with an unsatisfactory status quo, with commission following commission and manpower czar following manpower czar. The War Department, the Selective Service, and the War Manpower Commission pulled and tugged, resembling nothing quite so much as a Siberian *troika* powered by three untrained and fractious horses. Clark swung into action, organizing a Citizens Committee for a National War Service Act.

Possibly as a result of a surreptitious communication from Clark or, more probably, as a consequence of the sheer intolerability of the situation, Franklin Roosevelt included a recommendation for national service legislation in his annual message to Congress in January 1944.

Warren Austin in the Senate and James Wadsworth in the House promptly introduced enabling legislation, which Clark enthusiastically supported with congressional testimony and the formation of a grass-roots citizens committee. The initial bill never got out of the committee, and a second effort was beaten down on the Senate floor. Undeterred, Clark pressed the matter in his New Year's letter to FDR: "I'm hoping, of course, that your recommendation of a year ago will be renewed. It's not too late, I believe, to shorten the war and save lives." But again, nothing happened, and Henry Stimson lamented that the voice of the American conscience was not heard.

Needless to say, Clark was also bitterly disappointed by the repetition of the earlier failure in officer procurement, as he wrote to Frankfurter on September 29, 1944:

It's a real tragedy, I think, that we couldn't get National Service. I believe the German war has been prolonged somewhat by the lack of it and the Japanese war by at least a year—very likely much more. For with the National Service we could have mobilized on a much greater scale and faster, so that it would not have been necessary to permit the Japanese to make still further inroads in China this year. It was not hard to see *two* years ago that this would occur unless we mustered enough strength—ships and planes especially—to make a push through China by now as well as conduct the war in Europe. But an effort in that sense was impossible without legal power under a national service law to shift workers and mitigate strikes, absenteeism and turnover. So the inevitable result is coming to pass. However, it seems the milk has been spilt and it's now too late to remedy it. We'll just have to reconcile ourselves to a longer war and greater loss of life than there needed to be. At least that's my present view and consequently I'm proposing to wind up our Citizens Committee for National Service Act this November. If you have any different ideas please tell me.

But there was more to the letter than lamentation, even though national service meant much to Clark (interestingly, he had used it to describe his war service on a Harvard questionnaire: "Secretary-Treasurer of the Citizens Committee for a National War Service Act . . ."). The Citizens Committee was probably the biggest failure of all national efforts Clark attempted to organize, but defeat only spurred Clark to new efforts: "For the past 4 months I've worked away at my ideas on world organization (you may or may not remember that in the autumn of 1939 I wrote at the Harvard Law School quite an ambitious pamphlet with a proposed Constitution for a Federation of Peoples—so with my efforts for National Service having come to a standstill last June I want to turn back to the other)."

There was a perverse consolation. While war service legislation was of immediate tactical importance, its permanent necessity was zero. For, as Clark doubtlessly knew from his association with the development of the atomic bomb, World War III would involve neither winners nor losers, nor allow any time whatever for a belligerent to mobilize.

Forestalling Apocalypse: World Peace Through World Law

Go home and try to figure out a way to stop the next war . . .

—Henry Stimson to Grenville Clark, June 1944

The Great Commission

Clark had written Frankfurter in September 1944 about his work on world government from Dublin, New Hampshire, where he had been since June, well before D-Day. His pre-victory discharge had been both honorable and authorized. As he later told the story, with typical laconic modesty: ". . . I became cognizant of the A-bomb, the development of which was Mr. Stimson's responsibility, and when it seemed that it would succeed as a weapon that would end the war within a year or so after the June 1944 successful landing in Normandy, I ceased this relation as Stimson's confidential consultant in June 1944 and with Mr. Stimson's consent, in order to devote myself to efforts to prevent future wars, the appalling results of which on the assumption of nuclear weapons were already apparent in 1944. Therefore I ceased my residence and frequent visits to Washington in June 1944 and wrote my first article on the subject of peace—'A New World Order—The American Lawyer's Role'—in the *Indiana Law Journal* in July 1944."

Clark went home a year too soon. His June 1944 departure caused him to miss the meeting on June 18, 1945, when the top policy advisers gathered in the White House conference room to resolve how the new atomic bomb should be used to bring the Japanese war to a close.

The Assistant Secretary of War, New York lawyer John J. McCloy, noting that Japan had scarcely a warship still undamaged or unsunk or a major city unscathed by the dreaded fire bombing, strongly urged working toward full Japanese surrender without using the awful weapon. McCloy favored an ultimatum disclosing American knowledge of the key to the bomb's manufacture and delivery, along with the threatened use of it if surrender were not immediately forthcoming. The proposal met the opposition of Assistant to the President James F. Byrnes and a liberal bloc, wishing to try to execute Emperor Hirohito as a war criminal. In the cut and slash of oral argument, the opposition carried the day and forced a consensus against forewarning about the bomb or leaving the emperor unharmed.

Although President Truman had indicated a disposition to attain surrender without employment of the bomb, the emergence of opposition to the idea caused him, in the end, to authorize its use. Typically, he accepted full responsibility.

It has always been McCloy's contention that President Truman sincerely sought a basis for ending the war without the bomb. Having been impressed with Clark's tenacity and drive during their joint War Department service, McCloy later mused: "The result might have been very different if I had had Grennie Clark alongside me to persuade the decision-makers."

Surely, apprehension about the potential of the new weapon had caused Henry Stimson to give Clark a new commission a year earlier with special bluntness: "Go home and try to figure out a way to stop the next war and all future wars."

When Stimson said "home," Clark had not understood him to mean Long Island. Clark's acculturation to his true roots came almost by serendipity. During the heavy war years, he had acquired the habit of stealing away to the rambling frame-and-brick farmhouse at Dublin, New Hampshire, which had belonged

Grenville Clark about 1940

ABOVE: *LeGrand Bouton Cannon, Grenville Clark's maternal grandfather*

LEFT: *Louis Crawford Clark, Grenville Clark's father (c. 1917)*

Grenville Clark about 1885

Grenville Clark (front center) and classmates at Pomfret School, Pomfret Center, Connecticut, 1895

Porcellian Club, Harvard College, about 1900 (Clark is in top row, right)

*Fanny and Grenville Clark
on their wedding trip to
California, August 1909*

Fanny Pickman Dwight, 1888

*Grenville Clark during
World War I*

ABOVE: *Mary Dwight, Eleanor Dwight and Grenville Clark, Jr., 1921*

LEFT: *Grenville with Eleanor Dwight Clark, c. 1915*

Root, Clark, Buckner and Howland office dinner at the University Club, New York, January 24, 1921. Seated, clockwise from lower left: Reed B. Dawson, Emory R. Buckner, George A. Steves, Maxwell Steinhardt, William P. Palmer, Alexander B. Royce, Mortimer Boyle, Vanderbilt Webb, Cloyd Laporte, Bernhard Knollenberg, Radcliffe Swinnerton, George E. Cleary, Loyal Leale, Hamilton Rogers, Clinton Combes, Alfred C. Intemann, Silas W. Howland, Senator Root, Elihu Root, Jr., Willard Bartlett, Arthur A. Ballantine, Grenville Clark, Clarence M. Tappen. Standing, left to right: Henry Jacques, Jerome Franks, Ashton Parker, Ralph Catteral, Leo Gottlieb, Ellis W. Leavenworth, Robert P. Patterson

Clark house in Albertson, Long Island, 1920s

President Franklin Delano Roosevelt and Grenville Clark at Harvard Tercentenary celebration, September 19, 1936

President and Fellows of Harvard College, 1943: Henry L. Shattuck, Grenville Clark, Henry James, President Conant, Jerome D. Greene, Charles A. Coolidge, Dr. Roger I. Lee, and Treasurer William H. Claflin

Recipients of honorary degrees from Dartmouth College, June, 1953. Back row: Dudley W. Orr, Beardsley Ruml, Sherman Adams, Grenville Clark, Governor Hugh Gregg of New Hampshire, Charles J. Zimmerman, Lloyd D. Brace, and Thomas B. Curtis. Front row: John R. McLane, Ernest M. Hopkins, John J. McCloy, President Dwight D. Eisenhower, President John S. Dickey, Lester B. Pearson, Joseph M. Proskauer, Harvey P. Hood, and Sigurd S. Larmon

Grenville Clark with Chief Justice Earl Warren and Justice Felix Frank-furter at Harvard Law School, September 22, 1955

Grenville Clark with members of Dartmouth's A Better Chance program, August 5, 1964

Grenville and Fanny Clark, Easter, 1959

Clark with John S. Dickey, his duck-hunting companion, in Vermont, November 1964

Grenville Clark, November 1963

to his wife's family for a century and a half. The house was to be his retirement haven. It lay in the shadow of Mount Monadnock, and like Clark himself, it was vintage New England.

Irving Dilliard has vividly recorded a visit to Clark's "Walden Pond" and the man who dominated it:

If you are driving from Boston, you come first to Peterborough where the McDowells started their colony for musicians, artists, and writers deep in the New Hampshire hills . . . Since you phoned ahead and are almost due at Outlet Farm, you will follow right along west through Dublin, one of the highest towns in New England, where a library was begun in 1793, where gold was discovered in 1875 and where Theodore Parker, Lord Bryce, Albert Bushnell Hart, and American Winston Churchill enjoyed many a summer holiday. Going out of Dublin toward Marlboro, you will want to watch for the turnoff because it drops down suddenly to the left into the trees. This narrow road winds a bit through the timber and then you are on the shore of Dublin Lake with the worn crown of Monadnock three miles due south.

A tall, rugged man bearing a long walking stick stands at the edge of the road to make certain that you are alert to the next and last turn . . .

Dilliard's journalist's pen also touched on the sheer beauty of the place—the scented summer evenings, the first green of spring with early bluebirds overhead, the October reflection of the emerald lake capturing a border of yellow, scarlet, and burgundy. Unquestionably, the stark contrast between Dublin verdancy and the reports Clark had seen of the horror of nuclear devastation must have spurred a continuing compulsion to forestall the ultimate Armageddon.

There was also something of an Antaean effort, for Clark was in large measure touching his mother earth. Quite apart from the long tenure of the Dublin farm in his wife's family were his own New England—or, more specifically, Connecticut Valley—roots. The progenitor of the Clark clan had first settled there; a strong, reinforcing strain came from his Crawford grandmother out of Putney, Vermont; and his boyhood had been profoundly shaped by the summers at Overlake, LeGrand Cannon's baronial Vermont estate.

The move north had yet another consequence, bringing Clark into the orbit of nearby Dartmouth College, for which he developed an expansive sunset affection and whose honorary doctoral alumnus he would become in 1953.

Just as the liberation of a domesticated animal may cause it to revert to ancestral type, the New Hampshire transplantation worked a mutation in Grenville Clark, turning the urbane New York lawyer into the classic Yankee Brahmin. Not that Clark became any the less the grand seigneur, but visitors commented on a subtle physical transformation which could have made him the square-jawed model for Saint-Gaudens' classic statue "The Puritan." Clark did possess the unique Calvinist amalgam of sensed predestination and humility, rectitude without righteousness, urgency, diligence, and transcendental concern. Indeed, at an age when most men were winding up their lives and careers, Clark had gone north to home to begin what he saw as the most urgent task of his life—saving the world from itself.

1940 Pamphlet: A Proposal for a Federation of Free Peoples

It could be fairly said that Clark was well at work at the *chef d'oeuvre* of his life long before he left the War Department pursuant to Henry Stimson's commission to go home and "stop the next war." The gathering war clouds of late 1939 had found him at the Harvard Law School engrossed in exploring the proposal which would dominate his sunset years.

The result had been a pamphlet, privately printed the next year, entitled *A Proposal for a Federation of Free Peoples* or, to give its full, long-handled, seventeenth-century-style title, *A Memorandum of New Effort to Organize Peace Containing a Proposal for* a *"Federation of Free Peoples."* The specifics still had to be worked out, but Clark, with James Conant's encouragement, had already enunciated the core concept underlying the word "new" in his title. This was a massive repudiation of the principle of sovereign parity, whereby every separate country was absolutely supreme within its territory and absolutely without constraint or account-ability unless it came under a victor's power by losing a war. The principle was the cornerstone of traditional international law, and had been the fault line that had split the League of Nations. Necessarily, by its logic, each country was the juridical equal of all others. It was—quite literally—a rule of international anarchy, and Clark's orderly, logical mind saw with a flash of insight that its perpetuation was utterly inconsistent with the continuity of peace and order in the atomic age.

Answering the Dumbarton Oaks Proposals

Clark must have watched with alarmed apprehension as the course of events through World War II suggested a repetition of the errors of the past. Then the victorious anti-Nazi powers issued their perceived vision of the postwar world, in the Moscow Declaration of 1943 and at the Dumbarton Oaks meeting of 1944. The Allies agreed that some international organization dedicated to collective security and peacekeeping was absolutely essential. But both declarations proclaimed what Clark saw as the impossible—achieving this objective while maintaining the principle of sovereign equality. From his New England sanctuary, Clark worked out his revisionist principles.

As an experienced, practicing lawyer, he leaned toward technique rather than philosophy, and, moreover, his successful opposition to Roosevelt's Court-packing plan had taught him the disproportionate power of the American Bar in American politics. Seeing the hitch in international affairs as something of a domestic constitutional crisis, not unlike the malaise of the 1780s, he made his appeal to his fellow lawyers: "It should require no argument that we of the legal profession have a vital and perhaps decisive part to play in shaping the new world order which is to come out of this war."

Clark wrote as lawyer to lawyer, his plea being published in the *Indiana Law Journal*. The *Journal* was probably chosen for its roots in America's isolationist heartland, and the author was identified only as a member of the firm of Root, Clark, Buckner & Ballantine. In the article, Clark took his first decisive step toward the modification of sovereignty and correspondingly attacked the structure of the future United Nations proposed at Dumbarton Oaks. In Clark's view, shaped in the crucible of war, it was patently absurd that Panama and Luxembourg should be coequals juridically and (within an international structure) organizationally with the United States, the Soviet Union, and China. The obvious solution and bridge to reality was a concrete formula for voting power based on population.

To be sure, there were other flaws as well. The lack of provision in the proposals for both executive and judiciary branches was scandalous to Clark's analytic lawyer's mind, but he did not have much time to ponder that. The Dumbarton Oaks proposals were announced on October 9, and if a response was to have any effect, prompt action was imperative. There was another factor, too: Clark was approaching his sixty-third birthday, and while he was in fair enough health, age would sooner or later take its toll. Surely the time had come for retreat and withdrawal, leaving to younger men the task of saving the world from itself.

Any such impulse was laid to rest as a consequence of a chance meeting with Justice Frankfurter the day following the Dumbarton Oaks announcements. Clark wrote of that meeting almost two years later:

Speaking of quotations, I forgot whether I have taken up seriously with you the origin and precise language of the quotation from Henry Cabot Lodge . . . which you read to me at the Carleton Hotel

[sic] on or about October 10, 1944. If I recall, what you read me with considerable dramatic effect was "Not failure, but low aim is the crime."

The quotation had its predictable effect. However Clark might dislike failure, low aim or a short putt were even more detestable. So, aiming high, he dispatched a powerful and persuasive letter to *The New York Times,* which was published on October 15. Given the time constraints, he must have written at white heat, but the product was nonetheless vintage Clark—lucid, logical, coherent, and devoid of intellectual and stylistic pretense.

Much as if he were arguing an appeal before the Supreme Court of the United States, he seized the high ground at the outset with a double-barreled presentation of issues:

Do the Dumbarton Oaks proposals offer reasonable assurance for the realization of the basic purpose—the maintenance of "international peace and security"? Or are they so deficient in principle and detail that they offer no such assurance, and should, consequently, be radically modified?

Again, the complete lawyer, Clark answered his own question:

With regret, I am constrained to the latter view. It is then my firm conviction that these proposals repeat the essential errors of the League of Nations, which so signally failed in its prime purpose; that the proposals are demonstrably ineffective to the end in view, and that drastic changes are imperative if we are to avoid failure and disillusionment.

The issues and conclusion stated, Clark proceeded to make his case. He first analyzed the three main organs of the proposed United Nations—a General Assembly, with one vote per member country; a Security Council of eleven—five permanent superpower members, and six temporary ones chosen by the Assembly;

and an International Court of Justice. Confining himself to the first two components, Clark hit hard at their deficiencies:

> It requires no argument that with the role of one vote for each country the proposed Assembly must necessarily be a subordinate organ. It would indeed be contrary to all reason and common sense to confer important powers in vital matters upon a body in which Panama and Luxembourg have an equal vote with the United States and the Soviet Union, and in which Costa Rica and Ethiopia have an equal voice with the United Kingdom, China, and France.

Clark noted that it was precisely due to this obvious fact that the Dumbarton Oaks proposals carefully excluded the Assembly from any direct participation in effecting measures to prevent or put down aggression; that is, the main body was excluded from the basic function of the new organization and confined to electing the temporary members of the Security Council.

Clark ridiculed this restricted role, duly noting the anomaly that the principle of sovereign equality necessarily led to functional inequality, whereby the Assembly was "subordinate to a super-directorate of the Great Powers." Clark also attacked the "unanimity, that is the veto provision, accorded the permanent members of the Council," foreseeing with prophetic clarity that "this arrangement, incredible as it may seem, is that anyone of the Big Five may, by its sole fiat, paralyze the whole world organization."

Clark next noted that the key to the strength of the proposed General Assembly could be found in its method of representation. He restated the proposal he had made in his *Indiana Law Journal* article of the previous June: apportion Assembly representation by population. His concrete formula proposed that the United States (population 138,000,000), the British Commonwealth and Empire (population 567,000,000), the Soviet Union (population 183,000,000), and China (population 457,000,000) would each have fifty votes. France and her empire (population 110,000,000) would have twenty. The other members of the United Nations would have one vote for each 2 million of population, up to 14 million, and one vote for each 5 million thereafter.

It was not quite one-man-one-vote, but it did sum up Clark's almost lifelong recognition of human worth as the fundamental organizational unit for future planetary structural arrangements.

But Clark was still realist enough to know that power counted as much as population, and he shrewdly offered his gambit to the holders of power:

> Under this formula, the 326 representatives of the Big Five would indeed have the controlling vote, as they should. . . . There would, however, be the vital difference that all the countries of the world desirous of sharing in the organization of peace could do so on a basis of full participation, and would take their part as a matter of right in approximate proportion to their population and resources.

Conceding that his formula was not perfect and was capable of improvement, Clark turned next to the other and more essential defect of Dumbarton Oaks:

> The underlying defect of the Dumbarton Oaks proposals, as was also true of the League of Nations, is not in their failure to grant ample nominal powers. It is rather that no machinery is proposed whereby the nominal powers can be exercised with any certainty in a time of crisis. The concentration of authority in a World Assembly, operating by majority vote, would provide the means for certain and prompt action. There would, it is true, be a Council. But it functions under delegated powers from the Assembly and purely as its agent.

Clark wound up with a seven-point agenda for further action:

1. Treat the Dumbarton Oaks proposals purely as tentative;
2. Give the forthcoming conferences (to be held in San Francisco in early 1945) a free hand in structuring the new collective security organization;

3. Allow sufficient time to pass before convening the forth-coming conference and allow it sufficient time for its deliberations;

4. Make the conference truly international via participation of the United States and neutrals. (Interestingly, Clark had earlier implied the eventual participation of Germany and Japan in the new organization, at some appropriate but unspecified date);

5. Do not hold the conference in Washington, "a city whose atmosphere is not conducive to a meeting which should be held at a site wholly free from political intrigue." (Clark suggested Philadelphia, because of its association with the American Constitutional Convention of 1787, and proposed that Washington's words there be inscribed as an aspiration of the conference's work: "Let us raise a standard to which the wise and honest can repair; the rest is in the hands of God");

6. Abrogate the U.S. constitutional provision whereby international engagements might be vetoed by one vote more than one-third of the Senate, "an anachronism . . . unfair to ourselves but capable of vast damage to the whole world."

Lawyer to the last, Clark designed his seventh point as a classical summation to court and jury, and he reverted to the 1787 analogy:

Finally, I emphasize that we need above all imagination and a creative spirit, capable of a great leap forward in the organization of a world now truly made one by modern invention. The founders of 1787 not only had the vision of this nation but also the practical skill to find the formulae that made it possible. If we cannot fully equal their mature political wisdom, we can at least try to rival their capacity for original and adventurous thought.

Perhaps in consequence of Clark's long friendship with Julius Ochs Adler, the *Times* gave the letter top billing and a special accolade to Clark: "The writer of the following letter is a New York lawyer of international proportions. He was the leader of movements that resulted in the presentation of the Burke-Wadsworth bill and the enactment of the Selective Service Act and was an organizer of the first Plattsburg Training Camp."

Felix Frankfurter was almost equally complimentary, perhaps more so: "the whole of it seemed to me important as a contribution towards the full discussion of these problems which you can say without using big words will affect the destiny of the world."

But ever the schoolmaster, obsessed with exactitude ("I feel about accuracy the way Queen Victoria felt about chastity"), the Justice could not forbear a correction:

> Next time you quote—and for my purpose you cannot too often quote them—those wonderful words of Washington at the Philadelphia Convention, I hope you will quote them in the most authoratative form. I should suppose that Max Farand is the most authoratative source and in his "The Framing of the Constitution," he quotes them as follows: "Let us raise a standard to which the wise and *the* honest can repair. The event is in the hand of God." p. 66.

However, here Homer nodded and poor Frankfurter was hoist on his own didactic petard. Clark, after explaining at length how reliance on a law student had led him to misquote Farand, closed with a Parthian shot: "By the way, whence comes the spelling of 'authoratative' twice used in your letter? I want to be sure to keep up with the times on such things."

Even though taken *in flagrante,* like a temperance crusader in an alehouse, Frankfurter was equally good-natured in his response:

1. "Authoratative" is not authoritative, of course. In your desire to keep up with the times please do not keep up with its errors.

The San Francisco Charter

The times, however, seemed to be more than keeping up with their own errors. The San Francisco Conference came and went in early 1945, launching the new United Nations largely along the lines envisioned at Dumbarton Oaks, but Clark went along in the hope that a built-in provision for charter re-examination and possible revision would bring the organization around. Clark's warnings of the previous autumn seemed to be love's labor's lost. He expressed his fears in a letter to the new President, Harry Truman, protesting, subtly enough, the administration's "containment" policy: strongly resisting the Soviet creation of a buffer zone of puppet Communist states between itself and a possibly resurgent Germany. The measure of his alarm could be seen in his willingness to understand how "Finland, Poland, Czechoslovakia, Rumania, Bulgaria, Hungary, Yugoslavia, and perhaps even Austria" would be consigned to Stalinist totalitarianism. Clark implied that such might be the sheer consequence of events:

> But what seems to be little understood is that these protective arrangements by Russia are the logical and necessary consequence of her experience and apprehensions, in the absence of any *commitment* by the United States to aid in preventing or suppressing still a third German aggression.

It was not that Clark had the slightest sympathy for expansionist Stalinism. Instead it was that Clark (the complete lawyer and founder of a firm in which it was a commonplace that an advocate was unfit to try a client's case unless he knew enough about the controversy to present that of the adversary) felt strongly that "hard as it may be, we must try to put ourselves in the Russians' place."

The fault, Clark insisted, was not in Russian intransigence or malevolent fate but simply in institutional arrangements which had been constructed with American acquiescence.

> ... as you know, the San Francisco Charter will carry no *agreement* on our part (or on the part of any of the Big Five) to apply sanctions no matter how clear or formidable the aggression ...
>
> It is a pity, I believe, that a more effective international organization could not have been formed ...

He then played the trump card of what became his idée fixe:

> Sometimes, if we are really to have world order, we (and others) will have to modify our ideas about "sovereignty" and make up our minds to relinquish the unilateral veto as to joining in cooperative action to maintain peace. We will have to consent to be bound by the majority vote in this respect of a World Assembly in which we have a fair and full representation. But, although I hope that day is not far off, it is evident that we must wait for it a while because we (and other peoples) are not yet sufficiently mature to release ourselves from the old shibboleths of "sovereignty."

From the nostalgic note, it was evident that Clark saw the current state of the world as drifting between rationality and catastrophe, and, almost in desperation, he proposed a multilateral defense treaty as a device to correct San Francisco's errors. Already the Russian putsch in Poland had triggered the Cold War and set in motion the beginnings of a new arms race, whose ultimate consequence could be the nuclear catastrophe of which Stimson had warned Clark but a year earlier. Hence, Clark closed with a reference to the man who had given him the great commission: "On this subject, I suppose that Secretary Stimson is being consulted. With his immense experience, there is certainly no one in the whole country better equipped to give wise counsel on this great question."

But what to do? The precedents of the Court battle, 1940 selective service, and Plattsburg necessarily suggested themselves to Clark. And, quite possibly, Felix Frankfurter supplied an item in the mosaic. In the letter explaining his "authoratative" gaffe, Frankfurter had added a third numbered paragraph concerning Clark's October 15, 1944, letter to *The New York Times* on the imperatives of any international peacekeeping structure:

> 3. I know Justice Roberts would not mind my telling you with what appreciation he read your N.Y. Times letter . . .

Like Clark, Roberts was a liberal conservative. A fearless prosecutor of Teapot Dome corruption, he had left the Supreme Court in dismay over its petty internal chicanery. His judicial record was impressive, for Roberts had the sure craftman's touch in navigating the tough and technical mazes of bankruptcy. His major civil liberty opinions could have been written by Clark himself. Typical were *Herndon* v. *Lowry*, 301 U.S. (1937), freeing a black Communist from a virtual death sentence under a vague "insurrection" statute, and *Schneider* v. *State*, 308 U.S. 147 (1939), protecting the right of Jehovah's Witnesses to solicit funds, which, with others, had been duly noted in Clark's *Bill of Rights Review*. Closest to Clark's heart, however, must have been Roberts' majority opinion in *Hague* v. *Committee for Industrial Organizations*, 307 U.S. 496 (1939), which virtually restated Clark's ABA brief on behalf of the union.

Roberts' "swing" behavior had often provided the one-vote majority by which certain New Deal legislation was invalidated, and thereby had incurred the acid criticism of Felix Frankfurter. However, Frankfurter later recanted, penitently asserting that no judge had ever served on the Supreme Court with greater moral sensitivity to the office than Roberts. President Roosevelt in effect validated that judgment when he named Roberts to head a postwar commission of inquiry into the debacle of Pearl Harbor.

So Roberts, without endeavoring to do so, had clearly made

himself Clark's man by virtue of his own intellectual and moral prominence. Also, Roberts had already gravitated toward an interest in that portion of the world government movement which paralleled, both existentially and analytically, Clark's interest in the subject.

Historically, the world government movement had several roots. There remained a pathetic remnant of Wilsonians, still dedicated to a League of Nations. Roberts had intuitive ties with another. This was Clarence Streit's Federal Union, Inc., persuasively argued in his immensely popular book, *Union Now,* which had been launched in 1939 and which proposed building on the American experience by forming a federal union of the North Atlantic democracies in which the member states would largely retain internal sovereignty and autonomy. A mélange of other groups completed the spectrum, including Walter Lippmann's followers, concerned with bloc rather than collective security and endorsing the balance-of-power concept. Also extant was a component of extremists who advocated immediate abolition of national boundaries and the institution of a homogenized world state. But the huge force of American public opinion was uncommitted.

Clark saw two problems. The first was to catalyze public opinion, which, thanks to wartime experience, had been tilting toward collective security; the second was to establish the dominance of his own solution within the forces of reform. On the second front, the solution necessitated grappling with—and breaking—an ally, for the Streit solution, while commanding a superficial allegiance, seemed to incorporate a basic racial and class bias and thereby to hold the seeds of World War III.

Dublin One

Setting the stage for a showdown, Clark acted with characteristic anonymity and decision. The triggering event was to be a conference on his home turf in Dublin, New Hampshire. The meeting, the first of its kind on that spot, was to bear the name of his telephone number, Dublin One. The meeting was given a special thrust and impetus by the first use of an atomic weapon, which closed the war against Japan and signaled the arrival of a new order.

The lessons of Plattsburg showed in the careful selection of the fifty participants. Clark did not get quite the stars he wanted, with Reinhold Niebuhr, Henry Stimson, and Cordell Hull declining invitations. Nonetheless, the list of accepters was impressive. Each held some special credential as a molder of opinion. Issuing the invitations along with Clark as sponsors were Justice Owen Roberts; the former governor of New Hampshire, Robert P. Bass; and Thomas H. Mahoney, Boston lawyer and chairman of the Massachusetts Committee for World Federation. Responding were men of the caliber of Thomas K. Finletter, future Secretary of the Air Force; atomic physicist Robert D. Smythe; Senator Styles Bridges; and newsman Edgar Ansel Mowrer. Clark's eye for potential was proven by the presence of young Kingman Brewster and equally young Norman Cousins.

Formally, Justice Owen Roberts presided, despite his ideological predilection toward the Streit camp. Functionally, it was future U.S. senator Alan Cranston who was "chairman of the Dublin Conference Committee." ("It became clear," Cranston later wrote, "that my principal responsibilities were to help execute Clark's strategies.")

On October 11, 1945, two months and six days after the bomb fell on Hiroshima, the conference opened, with Clark serving as secretary. He also took the job of keynoter, a job too important to be delegated. Norman Cousins has left a reminiscence of "the unforgettable experience" of Clark's remarks:

> ... He was looking ahead twenty years or more. He said he thought it unreasonable to assume that the wartime alliance between the United States and the Soviet Union could hold up under the pressure

of events. He forecast a struggle for the balance of power under conditions of uncertainty and insecurity for both countries. He saw the emergence of a world atomic armaments race. Despite published assurances to the contrary by U.S. government spokesmen, he anticipated the development within a few years of nuclear weapons by the Russians and by other countries within a generation. He said it would be difficult to keep the atomic holocaust from leading to a world holocaust unless strong measures were taken to create a world authority with law-enacting and law-enforcing powers.

He believed the moment in history had come for creating the instruments of workable law. He spoke of the need for a world government which would have "limited but adequate" powers . . . In short, he proposed world law as the only alternative to existing world anarchy.

The lofty peroration of the keynote almost necessarily set the stage for the conference's next major step, which was breaking the back of the opposition. Clark felt that on the critical pressure point of residual sovereignty there could be no compromise whatever, and, by logical inference, there could be none on the universality of allegiance to the new world government. Already he had moved well beyond his 1939 proposal for a federation of *free* peoples and had reached the bedrock proposition that the federation had to comprehend *all* peoples, free and otherwise: "We cannot start with just a small group of nations discriminating against the rest of the world." (Interestingly, Clark's grandfather had thought otherwise, ascribing the Civil War to the Founding Fathers' "effort to establish a system of government under two widely different forms of civilization . . ." Hence, the keynote speech of Dublin One marked a critical stage in Clark's intellectual development, as it pushed him beyond LeGrand Cannon's conventional wisdom and set the stage for still more radical mutations to come.)

Not all was peace and harmony. The participants were to be formed and molded. Stringfellow Barr confessed shock at the speed with which the anti-sovereignty, pro-universality forces took over. Suspecting that this was Clark's work rather than the random sequence of events, Barr says he protested, making "some pretty biting remarks." Barr remembered especially how "Mr. Clark flushed and prepared for battle." Barr also recollected how Clark caught himself and made such a handsome apology that Barr felt thoroughly unjustified in his criticism and thoroughly won over to Clark as a person.

One other episode of Dublin One served to facilitate the final result. During the heat of the debate between the pro-sovereignty and the pro-universalist forces, young Alan Cranston quoted (correctly) the words of Washington at Philadelphia, in mild reproach to those who felt the creation of a more perfect union was an impractical dream: "Let us raise a standard to which the wide and the honest can repair. The event is in the hand of God."

Little wonder that the conference was able to end its work on October 16, 1945, with a note of high consensus. The closing declaration was a virtual restatement of Clark's keynote speech:

> Whatever may have been the efficacy of the United Nations Organization for the maintenance of peace before August 6, 1945, the events of that day tragically revealed the inadequacy of that Organization thereafter to do so . . .
>
> Believing that the mounting waves of distrust and fear that threaten mankind may engulf us in a war which, in this atomic age, would destroy civilization and possibly mankind itself, and being convinced that the United Nations Organization is wholly inadequate to prevent war, a large majority of the conference proposes:
>
> That a World Federal Government be created with closely defined and limited powers adequate to prevent war and strengthen the freedoms that are the inalienable Rights of Man.

There followed eight specific measures which had been passed as resolutions of the conference and which ranged from a cry of alarm "that there is no time to lose" in creating effective war-preventing arrangements to the coda that the American people should urge their own government to promote the formation of a World Federal Government by drastic amendments to the United Nations Charter or by rewriting that document altogether.

The pro-sovereignty forces (perhaps pro-Nordics would be a better word) were not wholly scotched, however. Five participants (including Justice Roberts) declined to sign. Clark had persuaded Roberts not to bolt the conference and, gentleman loser to the end, Roberts offered a dissenting opinion:

> We do not join the statement for these reasons: We agree with the object and, with some reservations, with the structure of the organizations envisaged in the resolution. We think, however, that simultaneously with efforts to attain a world federal government, the United States should explore the possibility of forming a nuclear union with nations where individual liberty exists, as a step toward the projected world government.

Copies of the report went to the President, the Cabinet, and the governors of all the states.

The New York Times duly reprinted the declarations and, in its report of the conference, said of the man who had conceived, assembled, and overseen the whole thing: "Grenville Clark served as Secretary."

Princeton One

The Dublin conferees met again within a short time of their first meeting. Doubtless because of his ongoing sense of urgency, as well as his longtime friendship with Princeton president Harold W. Dodds, Clark summoned the Dublin group to Princeton in January 1946. It was an amplified group; the forty-eight attendees of Dublin had grown to sixty. In a sense, the reconvocation was something of a homecoming, for it was to Princeton and Dodds that Clark had taken his *Federation of Free Peoples,* in late 1939, for extended analysis and review. Now he was back, with extended and radically different ideas. So were the Dublin conferees, but with a distinguished addition. Albert Einstein, in residence at the unaffiliated Princeton Institute for Advanced Studies, attended.

Clark had been presiding at an early session when he received a folded note. Rising, Clark told the asemblage that the great Einstein wished to join the deliberations. There was a certain poetic justice in the request. It was Einstein's work in theoretical physics which had let the atomic genie out of the bottle in the first place. Moreover, it was Einstein's letter of August 1939 to Franklin Roosevelt, pointing out the weaponry potential of the split atom, that literally triggered the American effort to build the atomic bomb.

As confidential assistant to Stimson, Clark must have been implicated in the bomb effort all the way, from shepherding the gargantuan but disguised appropriation through Congress, to riding herd on the production effort, and, finally, to prophesying what terrible holocaust the weapon would produce when it was used. In a significant understatement, he later described himself as having been "cognizant" of the efforts. But, as was Einstein's, Clark's sense of personal involvement was probably deep and abiding.

It was at Princeton that the great scientist made his famous remark to Clark that politics was infinitely more difficult than physics. Felix Frankfurter recalled the incident: "But my dear classmate Grenville Clark . . . a Harvard man known to many of you, recalled the day after Einstein's death, what Einstein said. They had a meeting . . . and someone went up to Einstein and said, 'Dr. Einstein, how is it that the brain of man is able to evolve these wonderful theories and translate them into practice in the world of physics, and yet we stumble along at the razor's edge of the abyss of destruction . . . Why can't the human brain answer these questions of government and politics?' And the profound Einstein in his loveable, childlike way, the childishness of great profundity, said: 'The answer is very simple: politics is so much more difficult then physics.' " (Indeed, Einstein had already proven that point, for surely the nadir of the Einstein writings was the totally forgettable *Why War?*, turned out in 1933 with the collaboration of the equally formidable Sigmund Freud.)

Einstein exhibited much the same nonscientific naïveté at Princeton, where Clark's daughter recollected how the great man successively stood to vote for and then to vote against a proposition, as Clark put the question to the house. She also recalled saving the scientist from falling down a scullery staircase at the Princeton Inn. The scope and character of Einstein's participation were epitomized in a second note which he sent the chair and which Clark read to the assemblage after the Nobel laureate had taken his departure: "I will be happy to vote for any conclusion at which your conference arrives."

Notwithstanding the enormously newsworthy aspect of Einstein's participation, the Princeton Conference made little dent on the media or upon public consciousness generally. Indeed, the set and drift of public opinion seemed but to vindicate the twofold reservation of Princeton's president Dodds to Clark's grandiose vision: first, that fear of nuclear bombs would not suffice to drive nations to accept world government as the principal instrument for attaining national goals, and, second, that a common ideology —that is, an inherited faith in the democratic process, especially of courts and parliaments—was an indispensable cement of union.

Clark's foresight seemed particularly beset by the historical ill fortune which attends any idea whose time has not yet come. Even a flight by Alan Cranston in a wholly private capacity to the London UN meeting was totally unproductive. Things seemed to go from bad to worse as 1946 unfolded.

On February 9, Stalin made a classic restatement of the Soviet fear of capitalist encirclement. Justice William O. Douglas, who had become a world government sympathizer, labeled the speech the opening gun of World War III, and on March 5, Churchill responded in kind with the famous Iron Curtain address at Fulton, Missouri. The pressure of events seemed so disruptive, and the possibilities of success so uncertain, that Clark even disbanded his Dublin committee. Half the trouble was the momentum of events. Almost as bad was the internecine squabbling of the internationalists.

The Baruch Proposal

On June 12, 1946, a new dawn seemed to break in the form of Bernard Baruch's proposal that the United States transfer its nuclear monopoly to an international authority in which all nations would be afforded a means of control and participation. Clark, with an uncharacteristically bravura letter to the *Times,* enthusiastically seconded the proposal. Always the complete lawyer, he put the questions at the outset:

> Will the effort to create a limited world government succeed in time to forestall World War III? Will the recent proposals of the United States for an International Atomic Development Authority, the first great official plan for limited world government, become a reality? These are the great questions of our time. They transcend all other questions, foreign and domestic.

Framing the major premise of his answer, Clark was again every inch the man of law:

> The essence of government is law—law in the sense of rules binding upon individuals and enforceable by sanctions imposed by the law-making authority. The American plan contains these essentials. Thus, when Mr. Baruch calls for a world agreement for "renunciation of the bomb" with "condign punishments set up for violations of the rules of control which are to be stigmatized as international crimes" he is speaking of nothing less than branding world war. In a word he is speaking of limited world government.

Clark went on to point out that the Baruch proposal was not a false dawn:

> We should not be misled by the fact that the field of federal jurisdiction is at the start to be restricted to atomic energy only. It remains true that within that field the plan calls for government in its true sense and with all its implications.

Clark then passed to his dominant concern—reconstituting the General Assembly of the United Nations on the basis of power and population and abolishing the big-power veto in the Security Council. He also seized the nettle which Bernard Baruch had carefully avoided—whether the proposed atomic authority should be subordinate to or independent of the existing United Nations structure. He conceded the inefficiency and confusion that would result from having two world authorities functioning in closely related areas. But he also emphasized that integration of the authority with the United Nations would only spread the latter's paralysis and inefficiency to a new field.

Quoting Holmes, he closed with a jury-impressing flourish. As he noted that, with a few changes, the Baruch plan could be made his own, he cautioned against both overoptimism and despair:

> It would be folly to ignore, however, the formidable obstacles still to be overcome. Cynicism and defeatism still persist. Vestiges of isolationism survive. There remains a chasm of suspicion and mis-understanding between Russia and ourselves, for which we are equally at fault and which must be bridged by mutual forbearance.
>
> There may be some to say that the necessity of world government is so plain that its coming is inevitable. It is probably true that world government is on its way. But the question remains whether it will come soon or only after mankind has been still further chastened by another and yet more frightful war.
>
> It is only a combination of clear political thought and of persistent work that can prevail in time. There was never a better moment

to recall the famous saying of Mr. Justice Holmes, "The mode by which the inevitable happens is effort."

Predictably, Felix Frankfurter applauded the effort but corrected the quotation. Clark good-naturedly replied:

> I noticed your letter dated *Sunday*. It gave me quite a "kick" that you had had your *Times* and been over the editorial page by 10:30. Too late to change; you'll always do it; good habit.
>
> Well, I knew it was 50 to 1 my quotation was wrong. They always are unless you go to the original. But I had it from a source that looked pretty good when I copied it off a few weeks ago (though I can't remember now what it was). However, I had hopes —indeed I was pretty sure—that within a short time I would get an authoritative version. And sure enough, it came along right on schedule, even quicker. Really, this delighted me immensely by indicating that you are running right true to form. Also it puts me in a properly chastened mood, although I expected it.

Clark had every reason to be indulgent. His letter had been an immense success. Senator George placed it in the *Congressional Record,* entreating his colleagues in Congress to read it. Requests for copies poured into Dublin, and Clark made reprints (as he explained to Frankfurter) with two changes: "(1) In the quote to conform to your text; and (2) in a single sentence where a too-smart editor, without consulting me, changed seven words and altered the sense materially." Clark closed with a potpourri of items of family news and verified his New Hampshire transplantation:

> I am staying up here all summer and hope to do some more or less systematic writing. I have brought all my personal papers of 40 years up from New York—three and a half tons—and have a nice little office and am really getting organized.

Organized for what? Already, at sixty-five, his body was at the threshold which the Social Security Act had selected as the point of most people's retirement. More than this, his powerful heart was already sending signals that six and a half decades of strenuous activity had pushed it to the point of exhaustion. Indeed, by 1947, the adverse medical verdict would be in, and complete retirement enjoined.

But "complete" can be a relative rather than an absolute word and admits of a variety of shadings. As Clark noted in his letter to Frankfurter, one activity completely compatible with sedentary New Hampshire seclusion was writing. And one item particularly waiting to be written was his own memoirs. As he himself later said, there were things which he alone knew and which deserved to be noted in the historical record. And to this end, Samuel Spencer, the future president of Davidson College, but then a graduate student in history at Harvard University, was summoned to Outlet Farm to serve as amanuensis and research assistant. Spencer's initiation to the job was a skinny-dipping foray with Clark into the cold waters of Outlet Pond. The episode graphically impressed Spencer that whatever the medical verdict, inactivity was utterly alien to Clark.

Spencer worked with Clark for the next two summers, but the memoirs never got written, and the only visible product of their collaboration was Spencer's doctoral thesis at Harvard, "Cornerstone of Defense: A History of the Selective Training and Service Act of 1940." The opening sentence told the story of the statute and Clark himself: "Actually the Selective Training and Service Act was conceived, written, and pushed through Congress by a determined group of private citizens who had no connection whatsoever with the government."

The failure to complete a self-assigned task was highly unusual, but the inaction emphatically did not mean that Clark's tenacity and drive were falling victim to advancing years or physical disability. Rather it was quite the contrary and exemplified the sense of *ars longa, vita brevis* which would haunt the next two decades of life that were left to him.

14

Harvard Sunset

The fairest things have fleetest ends,
Their scent survives their close:
But the rose's scent is bitterness
To him that loved the rose.

—Francis Thompson, "Daisy"

Power Struggles

Before the war Harvard had largely pre-empted Clark from the practice of law, and after the war it threatened to divert him from his obsession with world peace through world law. There had been a gravitation of power within the Corporation toward a faction of wealthy Boston alumni, which coalesced around the Harvard Treasurer, the only University officer, besides the President, specified in the institutional charter. A cancer-enforced retirement of an incumbent Fellow precipitated a power struggle. Clark had his own candidate for the vacancy, Marylander William Marbury. Marbury was, in Clark's words, an excellent man. He had served as secretary to Clark's National Committee for Independent Courts in the thirties and, during World War II, had worked alongside Clark in Stimson's War Department. Unfortunately, he was not a Bostonian (although the argument might be made that Baltimore was the Boston of the South), and, worse yet, although he was a graduate of the Harvard Law School, his undergraduate training had been received at the University of Virginia rather than at Harvard College. President Conant literally laid down the law to the Overseers:

The question is in fact one between the President and the University together with a majority of the Corporation on one hand and the Treasurer on the other. If this election is not confirmed, it will be apparent to the Treasurer and to the President that a majority of the Overseers think that the Treasurer and not the President ought to run the University.

A historian might have an easier time reconstructing the history of the Texas Railroad Commission or the Soviet Politburo than that of the President and Fellows of Harvard College, if such a task were to be done by records alone. A mandatory fifty-year lag in the release of Harvard records guarantees the effective severance of memory and archive. The severance is ensured by a procedure which records votes but not discussion. Hence, it will probably never be known by what advocacy Grenville Clark put the name of William Marbury through the Corporation itself and thence through the Supervising Board of Overseers.

It was a hard fight on tough terrain. Marbury was up against a candidate of the State Street faction, an eminent and respected member of the Boston financial community. Also, the milieu of the contest was the Cold War, and the tensions of that contest had at last penetrated the staid and paneled boardrooms of Harvard. As President Conant recollected, the issue of academic freedom ranked high on the agenda of the biweekly meetings of the Harvard Fellows. Manifestly, the pro-Soviet predilections (or at least the disposition to insist that there were two sides to the Cold War) of some of the faculty had ruffled some feathers in the ruling mechanism. Marbury's nomination assumed a disproportionate significance, much as that of the horseshoe nail, and both sides bowed their necks accordingly.

Possibly the least appreciated and least conspicuous of Grenville Clark's victories was the one that he won (by telephone?) from Dublin in securing the appointment of William Marbury to the Harvard Corporation over à determined and powerful opposition. Typically, the Overseers' approval was announced in a telegram to Marbury by Judge Robert Patterson, Clark's coadjutor in the fight. Clark, however, did get to savor his victory at a luncheon for Marbury at the Somerset Club.

Academic Freedom—The Ober Letter

Had Clark been serious about retirement and memoir writing in 1947, the momentum of events—particularly in the context of his Harvard connection—ensured that even in New Hampshire seclusion he would continue to participate in affairs of the moment rather than write about those of the past.

One particular affair was the Cold War, the classic Leninist maneuver of subversion and co-option which had already touched Clark's life in many ways. His high hopes for the Baruch plan as a beginning of world government had ended when the plan broke and shattered because of what its opponents saw as Stalinist paranoia, but what Clark perceived as the natural consequence of Soviet political and geographical vulnerability. No specific acts of repudiation had been involved—only the basic antipathy of the two superpowers, as the Soviets invited America to destroy its bombs and share its secrets, while Americans only reiterated their original proposal.

As America in general came to fear anything "Red," Clark's position as a member of the Harvard Corporation brought him into immediate contact with the attraction that radical proposals for social reform held for the intellectuals. The participation of Harlow Shapley, world-famous astronomer, at the overtly Stalinist Cultural and Scientific Conference for World Peace, held at the Waldorf-Astoria in April 1949, seemed at least inappropriate to some patriotic citizens. Equally offensive to some was the presence of John Ciardi, assistant professor of English composition, at a "Progressive Party" rally in Baltimore.

An outraged Maryland alumnus, Frank Ober, who was also something of an anti-Communist and the author of a Maryland anti-subversion statute which bore his name, wrote Harvard president James Conant and asserted his intention not to contribute to the Harvard Law School Fund as long as such a scandalous state of affairs persisted without University action or response. Conant turned to Clark for assistance. "Ordinarily, I do not trouble the members of the Corporation with my fan mail. In this case, however, I was wondering if you would not care to take Mr. Ober on."

Conant had made the perfect choice. He had taken as the theme of his own Harvard presidency the continuation of the Eliot policy of free inquiry, a thesis close to Clark's heart. The rise of Cold War tensions only confirmed Clark in his views, and made him the perfect exponent of them. Also, it would be utterly absurd to suspect a wealthy, patrician establishmentarian of latent Communist sympathy. Clark's own deep-seated sense of social and economic security radiated an almost contagious contempt for the squalid and pathetic Communist ideas of takeover, as well as for the pathetic, petit bourgeois tincture of contemporary anti-Communism.

The commission to respond to Ober afforded Clark not so much a debater's opportunity to score points as the medium of expression of a personal credo which had been building and gathering momentum since the Hague controversy of the late 1930s.

For all its ideological overtones, Clark's response to Ober was still a lawyer's brief, and it followed formally the sequence and style which had become Clark's cachet. First came a summation of the issue, stated precisely the way Clark wanted it seen:

> You first state your intention not to subscribe to the Harvard Law School Fund because of the part taken by Professor John Ciardi . . . and by Professor Harlow Shapley in two recent public meetings. It seems you want them both disciplined. And then you go on with some general observations and recommendations for basic changes in Harvard policy in respect of the "extracurricular" activities of all professors.

With not-quite patient patrician hauteur, Clark described the context of the professorial activities—"Both . . . meetings were on public issues and open to the press. You do not question the complete legality of either meeting. And yet you seem to say that the two professors committed some sort of grave offense . . ." Clark then moved into position to deliver his coup de grace: "On this basis you appear to recommend, although your letter is not absolutely explicative of the point, that these two professors should somehow be disciplined—presumably by dismissal or at least by rebuke." Much as if he were cross-examining a hostile witness, Clark then delivered his coup:

> It is hard to believe that you intend to go to such lengths. But on rereading your letter again and again, one is forced to this conclusion. For you seem directly to identify engaging in such public meetings with "other types of conspiracies looking toward other crimes as part of their extracurricular activities" (I suppose, for example, arson or robbing) and ask: "Why then the distinction because the conspiracy is directed toward the forcible overthrow of our government—in short, sedition or peacetime treason?"
>
> I do not see how you can expect reasonable men to think of participation in open and legal meetings on public subjects as the equivalent of secret plotting to commit crime, merely because Communists or "fellow travellers" take part in such meetings. On this line of reasoning, literally thousands of reputable citizens would have offended. By no possibility could Harvard adopt a view which, to put it mildly, is so extreme. To do so would, I believe, call for conclusions which would be out of place anywhere in our country and are inconceivable at Harvard.

Clark (while he never explicitly broke with the Truman administration on the point) next let it be known what he thought of Executive Order 9835, which had reversed the historic burden of proof and countenanced the discharge of government employees where "reasonable grounds" existed to suspect loyalty:

Concerning your broader proposals for control of the outside activities of all professors, you want all the present agreements for their services so construed and future agreements so drafted that "aiding and abetting sedition or peacetime treason" shall be cause for discipline. Thus you say that in "future contracts, including any required by a raise in salary," there should be "appropriate conditions" on this subject. You also mention that: "reasonable grounds to doubt a professor's loyalty to our government should disqualify him . . ." and "see no reason" why professors should be treated any differently in this regard than government employees . . .

Having characteristically seized the high ground, Clark proceeded to an evisceration of his opponent's case. His first stab was historical. He began by quoting Eliot's 1869 inaugural address (as he would in a telecast years later): "A great university . . . must be rich, but, above all, it must be free." From this point, Clark passed to Eliot's successor, A. Lawrence Lowell, and his defense of faculty freedom of speech in World War I, and cemented his major premise with a quotation from James Conant's tercentenary address of 1936 (to which both he and Franklin D. Roosevelt had listened in the rain): "We must have a spirit of tolerance which allows the expression of all opinions, however heretical they may appear." From this threshold, Clark extrapolated a four-point conclusion: (1) that Harvard, per Oliver Wendell Holmes ('61), believed in the free trade of ideas; (2) that professors had the same rights of self-expression as other citizens; (3) that the limits of self-expression were wide; and (4) that Harvard would accept no gift conditioned upon the compromise of such conditions.

He then passed from history to significance:

The professor's right to speak his mind and to espouse unpopular causes should not be regarded as something separate and apart from the maintenance of civil rights in general. I think what is usually called academic freedom is simply part and parcel of American freedom—merely a segment of the whole front.

I believe, however, that it is an especially vital segment because it concerns the students as much as the professors. If the professors are censored, constrained, or harassed, it affects not only themselves; it also affects them when they teach—the future voters and leaders upon whose integrity and independence of mind will depend the institutions by which we live and breathe a free air. For if the professors have always to conform and avoid unpopular views whether in class or not, what kind of men will they be? And where will our young men and women go to hear and weigh new ideas, to consider both sides and acquire balance and integrity?

Clark next explored the practical implications of the proposal —the thin line between surveying meeting attendance and censoring. "What sort of a place would Harvard be if it went down this road?"

Saving the truly practical note for the last, he closed on the theme of Harvard money and Harvard freedom. Professing ignorance as to whether fidelity to the Eliot tradition would gain or lose money, he restated Eliot's theme that a great university should be rich, but must be free, and then came as close to an *ad hominem* thrust as he ever permitted himself: "I am under no illusion that this letter, or any similar argument, is likely to affect your attitude, at least for some time."

He closed by appealing to the longer view;

I hope, though, that I have convinced you that there is another side, and there is a deep-rooted tradition at Harvard opposed to your view—a tradition that must and will be upheld as long as Harvard remains true to herself.

Clark had had some help on the letter from William Marbury, who had proposed excision of some pejorative nuances, but who nonetheless rendered a detached judgment: "It is a superb piece of work which will undoubtedly be read as long as academic freedom means anything in this country."

Ober and Clark's exchange was duly published in the *Harvard*

Alumni Bulletin, although not with Mr. Ober's enthusiastic consent. He had insisted that his original complaint had not been written for publication and that the broadside disposition of his views and of Clark's formidable reply raised the issue of the confidentiality of alumni-university communications. However, some long-distance telephone advocacy and persuasion from Grenville Clark had wrung Ober's reluctant agreement, but *The New York Times*'s epitaph on the whole affair did indeed suggest the hazards of convincing one against his will. Under "Harvard University," the cryptic headline told the story in half sentences: PRESIDENT CONANT AND G. CLARK REFUSE FUNDS INVOLVING COMPROMISE ON ACADEMIC FREEDOM . . . CLARK DEFENDS RIGHTS OF FACULTY AS CITIZENS.

Felix Frankfurter, however, supplied the real *postscriptum:* " 'I have done the state some service' is something you can say, Grenny—and on more than one occasion. But never more so than your correspondence with Ober." John Ciardi, not Shakespeare's Othello, supplied the poetic epigraph, ". . . Grenville Clark. I never met him in person, but I once had a brief correspondence with him and knew instantly that he was a great man."

The Alger Hiss Case

Vitality and special interest were lent the Ober controversy by the fact that it was played out against the background of another controversy enmeshing Harvard, the establishment, and the worldwide Stalinist conspiracy. This was the Alger Hiss case, which even now admits perceptions which are varied and utterly unreconcilable. One permissible view of the matter is to see it as pure Sophoclean tragedy and monstrous miscarriage of justice. Another accommodates a perception worthy of a scenario by John le Carré, of a conspiracy of incredible dimensions. Grenville Clark never explicitly stated which hypothesis he believed in, but he did indicate a belief by his actions.

Possibly, Clark had been privy to wartime military intelligence which had, before and during World War II, pointed a finger of suspicion at Hiss as a conscious and accomplished instrument of Soviet espionage. One could predict Clark's instinctive rejection of the charge, drawing on two of the strongest elements in his personality. One was the revulsion that his ever-rising liberal impulse, especially when combined with his inherited Anglo-Saxon sense of fair play, would have for unsubstantiated denunciation. This became acute in the summer of 1948, when a shabby *Time* editor, Whittaker Chambers, told the House Un-American Activities Committee that, as a longtime Soviet courier, he knew establishmentarian Alger Hiss as a conscious and dedicated instrument of Soviet espionage. Closely related but distinct would have been Clark's reaction based on class and social allegiance. He would have seen as self-evidently absurd the proposition that the reputation of a graduate of the Harvard Law School, onetime law clerk of Mr. Justice Holmes, and experienced public servant could be demolished by the unverified accusations.

Nevertheless, Clark's broad intelligence caused him to keep his options open, and, given his long-established ties to the Carnegie Corporation, whose legislative charter he himself had drafted, it is quite conceivable that he could have been the discreet agent who, with John Foster Dulles, removed Hiss from the State Department and installed him as the successor of Nicholas Murray Butler as president of the Carnegie Endowment for International Peace.

The subsequent story is a staple of American history—Hiss's denial of Chambers' charge, which put the *cause célèbre* of the decade at issue.

The reverberations of the confrontation continued, as William Marbury flew back from Europe, going to Cambridge after landing in New York. He spent a Sunday in the middle of September 1948 with President Conant. Grenville Clark came for dinner, and after the meal the three sat in the garden and, naturally enough, discussed the Hiss affair. Both Conant and Clark were dismayed by Hiss's failure to file a vindicating lawsuit, and both felt that the failure would be perceived in the court of public opinion as an admission by Hiss that he had lied in denying membership in the Communist Party. Clark, Marbury recollected, was particularly vigorous in urging that such action be undertaken and that Marbury contact Hiss as soon as possible.

On his return to Baltimore, Marbury received a long, handwritten letter from Clark, outlining the legal strategy and tactics he recommended. Since the controversy involved the intricate legal complexities of multi-state media defamation, Clark's virtuoso analysis was especially needed about where suit should be filed, who should be counsel, and the measure and nature of damages. Clark advised on all points, and his dominating personality may well have pushed a reluctant Hiss into filing a defamation suit.

In preparing his defense of the suit, Chambers produced previously secreted photostats of papers which Hiss had allegedly purloined, copied, and transmitted. Subsequent analysis documented the reproduction of State Department material on Hiss's typewriter.

Late in 1948, Hiss was indicted for perjury before the House Un-American Activities Committee, and, exemplifying his own tenacity of purpose and strength of will, Clark moved to the defense. A pair of letters sets out the rest of the story:

Carnegie Endowment for International Peace

March 25, 1949

Dear Mr. Clark:

Richard Field of the Law School has just sent me a list of individuals who have been good enough to make financial contributions through him to help defray my legal expenses. I was very pleased and honored to see your name on the list and I recall that last fall Bill Marbury had told me that you had made inquiry of him as to whether any arrangements were being made for contributions to help me meet my expenses. I should have asked Richard earlier about this matter and suspect that I am very late in thanking you for this evidence of your support. I want to add what I have told others who have helped—that I regard these contributions as personal loans to me, even though without interest and even though I recognize that it will take me some time to repay them in full.

Very sincerely yours,
Alger Hiss

March 31, 1949

Dear Mr. Hiss:

Thanks for your note of March 25 about the very moderate check I sent you for legal expenses.

I appreciate what you say about wanting to treat any such contributions as personal loans and I remember Richard Field said that you had mentioned this to him. However, I told Field when I sent my check that I didn't wish it to be so treated because I had no personal acquaintance with you and wanted to do something solely as a public matter in the belief you were the victim of circumstances and ought to be supported in the public interest in an effort to clear the matter up. I still believe that you have got into this trouble through a combination of unfortunate circumstances and have no personal guilt, and I very much hope that this will be established in the court proceedings.

Sincerely yours,
Grenville Clark

Hiss, who was spared by a divided jury at his first trial, was convicted by a unanimous one at his second. Thanks to his own steadfast silence, his spectacular decline, fall, and degradation have given his case the dimensions of an American Dreyfuss or latter-day Sacco and Vanzetti case.

Perhaps an American Oscar Wilde case would be closer to the truth, for not only did both cases follow the same course—an initial libel suit that eventually brought a criminal prosecution upon the head of the complainant—but both also involved a squalid and bizarre episode where *post hoc* disclosures and explanation would only make matters worse.

Nonetheless, a substantial body of American opinion remained resolute, after the evidence was in, that Hiss was the victim of a miscarriage of justice. However, Clark's volunteering to contribute to Hiss's legal expenses cannot properly be regarded as evidence that Clark was convinced of Hiss's innocence, but only that he believed he was entitled to a fair trial and should not be prejudged. The situation illustrated Clark's instinctive sense of fair play and respect for the rule of law.

Similarly, the possession by Clark of these qualities was illustrated later in connection with the 1952 presidential election. Clark joined a number of prominent lawyers (22 LAWYERS UPHELD STEVENSON ON HISS) to deprecate the attack of vice-presidential candidate Richard Nixon on the action of the 1952 Democratic nominee, Adlai Stevenson, in testifying, via deposition, as to the good reputation and the veracity of Alger Hiss:

> We as lawyers, without regard to our political affiliation or personal preference in the forthcoming Presidential campaign, deplore any effort to criticize or reproach Governor Stevenson for testifying by deposition in the Hiss Case.

The list of signatures seemed like a partial roll call of the Grenville Clark cabal—C. C. Burlingham and "Wild Bill" Donovan were paired, along with John W. Davis and a galaxy of Wall Street lawyers. A scattering of signers came from the hinterlands, including "Grenville Clark of Dublin, N.H."

The Arboretum Controversy

Beneath the eruptions of the Ober and Hiss controversies, the routine of academic life flowed on at Harvard, that process alone guaranteeing to keep Clark's retirement active and the memoirs unwritten. One perennial item on the agenda of the Corporation was the matter of the Arnold Arboretum.

Established in 1872 at Jamaica Plain, the Arboretum was celebrated for its display of trees, shrubs, and flowers. An ambiguous bequest seemingly placed it under the formal governance of Harvard, but the Arboretum had grown into a virtually self-contained unit with grounds, library, and 1,200 "members." There were those who loved it (including Mrs. Grenville Clark, whose girlhood memories included her trips there on Lilac Sunday, a Boston rite, when the grounds were an explosion of color and fragrance). Affection notwithstanding, the gardens' physical separation from Harvard entailed duplication and waste, and a 1944 report, prepared by Professor Irving Bailey, had proposed institutional consolidation with Harvard's existing botanical facilities. Clark was one of the report's opponents during the nine years the plan was under discussion, but from inside the Corporation he had difficulty in making his will felt.

In general, Clark's sunset years on the Harvard Board were ones of frustration. In the spring of 1948 he had written Frankfurter:

> There seems to be all sorts of difficult matters at Harvard this year. I am struggling to find a man of really first-class caliber who is willing to be Treasurer. It isn't too easy and the effort may not succeed but I am putting considerable time at it. As I told you, I shall be getting off the Corporation in not more than 18 months and maybe sooner, depending on how things develop. And I am quite ambitious to do what I can to have an enlightened and strong group of younger men for the four places which will have to be filled in the next two years. As you can imagine, there are difficulties (1) in finding them and getting their assent to serve and (2) in getting them elected. I think we have made a good start with Marbury. Any suggestions gratefully received.

In early 1949, he wrote Conant of his "definite intention to retire in the autumn–winter of 50–51 upon my successor's appointment. You know my reasons are not age or health . . ." Clark resigned from the Corporation in November 1950. The old guard was firmly in the saddle but nonetheless under Conant's control, and the Arboretum matter remained unsettled. Doubtless Clark's commanding personality over the decades of his service had provoked a subtle undercurrent of resentment and opposition among the Corporation Brahmins who were not accustomed to being led, and in all probability, something of the same reaction may have tinctured the enigmatic blandness of James Conant.

Leaving the Corporation freed Clark to fight the Arboretum proposal with new weapons. Corporation approval of the Arboretum removal in January 1953 came over his strong letter of opposition. Subsequently, as chairman of the Finance Committee of the "friends" group, Clark proposed that Harvard cooperate in obtaining a judicial hearing and a legal decision as to whether the University really had the legal power to do what it proposed. His prestige must have sufficed to influence the Overseers' committee to visit the Aboretum and to adopt a supportive resolution. That was the high point of the relationship and the commencement of a sad ending to Clark's distinguished Harvard service, a departure occasioned by both his strong ideas on trustee behavior and Fanny's love for the traditional Arboretum.

After the Overseers' resolution, the dispute regressed in an exchange of letters marked by incivility, bad temper, and recrimination. Clark fired the opening volley on September 18, 1953, by asking Bradford Washburn for permission to publish the pro-litigation resolution which Washburn's committee had unanimously adopted; i.e., "That the Harvard Corporation should cooperate in obtaining a judicial hearing and decision on the legal issues . . ." Even though Washburn had presumably voted for the resolution, he was less than sympathetic to the proposal to print it, and patronizingly responded on September 23 that Clark's "long experience" on the Harvard Corporation should suggest that such proceedings were not made public, especially in inaccurate and incomplete form. He added that any reproduction should be verbatim of a complete record which he offered to supply under commitment to print as received.

Predictably, only four days later, Clark replied that any blan-
ket agreement was completely unacceptable. On October 3,
Washburn renewed his offer, now barbed with the comment that
he did not wish to debate with Clark, and added his surprise that
a professed champion was doing great harm to the Arboretum.
On October 7, Clark responded, using examples from the Dreyfuss case to contemporary Little Rock, insisting that the epithet
of "troublemaker" was an old tactic used to slander those protesting injustice by those persisting in it.

On October 9, poor Washburn, seeking to end the controversy
("any further correspondence between us would be futile . . ."),
added insult to insult by insisting that the Arboretum supporters
were "attacking Harvard." Five days later, he drew his comeup-
pance in Clark's rejoinder that his Arboretum allies were "responsible persons of equal standing with yourself." Clark quoted an
unnamed lawyer friend who said that Harvard's conduct violated
every axiom of trusteeship, and indicated his intention to make
the letters public.

The last two letters put the matter at issue, and the controversy
spilled over into the pages of *The New York Times:* HARVARD
ALUMNI FIGHT PLAN FOR ARBORETUM; WANT IT KEPT ON OLD SITE IN
BOSTON. Former Harvard students got a more detailed picture in
the December 1953 *Harvard Alumni Bulletin,* as both proponents
and opponents of the change stated their cases in contending
parallel columns. Clark's group bore down hard on the "legal
breach of trust . . . breach of moral obligation," while the
University president—now Nathan Marsh Pusey—and Fellows
(all Clark's old associates were ranged against him) could only
respond with the advantages of centralization and consolidation, as
well as long consideration and probatory legal advice. Even Judge
Learned Hand entered the controversy, describing Clark's position
as "frivolous." A countering blast from Clark forced a retreat. "B's
intervention in the Arboretum controversy is one of those things
which would be unbelievable if it were not evident. You certainly
made him eat crow," wrote Frankfurter two years later.

True to their principles, the protestants had previously filed a petition in the Massachusetts Supreme Judicial Court to review a decision by an assistant state attorney general refusing permission for a test suit. Interestingly, Fanny Dwight Clark (doubtless prompted by memories of her Boston girlhood) added her name to the petition as a plaintiff, in a rare display of formal association with one of her husband's causes.

Clark lost when a divided court upheld the Harvard action. It was a bitter pill after almost three decades of service, and his long friendship with Conant—who had asserted that appealing an internal University decision to the law courts was "dirty pool" —was at an end. Nonetheless, Clark bore the adversity with good countenance.

Distressing as it was, the Arboretum episode deserves the foregoing full narration because of the illumination it affords on Clark's character and personality. Superficially, the episode ranks with his major failures—the War Service Act, the Long Island parkways fight, and bringing about an effective world government. Essentially, however, it is all of a piece with the Ober controversy; it also shows how Clark embodied Cardozo's canon of trustee responsibility by his insistence that Harvard exhibit "the punctilio of an honor the most sensitive" in its fiduciary obligations.

That punctilio had already been made evident way back in 1930 with Clark's organization of the Fiduciary Trust Company, where, contrary to the lax Babylonian standards of pre-Crash Wall Street, interlocking directorships were especially proscribed, and all investment decisions undertaken on intrinsic merit rather than on the consequence of intercorporate relations.

Another college president wrote a felicitous epitaph on the sad Harvard controversy. John Dickey of Dartmouth, Clark's frequent duck-blind companion, expressed the hope that the fight had had beneficial ecological consequences:

I can personally bear witness that it contributed to the preservation of the black duck population. There was no other subject, not even that of world peace, that produced quite the pre-occupied concern on Grenny's part that this one did. When we spoke of it neither of us paid much attention to the ducks until at some point he would abruptly rise to his feet, take a shot at a departing duck, and conclude that year's installment of the Arboretum story with the half-chuckled observation: "We haven't been paying much attention to business, have we?"

Dickey was not quite right. Much as the Arboretum controversy shook Clark's equanimity, nothing displaced world peace from the focus of his vision. Indeed, that worry, never far beneath the level of consciousness, may have contributed to his Arboretum reaction. The provocation was real enough, an academic, bureaucratic proposal to obliterate an authentic and organic institution in the interest of tidy organization charts. But far more important was the fate of the earth, rather than a narrow corner of it.

The Harvard Divinity School

Clark did leave another farewell mark upon relinquishing his Harvard service. Irenic rather than hostile, it was of a very different tone from that of the Arboretum controversy, although both episodes may well have sprung from the same root—an internal administrative impulse to regroup and consolidate Harvard's manifold activities. This brought a change of location for the Arboretum, but it also portended extinction of the Divinity School, which President Conant's humanist mind may have perceived as not only an anachronistic vestige of superstition but one impermissibly below Harvard's standard of intellectual excellence. Beset with falling enrollments and declining clerical placements, the moribund institution's demise seemed imminent in early 1946, when a committee was appointed to decide its fate.

In early 1947, the group responded with the recommendation that the school not be abolished or allowed to die but be moved into an ecumenical future with the aid of a six-million-dollar rehabilitation. With a powerful assist from Clark, via both personal contribution and telephone solicitation, the campaign succeeded and the school passed into an invigorated renaissance. "Grenville Clark," recalled onetime divinity dean George Williams, "was the major force behind the drive for the expansion or renaissance of the HDS."

The triumph was festively noted when the new Harvard president, Nathan Pusey, chose to deliver his first official address at a Divinity School convocation in Andover Hall on September 30, 1953. Dean Williams recalls delivering a long introductory prayer and being pulled up short by a nettled glance from Clark in the first pew, which telegraphed clearly: "A few hymns perhaps, but we've come to hear Pusey."

Clark was entitled to frown, for it was *his* day. His accomplishment had been duly prophesied when the fund drive was trembling in the balance and John Lord O'Brian had written Reinhold Niebuhr: ". . . if this undertaking succeeds, it will be largely due to help given by you and Grenville Clark."

Writing for Peace

After 1937, Clark certainly understood the nuances of Frankfurter's mind-set, and probably sympathized with them.
Nonetheless, Frankfurter's aloofness from what seemed to Clark
the compelling and civilized case for world government was not
without a special significance. If a cultivated, subtle, and sensitive
mind like Felix Frankfurter's could not be brought around,
clearly new tactics were in order; the instrumentalities of Plattsburg, Supreme Court defense, and conscription were demonstrably unavailing. The passage of time only confirmed Clark in his
initial decision to turn to the written word as the medium to
execute Stimson's great commission.

By the end of the 1950s the hour for another decision—that
of writing a book about peace—had arrived, and the memoirs
were again deferred to a back burner. The book decision was
actually but a way station on a continuum which stretched back
to 1939, when Clark, at the outbreak of World War II, had
thrown together his ideas on the institutionalization of peace.
One thesis at that time seemed to him self-evident, and he never
lost sight of it—that securing peace was essentially a collective
rather than an individual effort. Another idea which he would

sift, test, and eventually transmute was the necessity of a free institutional ethos permeating the structure.

In 1940, he wrote as a preamble to the constitution of his proposed Federation of Free Peoples:

> By free institutions . . . we mean: *First:* Institutions resting upon the consent of the governed, by which is meant the free choice of their rulers by the people under a reasonably extensive franchise exercised in uncoerced elections. *Second:* Institutions that recognize and protect certain inalienable rights of the individual which should be held inviolate by government, even though representing a majority for the time being, among which rights are: religious liberty; a reasonable freedom of expression through freedom of the press, of speech, of assembly and of petition for a redress of grievances; and the assurances of fair trial in both civil and criminal cases. We mean government by known law through freely chosen representatives as opposed to government by will and arbitrary decree.

Citing Kant's 1795 *Zum ewigen Freiden* (*Towards Eternal Peace*), Clark laid down a blueprint of an Anglo-Saxon, or at least a Nordic, League of Nations:

> . . . as a practical matter . . . the membership of the Federation at the start should be confined to the United States, France, the United Kingdom (including Northern Ireland), Canada, Australia, the Union of South Africa, New Zealand, Ireland (Eire), Finland, Sweden, Norway, Denmark, Holland, Belgium, Switzerland and several of the countries of Central and South America most advanced in the practice of stable, popular government.

However, even at this point, Clark was touched by the universalist vision:

> This is emphatically not to say, however, that the *Federation of Free Peoples* should be highly restrictive in its membership. To the con-

trary, the policy should be to welcome new members as *fast as they qualify by being in sympathy with the fundamental purposes of the Federation*—a test that will consist of their solemn declaration of adherence to the simple purposes of the Federation.

There followed the substance of what was to be Clark's unique mutation of the American constitutional design—a Congress structured on weighted, popular voting, a Supreme Court, no Senate (bicamerality was to become Clark's special *bête noire*), no Executive to speak of. In sum, it was the late-twentieth-century expression of Tennyson's parliament of man and federation of the world, expressed in the form of supranational world government of closely defined and strictly limited powers.

Truly, it was a grandiose vision, but Clark, in the sunset of life, was still inspired by the example of one man who had profoundly touched him. Senator Elihu Root, he noted, never wavered in his efforts to organize the world for peace, even into his eighties, despite disappointments at home and abroad.

1950 Book: A Plan for Peace

The global struggle of World War II against an enemy whose ethos was explicitly founded on race and blood undoubtedly changed some of Clark's perceptions. Initially, these had not been too far removed from Clarence Streit's Union Now movement, which, in the shadow of an approaching World War II, stirred deep enthusiasm by proposing an organic Atlantic Union under a supranational government with wide purposes and extensive powers. Nonetheless, experience and reflection convinced Clark that the elitist and ethnocentric approach was basically and tragically wrong; at the Dublin Conference he had reserved for it an opposition more formidable than that he had reserved for total nonbelievers, even though this had meant setting his face against Justice Roberts.

Even before his formal retirement, Clark found his writing

collaborator in Professor Louis Sohn of the Harvard Law School, and the creative tension of their relationship was such as to tilt Clark in the direction of universality. The intellectual initiative had been Sohn's, and his appeal against an elitist and exclusionary founding group evidently struck a responsive chord in Clark: "No, I cannot stand discrimination. I have always fought against it in this country. I cannot promote it internationally."

Clark and Sohn were united not only by this vision but also by a shared approval of weighted voting in the democratic process. (Indeed, it was that view that had brought them together.) Step by step, between 1945 and 1949, they proceeded to extrapolate their common ideas to a structure, the result being unveiled in a book, *A Plan for Peace,* published in 1950 by Harper & Brothers.

The *Plan* embodied the basic propositions of Clark's evolving political and philosophical thought, which reduced themselves to five bedrock principles, all shaped in the writing process and buffed by the subtle and astute collaboration of Sohn. These were: (1) an initial injunction to think through the unthinkable, particularly reflecting on the shocking moral and physical consequences of World War III; (2) that disarmament is the key to any stable world settlement, and that universality of membership in a reconstituted United Nations is an equal component; (3) that there should be a programmed prelude to disarmament and to reconstitution of the UN; (4) that continued American military strength and resistance to Communist expansion are imperative, pending permanent resolution of international tensions. The fifth and final point was a surprising one, stressing the obvious—that existing governments could not be counted upon to produce the new ideas necessary to deal with unprecedented problems.

On the last proposition, Clark cited with appropriate modesty his own experience with Plattsburg preparedness and pre–Pearl Harbor conscription. The thrust of the message, however, lay elsewhere, and Clark relentlessly hammered home his twin imperatives—no peace without disarmament; no disarmament without limited world government. To these two points the rest of Clark's gospel was ineluctably linked, as either indispensable premises or inevitable consequences.

Generalities are stirring and came easily enough to Clark, but he was also ready with the specifics. First, as to the UN, came proposals for universal, compulsory, and nonresignable membership, for a UN Bill of Rights and for dual national and UN citizenship for every inhabitant of the planet—all the consequences of further revision of the UN charter toward the end of providing binding and enforceable world law and planetary preservation. An even harder nut to crack was the issue of the logistics of disarmament. Clark saw, with customary clarity, that the process must be universal, synchronous, and absolute. The disarmament process was to be phased in over a twelve-year period, in four-year increments. The plan was a masterful lawyer's document calculated to find the largest common ground between adverse parties.

1958 Book: World Peace Through World Law

For years Clark and Sohn had proceeded through the agonizing tension which inevitably besets joint undertakings. The process was not easy. As Sohn wrote later, what stood out in his memory was the amount of sheer work that went into the first book. At least one month of each summer between 1950 and 1957 was devoted to hammering out the draft, and during the academic year Sohn commuted to Dublin. Each stint involved four hours of cooperation, with the patient secretary creeping out to type mutually acceptable portions of the text as the co-authors debated. Clark undoubtedly lived up to his student nickname of "Wrangler."

The first collaborative product was essentially an update of Clark's 1939 *Federation of Free Peoples.* As noted, it made its appearance in 1950 under the title *A Plan for Peace.* The internal dynamics of the text produced a sequence of extrapolations—a

1953 effort (truly Herculean) outlining a chapter-and-verse revision of the UN charter. That effort was itself revised some three years later with further suggestions. Then, in something of a symphonic coda, embodying all the hard thinking of many years, the definitive *World Peace Through World Law* appeared, to which all prior efforts had been the prelude. As Clark wrote Frankfurter in midsummer of 1957:

> Louis Sohn and I put on a big spurt and finished our "World Peace Through World Law" to the point of sending it all to the printer for a page proof (600 pages). Very hard work for several months and I am still recovering. It will be published six months or so hence; still some revision and arrangements to be made. Hope it will do some good; it is no doubt a few years ahead of the times but perhaps only a few.

The finished product was truly remarkable, and masterfully presented Clark's longtime ideals—a truly international world state, a unicameral parliament chosen on the basis of weighted population bases, a vetoless executive arm, a world court, and a world police force.

There were some new and distinctively lawyer-like touches: for example, a World Equity Council to make recommendations on confrontations of an extralegal nature. But what truly marked Clark's coming of age, as he entered the last decade of his life, was the explication and elaboration of the idea, previously touched on in his *Plan for Peace,* that the proper function of a world government was ensuring the economic and social welfare of the entire planet and every inhabitant of it. Hence, the most innovative and insightful item in *World Peace Through World Law* was its proposal for a World Development Authority and its contemplation of massive capital transfers from the Northern to the Southern Hemisphere, with a view toward mitigating economic disparities between nations and regions. However, LeGrand Cannon's grandson to the last, Clark resolutely resisted grass-roots intervention by the new agency, preferring to use the nation-state as the distributive mechanism.

The Clark-Sohn team was a true synergistic partnership. Reminiscent of Clark's law-office difficulty in delegating work was his reluctantly permitting Sohn (along with Clark's trusted secretary, Ruth Wight) to read proof. In something of a postscript to the book, the team expressed alarm over nonrevision of the UN charter to respond to the twin planetary perils of nuclear overhang and crunching economic imbalance. The response was to turn out, in the mid-sixties, proposals for a new international organization, supplementing but not replacing the UN, to concentrate on world disarmament and world development.

World Peace Through World Law was published in March 1958 and it got prominent billing. Thomas J. Hamilton reviewed it for *The New York Times* under the caption "Global Peace Through Global Government: A Blue Print." By singular (and Clark would say appropriate) coincidence, the review appeared directly below Lynn Montross' appraisal of *Soviet Strategy in the Nuclear Age* ("The Doctrine That Guides Russia's War Machine"). The review of Clark's work was surly and hostile, and attempted to gloss its venom by ending on a point that Clark had anticipated:

> In the past it has been customary to smile benevolently on the champions of world federalism, and to remark that, although their proposals are impractical, they are well meant. So, no doubt they are. Unfortunately, however, they have been seized upon by American isolationists to attack the United Nations itself. It is high time for Messrs. Clark and Sohn to turn their energies to the United Nations as it is the only international organization we have or can get before the millennium . . .

Clark had learned early in a long life that there never was a fair debate between a reviewer and an author (although the *Times* reviewer of *World Peace Through World Law* did catch a devastating counter-volley from Clark's cousin, Senator Joseph Clark of

Pennsylvania), and there is no record of even a private "memo to file" responding to the sour misstatement: "Can the authors really believe that the United States should disband its army, navy, and air force, hand over the nuclear bomb, surrender its veto and trust its very existence to a theoretical United Nations police force?" The silence exemplified what historian J. Garry Clifford called Clark's supreme indifference to ignorant criticism.

1962 Draft of a Proposed Treaty on General and Complete Disarmament in a Peaceful World

The other barb in the *World Peace* review, which counseled Clark and Sohn to turn their energies to the United Nations, was gratuitous, for Clark had already done so and done so with great effort. Indeed, the strongest words on the subject to be delivered on the UN floor had been drafted by him for utterance by his Filipino friend Carlos Romulo back in 1946:

> In all the history of mankind, it has never been possible for people, living in a state of anarchy, to keep the peace.

From that point, the question of Charter reform had been persistently on Clark's mind, and his concern grew with the advent of the tenth anniversary of the founding of the UN. It had been largely at his behest and because of his discontent with the original organization that Article 109, paragraph 3—providing for decennial review by the UN of its Charter—had been inserted in the Charter in the first place, but the glacial forces of inertia, drift, and indolence were too much even for him. Article 109 became a dead letter. Predictably, the General Assembly took no action aside from appointing a committee to study the matter. In keeping with his constantly enlarging intellectual and moral horizons, Clark responded by proposing a UN of his own—an alternative and coexisting world organization which imposed institutional obligations more far-reaching than those of the UN. The first draft appeared in the spring of 1962 under the caption *Draft of a Proposed Treaty on General and Complete Disarmament in a Peaceful World.*

Interestingly, Clark did not fare much better with Dwight Eisenhower than he had with the *Times.* The President's comprehension seemed as garbled as his syntax. Ike responded, when asked whether he had read Clark's book:

> Secretary Dulles and I and others, have discussed this matter frequently, and, by coincidence, only within the last few days. Now, I have not read this particular book, although I have read much of what Grenville Clark has written, and I have no doubt that it is on the same vein really a world of peace through world law.
>
> I, myself, quoting my favorite author, wrote a short chapter to conclude a book that I wrote back in 1947 or '48 and in it I pointed out there was going to be no peace, there was going to be no real strength among the free world countries unless each was willing to examine its—simple sole sovereign position and to see whether it could make some concessions, each to the others, that it could make a legal or law basis for settling disputes.
>
> Now I still think—I think that that is the gist of Mr. Clark's and, as a matter of fact, Justice [Owen] Roberts was of the same group —it is the kernel of his thinking.

Unlike the *Times* or the President, Dean Sperry of the Harvard Divinity School gave the book a handsome plug in his Dean's letter, urging readers to get and read the book. Alas, the recommendation came from a quarter which had neither pelf nor power.

Despite the worldwide acceptance of *World Peace Through World Law* as a classic of international relations, and its translation into many languages, the book had little immediate impact. But just as a blade of grass has the ultimate force to crack a concrete highway, Clark's appeal, necessarily to the intelligence of a future day, may still constitute his enduring memorial, to be vindicated (in the view of futurologist Herman Kahn) when an American President sends an inscribed copy to a Soviet Premier: "There's no point in reading this book; you will not like it any more than I did. I merely suggest you sign it right after my signature. This is the only plan which has been thoroughly thought out; let us, therefore, adopt it."

Freedom's Flag Flying

*He has helped to keep freedom's flag flying
and by his example has ever reminded his fellow lawyers
of their duty to uphold liberty and to expand support
for the Rule of Law.*

—Grenville Clark citation, American Bar Association (1959)

The Knife Edge of Holocaust

Clark had himself undergone the process he had urged upon others of thinking the unthinkable: if peace were lost and war came, what would the war and its aftermath be like? Like a man obsessed, he crisscrossed the world, speaking and holding conferences on the twin institutions of disarmament and world government, which he saw as indispensable to forestalling catastrophe: London in 1951 and 1952, Copenhagen and back to Princeton in 1953, New York and Minneapolis in 1954, and St. Louis in 1957.

Most of the effort was on behalf of the United World Federalists, an umbrella organization which Clark and others had formed at Ashville, North Carolina, in February 1947 to unite the quarreling world government ideologues into an effective national force—or perhaps international force would be more appropriate, for the membership included two Third World past presidents of the UN General Assembly and was founded on Clark's idea of reaching well beyond the industrial democracies. Again, Clark hung back from front-rank command. After Henry Stimson declined the presidency, despite Clark's extra effort of persuasion, he turned elsewhere. This time his target was young Cord Meyer, wounded Marine veteran and Dublin conferee. "I was persuaded," recollected Meyer, "by Grenville Clark . . . to take the job [of president] myself, with the understanding that they would serve as vice presidents and raise the necessary funds." Certainly far more than the UWF presidency, Clark deserved the accolade of "apostle of peace" which Archbishop Ignio Cardinale, Apostolic Delegate to Great Britain, bestowed upon him (much as his Unitarianism would have caused him to reject the theological implications of the term).

Conformity and Containment

The prospect of planetary incineration was but one of the impulses which drove Clark in the decade of the 1950s. Almost equally besetting (*nothing* could be equally besetting) was the rising repression at home, as America responded to the Soviet pattern of duplicity, mendacity, penetration, and subversion. In Clark's perception, the two problems were the Siamese-twin consequences of international anarchy and paranoia:

> The truth is that in "containing" Russia, we have gone quite a long way in imitating Russian ideas in respect to coerced conformity. We had better look this straight in the eye and realize that this result is just as adverse a consequence of the containment policy as deficits and trade restrictions.

Indeed, Clark's lawyer's capacity to see both sides of an issue had brought not a domestic but a foreign policy estrangement with the Truman administration in 1948. The President, in responding to Clark's plea for an accommodationist stance with the Soviets, had suggested that Clark read Peter the Great's will, which Clark knew was a fabricated blueprint of Russian expansion on a par with the *Protocols of the Elders of Zion*. Truman's patronizing tone sufficed to bring Clark out fighting, with the pugnacity exhibited in the Arboretum affair, and produced a thunderbolt telegram:

YOU WERE GROSSLY IMPOSED UPON IN BEING LED TO BELIEVE THE AUTHENTICITY OF THE SO–CALLED WILL OF PETER THE GREAT . . . IT WAS PUBLICIZED FOR PROPAGANDA PURPOSES SHORTLY BEFORE NAPO- LEON'S INVASION OF RUSSIA AND IS APPARENTLY BEING USED FOR SIMI- LAR PURPOSES NOW.

After much soul-searching, and consultation with Felix Frank- furter, Clark finally wrote the President in late June. By that time the issue was beyond retrieval, in view of Truman's March 17, 1948, message urging the arrows of renewed conscription and the olive branch of the Marshall Plan. When Stalin, during the summer of 1948, imposed a blockade on overland access to Berlin, occupied by the Russians, the confrontation which Clark had sought to prevent had become inevitable.

Before 1948 was out, the atomic confrontation which Clark had dreaded also seemed an accomplished fact. Indeed, even before the "Will" episode, he realized he had lost the battle with the inner circle of the administration, and had written Cord Meyer about the President and his advisers: ". . . really noth- ing of what we are struggling for can be expected from the Truman-Leahy-Marshall-Lovett-Kennan-Forrestal-Harriman combination."

Clark had never really hit it off with Harry Truman, whose personality and perspective on history were virtually guaranteed to irritate him. In early 1945, he had declined to support Truman for an honorary degree: "I believe there is a very strong argument for sticking to the idea of giving a degree only to presidents who have proved themselves in office."

For proof positive of the validity of his view of America's shortsighted conformity and containment, Clark needed to look no further than his own American Bar Association. At the 1950 convention, the president of that body declared: "We are faced with an attack from within on our form of government and our

American way of life by foreign ideologies." The convention responded by recommending a loyalty oath for members of the Bar—in the hostile perception of Clark's longtime coadjutor, Zechariah Chafee, "with less discussion than would have been devoted to the menu at the next annual banquet."

The mind-set of the ABA was further demonstrated the following year, with the establishment of a Special Committee to Study Communist Tactics, Strategy and Objectives, truly the polar opposite to Clark's Bill of Rights Committee, which had been instituted just nine short years earlier.

The lawyers' loyalty oath was an especially repugnant paradigm of what Clark called coerced conformity. Chafee declared, "If nobody stood up on his hind legs and yelled, I was going to do so." Possibly at Clark's behest, but probably on his own initiative, Chafee joined Clark and a number of prominent attorneys in denouncing the oath as "unfounded in its implications of widespread disloyalty." Zechariah Chafee, writing Clark, also quoted Ross Malone, who said: "I must confess that having had some small part in the glorious past of the Bill of Rights Committee I was perhaps [more] disturbed than the average person to see its perverted efforts on that occasion."

All in all, it was a bad time on the home front—nowhere more so, it must have seemed to Clark, than in the unwillingness of the national Bar to rally to the First and Fifth Amendments as it had to the defense of the Supreme Court in 1938. Not only did the national organization endorse ritual incantations of conformity, but its members were quite unwilling to defend accused subversives. In its report for 1952, Clark's Bill of Rights Committee put a brave face on matters by finding it "gratifying" that no cases warranting intervention had come to its attention, even though one lawyer, tarred with the Communist brush, had had his request for an *amicus* brief spurned as "not appropriate."

Little wonder that Clark's enormous tenacity and drive became tinctured with discouragement. In April 1952, he wrote Ross Malone that the "supineness" of the organized Bar "appalled" him, and, before the decade was out, he had, in a statement quite unusual for him, conceded failure of his Bill of Rights Committee.

Nonetheless, at its 1959 convention, the American Bar Association bestowed on Clark its highest award, the Gold Medal for Illustrious Service to the Law. Clark was the twenty-fourth recipient of this medal, following men of the caliber of Oliver Wendell Holmes, John Wigmore, and Charles Evans Hughes. In this case, a touch of bad conscience peeped through the florid language of the citation, which ran the roll call of achievement from Plattsburg to efforts for world law, and concluded:

> Through his dedication to the discharge of the public responsibility of the Bar during a long and distinguished professional career, he has rallied many others to that noble concept [of the Rule of Law between Nations]. He has helped to keep freedom's flag flying and by his example has ever reminded his fellow lawyers of their duty to uphold liberty and to expand support for the Rule of Law.

It was Felix Frankfurter who provided an appropriate *postscriptum* in a letter in his own beautiful copperplate handwriting, putting the best face on the laurel of a group that Clark felt had let him down:

> Dear Grenny:
> The American Bar Assn. couldn't honor you, but it honored itself by formal recognition of your intrinsic worth and the high uses to which you have put it. In crowning you, the ABA has done a valuable thing in advertising you as a symbol of what is honorable and distinguished in the eyes of our profession.
> > Affectionately and fondly yours,
> > Felix

The Fortunes of the Firm

The ABA award was duly noted in several places. One was, of course, *The New York Times,* which observed:

> Mr. Clark has been a lawyer in the grand tradition, dedicated to the public service and the uplifting of our legal ideals, fighting for freedom, against our enemies abroad in time of war and against those at home who would have undermined our Bill of Rights.

Another reference came in the first issue, dated September 15, 1959, of the *Cleargolaw News,* which was the office newspaper of the firm of Cleary, Gottlieb, Steen & Hamilton. The Cleary, Gottlieb firm, as it was generally known in the argot of the Bar, was founded in January 1946 by four former partners of the Root, Clark firm, a former associate of the firm who had become an Assistant Attorney General, and two other rising young lawyers who had been serving the United States war effort.

When the Cleary, Gottlieb firm was started, Clark had retired from Root, Clark and had moved to Dublin to work full-time for world peace. His fellow founder of Root, Clark, Elihu Root, Jr., had remained with the firm, and he and Arthur Ballantine became the only two survivors of the original five partners, Howland having left the law in 1930 to become a partner of Guggenheim Brothers (he died in 1938) and Buckner having died in 1941.

In March 1946, the name of the firm, which had been Root, Clark, Buckner & Ballantine since May 1933, was changed to Root, Ballantine, Harlan, Bushby & Palmer. The three new names, Harlan (later a Justice of the United States Supreme Court), Bushby, and Palmer, were those of younger partners. When Felix Frankfurther received the announcement of the change of name, he scrawled across it: "Isn't this wonderful! Now A.A.B. is cock of the walk, but the walk is a very different walk!! Love to you both," and sent it on to Clark in Dublin. (Frankfurter's hostile attitude toward Ballantine dated back at least to the Harvard *Crimson* dinner of 1935, which—so Frankfurter wrote FDR—had been manipulated by Ballantine to exhibit New Deal sympathizers to worst advantage).

In 1954, Elihu Root, Jr., decided to sever his ties to the Root, Clark firm and become counsel to Cleary, Gottlieb. Clark was also invited to join with Root as counsel, and he accepted with pleasure in renewing an old companionship with Root. However, Clark made it clear that his relationship to the new firm would differ from Root's and be more form than substance. He told them that he welcomed the chance to renew old contacts but would not curtail the work on public causes which had taken all his time since moving to Dublin. He also made it clear that he would not move back to New York and that there was no need to supply him with an office and secretary as the firm had done with Root.

Clark did come to New York from time to time after he became counsel to Cleary, Gottlieb, and whenever he did he made the firm's offices his headquarters. On one occasion, the firm gave a dinner in honor of Clark at the Knickerbocker Club. On November 5, 1962, the *Cleargolaw News* carried a seven-page biographical sketch summarizing Clark's life, career, and contributions to national defense and world peace, as a tribute to him on his eightieth birthday. In 1965, Clark came to New York for the presentation of an award by the Metropolitan Committee of United World Federalists for service to world peace, and the award dinner was attended by eight partners of Cleary, Gottlieb.

Frankfurter's Changing Views

In spite of the encouraging award of the ABA Gold Medal, it must have seemed to Clark that things were going badly everywhere. At home, concern over domestic subversion manifested itself in increasing constraints, surveillance, and reprisals on suspected dissidents. Abroad, the Cold War deteriorated to subpolar lows with atomic exchange an ever-increasing possibility; in addition, the newly Communist state of China, containing almost half the human race, seemed frozen in an icy hostility to the U.S. Resolute nonrecognition of and by China (at least the U.S. and U.S.S.R. talked to each other) made Soviet-American relations seem, by contrast, an *entente cordiale*. The world security movement was a gaggle of quarreling ideologues, apparently immune from unity or harmony.

Felix Frankfurter was almost a case in point. Remarkably, a different aging process had affected the two old friends. Clark, the Fifth Avenue aristocrat, grew more open-minded as time passed; in contrast, Frankfurter, the child of the cold-water tenement, became increasingly bitter, conservative, and insecure.

Still very much concerned with Clark's good opinion, Frankfurter was in the habit of sending a highly selective ordering of his opinions up from Washington. Typical was the dispatch of what he had had to say in *Watkins* v. *United States* and *Sweezey* v. *New Hampshire*. Both cases were decided on the same day in 1957 and involved legislative inquiry into subversion: *Watkins* concerned Congress, *Sweezey* Clark's New Hampshire legislature.

In the first case, the Supreme Court reversed the contempt conviction of a closet Communist who, while admitting his own activities, had refused to identify his associates. The grounds were Watkins' lack of opportunity to appraise whatever right of silence might be his and the vagueness which had tinctured the whole proceeding. Frankfurter, concurring in a baroque opinion, limited his agreement to the circumstances of the case.

Sweezey, a leading American Marxist, had refused to disclose his associations with Henry Wallace's Progressive Party and the context of a lecture he had delivered at the University of New Hampshire. His state contempt conviction was overturned as violative of the due-process clause of the Fourteenth Amendment because the state attorney general had asked irrelevant questions. Frankfurter again concurred, this time on free speech grounds, but with apprehension.

Clark responded almost noncommittally:

> Many thanks for sending me the Watkins-Sweezey opinions. Very good of you. I had read Watkins in the *Times,* mostly aloud to Fanny, but not Sweezey, and was very glad to get it.
>
> Of the group of decisions, I incline to think Sweezey will prove most important. I think your concurring opinion very fine; one of the best things you have ever done. I have just written to Sweezey (copy enclosed). Please note and give me a good mark for predicting the reversal to the President of the University of New Hampshire. I now hear he *did* let Sweezey speak soon after he phoned me.

Significantly, some eight years earlier, Frankfurter had not sent Clark a copy of his dissent in *Terminiello* v. *Chicago,* where—on a technicality, to be sure, but nonetheless clearly—he had turned his back on the proposition which he and Clark had jointly forged back in the easy, uncomplicated days of 1938, to the effect that the proper constitutional response to foreseeable public tumult is protection, not suppression, of the speaker.

Clark was able to close out a generally disheartening decade with two achievements ("triumphs" would be technically incorrect) which came at a psychologically propitious moment and were undoubtedly necessary to buoy and fortify his spirits. One was in the newly emerging area of civil rights; the other involved a more traditional liberalism in which Clark had long been involved.

The Black Minority

On February 1, 1960, four black freshmen from North Carolina Agricultural and Technical College "sat in," demanding lunch-counter service at the Woolworth dime store in Greensboro, North Carolina. By design, they had chosen an anniversary of the Fourteenth Amendment to mark the initiation of their quest for equality of life. Their social position had remained essentially unchanged despite the landmark decision of the Supreme Court some six years earlier abolishing segregation in education.

With respect to the Fourteenth Amendment, as Judge Francis Rivers later pointed out, there was little evidence prior to 1960 that Clark "revered the guarantees owed the Negro under the 'Equal Protection Clause' as much as he did the First Amendment freedom owed to every citizen." It was fair to question Clark's thought on Negro rights, for he was not a self-starter; his powerful mind did require a galvanic impetus. It took the *Lusitania* sinking to produce the Plattsburg movement (although the need for national preparedness had seemed obvious since Sarajevo). Similarly, it had required the defense of the Supreme Court against FDR's proposed reorganization to underscore the necessity of independent judicial safeguards from majoritarian tyranny à la Frank Hague. And in terms of the meaningful sociological assimilation of the African minority in the United States, unquestionably the Freedom Riders and sit-in demonstrators were needed to galvanize Clark's latent conscience, probably in concert with Allan Nevins' *Emergence of Lincoln,* which constituted his reading of the time.

The latent moral commitment had been there for a long time. As Clark subsequently told Jack Greenberg, general counsel for the NAACP Legal Defense Fund, a boyhood visit to South Carolina had shown him "black people being treated quite literally no better than dogs . . ." and had induced in him a desire to change circumstances for the better.

But if Clark did require some impetus, it was comparable to the trickle of gravel which precedes an avalanche. By May 1960, he had already analyzed the issue and was moving to meet it head on with resolve and glacier-like formidability. As he wrote Allen Knight Chalmers of the NAACP:

> . . . Like so many others I have been thinking hard about the future course of our Negro problem, by which I mean especially the best

strategy to use in the necessarily long and bitter contest which lies
ahead . . .

Having in mind that the effort to obtain anything like equal
opportunity for our Negro population in the numerous fields in
which they are disadvantaged (housing, jobs and pay, voting, education, recreation, etc.) will undoubtedly be long and hard. The key
to ultimate success obviously lies in sustaining a *steady, persistent, and
if possible, increasing* effort over a long period. In part, this means
psychological preparation in much the same way as Churchill, after
Dunkirk, made it so clear to the British people that their only chance
was to stick it out for an indefinitely long time. However, of equal
importance, is the making of long-term strategy plans of a material
sort, which means a long-term financial plan.

Clark went on to specify the logistics of his plan—100 persons
subscribing $1,000 per annum for ten years, beginning in 1961.
Such a plan, Clark suggested, would provide practical assurance
of at least $100,000 per year, which would be one-third of the
$300,000 per annum which he foresaw as the "absolute minimum
amount required by the (NAACP) Legal Defense and Educational Fund, Inc., during the next ten years."

The proposal was truly seminal. It led, recollected Jack Greenberg,

> to the development of the Grenville Clark Plan, in which we (the
> NAACP) enlisted financial support on that basis. The effect was
> substantial. What happened was that a number of contributors did
> pledge funds over a number of years. But their sights raised and, in
> fact, gave more and regularly. At the time of the great civil rights
> demonstrations, sit-ins, freedom marches, Mr. Clark became more
> convinced about the rightness of his proposal and urged it strongly
> upon us and others he could influence.

Greenberg also reported on the bottom line, which was that
sustained, systematic support enabled the NAACP to bring cases

over the years without the fear of starting things it could not finish.

Clark was not only strategist; he was also tactician. Here, his coadjutor was his onetime Root, Clark associate Louis Lusky, whom he commissioned to serve as an observer in the Freedom Ride cases. Lusky recalled how in October 1961 Clark had inconspicuously donated $10,000 to meet demands for exorbitant bail that threatened to stop constitutional litigation short of a final decision.

Clark's persistent optimism about the future of America also appeared in his sustained interest in Dartmouth's ABC (A Better Chance) program, which was designed to prepare disadvantaged blacks to study for college at ranking preparatory academies and eventually matriculate at Dartmouth and, in due course, at professional schools. John Dickey remembered how Clark had finished off one visit by taking dinner with the ABC group and reporting the incident as one of unusual pleasure for him.

Moreover, Clark never underestimated the sheer vastness of the job and the size of the return possible from the talented few. Indeed, on the threshold of his eightieth birthday, he foresaw "the slower but ultimately just as deep hardening of Northern sentiment." He correctly described the long-term character of the task he had set:

> You may ask why a ten-year subscription rather than five years or fifteen or twenty years. Certainly this is not because of any illusion that the effort for equality will even measurably succeed in ten years; for I believe it will go on for at least fifty years and, more likely, for a hundred years or even more . . .

But at least he seemed to be seeing more visible short-term success, and he was encouraged to—literally—put his money down on the side of history. Clark did more than ask others to give. He gave himself, and so did Fanny.

Fanny left two memorials. During her last illness, in conversation (or perhaps via note), she and Clark had resolved to assist with special—and anonymous—generosity the Defense Fund of the NAACP. The organization put out a specially printed announcement in 1964 to describe what they had done:

AN UNPRECEDENTED GIFT

On the occasion of the 25th Anniversary Convocation of the NAACP Legal Defense and Educational Fund, the Board of Directors gratefully acknowledges the receipt of the largest gift in the history of our organization.

The unexampled gift of $500,000 has been made anonymously by a long-term friend and his wife who desire that it shall stimulate the plan of generosity from other friends to meet the critical tasks which lie ahead.

The Christmas Card List

Hand in hand with the good fight over civil rights went the affair of Dr. Willard Uphaus, which provided virtually the last hurrah of Cold War tensions, repression, and insecurity. Dr. Uphaus, an eccentric idealist, was a New Hampshire neighbor of Clark, with a World Fellowship camp at Conway. He was an authentic American dissident in direct intellectual lineage to Thoreau. The guests at his camp came under no such cachet, however, and that circumstance attracted the attention of Louis C. Wyman, who was serving as a one-man "committee" of the state legislature to investigate subversion. Uphaus generally responded to the Wyman interrogation with completeness and candor. However, he drew the line at furnishing the names of guests and speakers at his camp. He was promptly cited for contempt and sentenced to jail for one year or until such time as he would comply and on December 14, 1958, began serving his term in the Merrimack County jail in Boscawen, New

Hampshire. The imminence of Christmas, the septuagenarian prisoner's age and obvious good faith, as well as the patent political hectoring he had suffered, seemed made to excite Clark's sympathy. "It's a shame to send an old man to jail because he won't give up his Christmas card list," Clark quipped. (Singularly, however, the same type of circumstance had actually emboldened Clark in his hope of traveling to Red China to reopen Sino-American relations, notwithstanding the Chandler Act's ban on private diplomatic negotiations: "They're not going to put an old man like me in jail."

Dr. Uphaus was put in jail, and when, in the spring of 1960, the New Hampshire Supreme Court upheld the sentence, Clark moved to bring the matter before the Supreme Court of the United States. Already older than the venerable prisoner, Clark, out of necessity, co-opted his New Hampshire neighbor, Robert Reno, and his old civil rights associate, Louis Lusky, to carry the burden of the manifold details of the appeal, perfecting the arrangements in one night and thereafter being virtually in daily touch by telephone with his coadjutors.

In a singularly shabby move, the state courts refused to admit the old pacifist to bail pending his ultimate appeal, and Justices Frankfurter, Black, and Douglas successively declined to exercise their extraordinary powers to keep the status quo by staying his sentence. On June 7, 1959, a divided Supreme Court upheld the imprisonment.

So Dr. Uphaus languished in jail, and, as *The New Republic*'s anonymous columnist, T.R.B., noted under the rubric "Poetry, Thoreau, and the Bible," because Dr. Uphaus was in jail for consorting with "oddballs and idealists" whom he refused to name, everyone else was figuratively in jail, too. Worse yet, Dr. Uphaus lay under virtually indefinite commitment, for it was quite possible that upon release he could be subpoenaed, reinterrogated, and returned to jail in an ongoing reprise of the initial miscarriage of justice.

Clark's effort in undertaking the appeal matched anything he had ever mounted for one of his corporate clients, and Reno described the qualities of Clark, the complete lawyer, in what was virtually his last effort at the bar: "patience; determination; careful thought; more determination; never losing sight of the desired end; not being deterred by obstacles, courage, and at the end, asking no credit for himself."

Alas, Clark's efforts for Uphaus seemed fruitless, for on November 14, 1960, the Supreme Court, in a brief anonymous opinion, declined to hear the Uphaus appeal.

There was one singular development: Justice Black wrote a characteristic dissent proclaiming the constitutional imperatives of free speech and free assembly. Clark, who had been outraged by Roosevelt's appointment of Black to the Supreme Court in 1937 and had corresponded with Douglas Arant about the possibility of aborting it, nonetheless was moved to send the Justice a congratulatory wire on his seventy-fifth birthday the following February:

ON YOUR SEVENTY-FIFTH BIRTHDAY, PLEASE ACCEPT MY RESPECT AND ADMIRATION FOR YOUR INSPIRING EXAMPLE ON THE COURT AND MY BEST WISHES FOR A FURTHER PERIOD OF FRUITFUL WORK.

He followed up with a letter, which closed

. . . you struck a strong blow for the rights of conscience with your superb opinion.

I wish you many years of health and vigor.

Black responded with characteristic courtliness:

I cannot tell you how much I appreciated the message you sent me on February 27th, my 75th birthday. While I have never had an intimate acquaintance with you, I have known through the years about the public service you have given so unselfishly.

And so, the Uphaus case ended with an exchange of civilities between two old gentlemen who, starting from diametrically different origins and taking startlingly diverse routes, had reached a common ground. Little wonder that Clark felt a surge of optimism, for the exchanged greetings had provided the perfect denouement to the unannounced and accelerated release of Dr. Uphaus by a court and officials anxious to avoid more adverse publicity.

17

The Arrow in Flames

*I find myself asking whether the human animal
is worth saving.*

—Fritz Von Windegger to Grenville Clark, November 26, 1946

Dartmouth Conference

Cut of the same cloth as his reaction to the UN inertia was
Clark's decision to meet the Russians halfway, even though he
made them come to New Hampshire for the occasion. The meeting bore the Grenville Clark cachet—a conference of cultural
(rather than political) leaders held at Dartmouth College. The
Soviet group was headed by Professor Alexander Myasmikov and
was there with official permission. Their presence was given a
special fillip by the recent advent of new leadership, that of John
Kennedy and Nikita Khrushchev. The fact that the meeting was
held at all was due to Clark's lawyerly capacity to see both sides
and to his perception of the Soviet's malaise as the inevitable
consequence of war-born insecurity and dissatisfaction with existing protective arrangements.

Even so, at the Dartmouth Conference the issue of inspection
to determine effectual disarmament separated the delegates as
sharply as it had ever divided their governments. When tensions
reached flash point, Clark took the floor. He had been silent up
to that point, and Norman Cousins recalls how Clark's deferred
contribution carried an impact all its own:

He began by saying he accepted fully the sincerity of the Soviet delegates to reduce and eliminate the dangers of war. He spoke of the enormous number of casualties suffered by the Russian people in the Second World War, some twenty million dead. He referred to the siege of Leningrad and the heroism of its people. He paid tribute to the Russian contribution to victory during the war. He spoke movingly and with great dignity. Then he told of the need to avert even greater wars in an age of nuclear weapons. He defined the basic principles that had to go into the making of a workable peace. He described the opportunity before leaders of public opinion in gaining acceptance for these principles. He called on both Americans and Russians to see the problems of disarmament in a larger and more historic setting than weapons alone. When he sat down, both sides gave him sustained applause.

Second "Dartmouth" Conference—Moscow

Clark's characteristic open-mindedness was the reason that he was enabled in 1961 to hold something of a follow-up "Dartmouth" Conference in Moscow itself. Were tolerance and civility capable of ending the Cold War, he would have been the mediator par excellence. At a time when the freeze was at its worst, in true family tradition (his grandfather had invariably referred to the sixteenth President as "*Mister* Lincoln"), Clark expressed the hope of going to the Kremlin to talk to "Mr. Stalin." For his proposed world government, he was willing not only to meet the Russians halfway but to walk the extra mile.

In his 1950 *Plan for Peace,* Clark had conceded the fierce ideological differences dividing—and potentially destroying— the planet, but insisted that an exchange of billingsgate was always better than an exchange of missiles:

Accordingly, the overall East-West settlement which I envisage would contain no restrictions at all on the right to propagandize. We could have our national and local restrictions on expression, if we wished, however unwise they might be. The Communist World would have its restrictions against the expression of Western ideas. But no charter or treaty would purport to censor or confine mere words coming from either West or East. Both would be free to persuade the other so long as the persuasion consisted only of words, however strong.

Beneath the seemingly free and easy unconcern was an almost Miltonian faith in the power of truth: "We can be confident that over a period of time this nonviolent competition in the free market of ideas will turn in our favor, if only we avoid complacence and self-righteousness." Clark was willing to leave the apparatus of Stalinist repression in place: "These provisions would not extend to any attempted protection of the individual against the action of his own government."

This was not appeasement, but a sober appraisal of the impending danger of nuclear holocaust, which could easily be escalated by exacerbating the insecurities of an atomic power. Nonetheless, Clark implied that one day the time would come for a world organization to guarantee every person on the planet protection against any authority whatever by granting a few fundamental rights—exemption from slavery, freedom from torture, and the right to be heard before criminal condemnation. However desirable this Utopia, man would have to wait for it. Clark's Calvinist perception had descended from the melancholy belief in an inherently sinful world that could be reformed only a step at a time.

Third "Dartmouth" Conference—Andover

The steps were incrementally small and maddeningly slow; a marginal movement might have been detected at the third "Dartmouth" Conference, held, not at Dublin or Moscow, but at Phillips Academy at Andover, Massachusetts. Clark's statement, printed in both Latin and Cyrillic alphabets, was accorded a hearing before both Russian and American delegations. Citing Kennedy and Khrushchev and appealing to the recent McCloy-

Zorin declaration, which had set forth an agreement in principle on the necessity of general and complete disarmament and supranational peacekeeping, Clark met the remaining difficulties head on, calling for American concessions in coordinating inspections. Lawyer-like, he put his finger on the issue underlying Soviet intransigence and restated his core case:

> On the other hand the USSR must recognize that nations cannot reasonably be expected wholly to eliminate their armaments unless adequate alternative means are established for peaceful change and the settlement of international disputes. This means a strong world police force . . . And it means also a well financed world development authority . . .

He concluded on a note of Enlightenment-style optimism:

> Accordingly, let discussions proceed until, through the pressure of sheer necessity and through increased mutual understanding, the great objective of general and complete disarmament is realized.

Ironically, the fine words were written against the near-miss of the Cuban missile crisis, and, as Clark celebrated his eightieth birthday, he had ample cause to ponder the answer which Albert Einstein had put to a questioner at the Princeton Conference sixteen years earlier about how politics was infinitely more difficult than physics.

Theoretically, the hairbreadth escape from nuclear incineration following the Cuban crisis of 1962 should have been a most powerful stimulus to the world to adopt Clark's twin plans for disarmament and world law. But in fact, no such thing happened, and the reason might well be found in physics.

Newton's first law proclaimed inertia as the critical element of mass and motion. Thus, in his *Plan for Peace,* Clark had imaginatively quoted Charles F. Kettering on the dangers of "groovology." Despite Newton, Kettering, and Grenville Clark

—and thanks to the ability of peasants to dance on the slope of Vesuvius—events went on as before, and, near-miss of 1962 notwithstanding, the superpowers seemed to maintain a steady planetary sweep and motion, even though the consequence, in Clark's apprehension, would—at best—be the descent of a new Dark Age.

The Ford Foundation

The Ford Foundation had been attracted early to Clark and his work. Initially, it had contributed $84,000 toward his research, and it subsequently pledged to grant an additional $2 million to give *World Peace Through World Law* the widest possible circulation and impact. Then, in midstream, the Foundation abruptly reversed itself. Clark underwent hectoring as to expenditures made from the original pittance allotted to him. (One item questioned was the purchase of a woodburning stove to properly accommodate a room at Dublin for the World Peace program.)

Adversity only confirmed Clark in his convictions and values. Associates flagged in the traces and grew fainthearted: ". . . I find myself asking," wrote Fritz Von Windegger of St. Louis, "whether the human animal is worth saving." But such counsels of despair, and even John Foster Dulles' private support and public silence, only vindicated Clark's long-standing decision to eschew politics and to influence public affairs by tenacity as a private man. As to the Ford ambuscade, he exemplified *noblesse oblige:* "We'll just carry on."

Dublin Two

The conferees at Clark's first Dublin Conference regathered in 1964, twenty years later, at the same spot. Their ranks had thinned. The world had changed and so had they. Their agenda suggested the mutations of two decades—it called for discussion of the significance of the shift from nuclear monopoly to nuclear proliferation, of the validity of the present United States position as contrasted with that of 1944, of the merits and limitations of the United Nations, and of the essential features of an effective world organization to prevent war and keep the peace. The intervening years had seen the dissolution of the high hopes of the mid-1940s and had produced the Truman Doctrine, the Marshall Plan, and NATO. (By singular irony, the latter was the *bête noire* of Clark's vision, since it was but an amorphous confederacy-in-arms organized around an avowedly ethnic base.) Owen J. Roberts was gone, and his place as chairman was filled by a rising young intellectual, Kingman Brewster. Norman Cousins was back, and so was Douglas Arant. Clark, a psychological constant in a world of change, once more served as secretary.

There were other changes. The composition of the delegates and the range of the invitation list suggested the constantly enlarging dimensions of Clark's world view. This time a Jesuit and a nun were in attendance, and invitations to the distinguished historian John Hope Franklin and a rising black lawyer, Derrick Bell, prevented the colloquy from being a totally Caucasian event.

From Friday to Monday, the participants reviewed, discussed, and argued, all the while being gently guided toward a final declaration by Grenville Clark, with the experience and the perspective of eight decades. Typically, the declaration seized the high ground with an Enlightenment flourish in its opening paragraph:

The rights of man and the conditions of life itself in this planet are imperiled by lawlessness among nations. World anarchy is manifested by the growing frequency of international crises as well as by the number of nations with the capacity to build arsenals of nuclear weapons. One serious adverse effect of that anarchy has been an increasing acceptance of violence and thereby, a cheapening of human life.

The declaration then moved to a point-by-point indictment of the status quo, concluding:

> The possession of nuclear weapons spreads. World tension does not subside. The arms race continues at an annual cost of $140,000,-000,000 (one hundred forty *billion* dollars). With world law, the massive savings from disarmament could be made available to close the dangerous widening gap between the "have" and the "have-not" nations.

The indictment passed from these generalities to a critique of the inadequacies of the United Nations—unrepresented nations, veto paralysis, the one-nation-one-vote General Assembly, the absence of an effective world court and reliable revenues.

All this was a prelude to Clark's commandments for world survival:

1. Universal and complete disarmament
2. Adequate world police force
3. Universal UN membership
4. World legislature
5. Responsible world executive
6. Competent world judiciary
7. Reliable world income
8. Safeguards to assure limitations of super-government
9. Charter adoption upon suitable planning

There followed unnumbered steps which set the slate for a revolutionary sentence tucked away in the baroque preamble: "The highest sovereignty on earth resides with the peoples who inhabit the planet." The two unnumbered points were that prevention of war requires a World Development Authority to mitigate growing economic disparities between nations and that appropriate steps should be taken to eliminate discrimination based on race, creed, color, or ancestry.

The world little noted nor long remembered Dublin Two; it was not even mentioned in *The New York Times*. Greater notice was taken of a second Clark pilgrimage—a gathering in San Francisco in 1965, the twentieth year following the founding of the UN in that city—at which Clark and twelve other "leading world citizens" proposed a radical strengthening of the world organization's mechanism and function.

The Bonds of Friendship

As he had been from Dublin One, Felix Frankfurter was absent, perhaps conspicuously, from Dublin Two. Felled by a stroke, beset with concerns for his invalid wife, Marion, and with the inadequacy of his judicial pension, Frankfurter's sturdy body had been bent and broken, and the bold, copperplate handwriting was now spidery and tremulous, as he wrote to Clark on the eve of their eighty-second birthdays. The state of his finances was indicated by the salvage of Supreme Court stationery, overwritten with his return address of 2339 Massachusetts Avenue.

> October 29, 1964
>
> My dearly beloved Grenny:
> I can certainly thus address Marion's hero. And the clock has ticked around another year [and] orbited you and me another year. And you are still my senior, and I still your respectful and devoted junior! Well, the Fates have not been kind to you and me. But our heads are still unbowed and both Marion and I are fortified by your devoted and generous friendship.
>
> Affectionately and in happy memory of Fanny's,
> Felix

The veiled thanks was for Clark's discreet action (all by telephone via Justice Harlan) of paying for the enormous medical bills of Justice and Mrs. Frankfurter after medical catastrophe and endemic illness had destroyed their resources. As 1965 approached, Frankfurter returned to the same theme, the tremulous manuscript underlining the poignancy of the message:

December 10, 1964

Our dearest Grenny:
    For such you are to Marion and me. You have been one of the most valued of friends ever since I encountered you in Austin Hall.
    Your friendship has greatly sustained me throughout these dark days. We send you and all your dear ones our most heart-felt good wishes . . .

Affectionately and gratefully,
Felix

Frankfurter died on Washington's Birthday, 1965. The last years had not been happy ones. The inflation virus of the welfare state Frankfurter had helped construct rendered his retirement income totally inadequate. Penury and destitution, averted only via Clark's discreet charity, lent a special poignancy to Frankfurter's references to "these dark days" and "the Fates have not been kind to you and me." Henry Friendly has left a record of Clark's appearance at the diminutive Justice's funeral: "He seemed much as when I first met him nearly forty years before—erect of bearing, quick of eye, correct of mien . . ." Yet the brave front was a façade.

Fanny

Judge Friendly's recollection also included a note that Clark seemed happy in his new marriage. Clark had married Mary Brush James on January 1, 1965. She was an artist who practiced her craft and was about as far from Fanny in style and personality as it was possible to get. It was a happy enough union, and was, in a sense, the product of Fanny Clark's dying injunction to the husband whom she knew better than he knew himself that he must marry again. Clark had described her passing in a handwritten letter to Frankfurter:

June 13, 1964

Dear Felix,

   The reason I didn't answer the very warm and kind letter of yours some months ago was that I was trying to do what little I could to make Fanny's last days as bearable as possible and found almost no time or energy for anything else.

   From being better for years until March 1963 she was quite suddenly afflicted with a muscle atrophy disease called amyotrophic lateral sclerosis—quite rare yet well known and for which the medical profession can do nothing whatever. She very slowly lost strength and died peacefully, just from weakness, it seemed, on May 3. We were on Long Island and she had hoped to get back here by ambulance on May 7, but her strength didn't quite hold out. Her mind was perfectly clear and alert right to the end although she hadn't been able to speak for months because of the paralysis of her throat, she could write briefly and did write many short very cute and humorous things, no matter how sick she was.

   Subsequently, in a spontaneous aside, Clark confirmed Fanny's judgment as to the second marriage: "You know how lonely you can be when you're alone. It's difficult: I need a helpmate."

   The New York Times of June 11, 1966, under the headline BOTANIC GARDEN, BROOKLYN, carried the story that Mr. and Mrs. Grenville Clark had donated the twelve-acre estate at Albertson, Long Island, where they had moved early in their marriage, along with appropriate funds to develop the site as a botanical garden in her memory. Thus the place beyond the city where Fanny had savored her flowers and plants was made available to all.

18
Nightfall

Keep thou my feet: I do not ask to see
The distant scene; one step enough for me.

—John Henry (Cardinal) Newman, "The Pillar of Cloud"

Judge Friendly's acute perception of Clark in February 1965—
"erect of bearing, quick of eye, correct of mien, happy in his new
marriage"—took in only externals. Beneath the urbane club-
man's exterior, things were quite different. The grand dream of
universal disarmament and world government was as short of
fulfillment as ever, and indeed it seemed that triumphs comparable to Plattsburg, the Supreme Court defense, and World War
II conscription were unlikely ever to be repeated. Moreover,
Fanny was gone and no second marriage, however felicitous,
could ever replicate the first. Worst of all, within the splendid
body, a cell had run wild. The enemy within had given its hostile
signal as early as 1959.

Clark's blessings had included not only inherited wealth and
station, but a fine body, which he had disciplined as he had his
mind—squash, rowing, golf, and boxing were favorite muscle
toners. Even in physical adversity, Clark's blessings included the
professional ministrations of the world-famous Paul Dudley
White, who counted Clark not only patient but friend.

Dr. White arrived in mid-passage so to speak, upon Clark's
rejection in 1936 for life insurance by reason of a heart murmur.

There had been difficulties prior to White's advent: scarlet fever and diphtheria in childhood, typhoid at twenty-one, and a tonsillectomy at the remarkable age of twenty-five. There had also been the nervous breakdown in 1926. Besetting but not disabling were varicose veins and pneumonia at the midcentury mark.

Death had never been far from him, having lost a child to meningitis and another at birth. But even though he wore a mourning band for the dead daughter for a year, possibly the first time Clark thought about death in immediate and existential terms was when he faced major surgery for gallstones in 1956. His papers of the time reveal plans for a funeral. The hymnal selection was truly lowercase catholic, opening with four from Whittier, termed "fair," "good," "good," "excellent," passing through No. 547, "Ten Thousand Times Ten Thousand," and winding up with John Henry Newman's "The Pillar of Cloud" ("Lead, kindly light . . ."). Earlier than that, in both 1945 and 1946, the abbreviation "D.V." (*deo volente*, "God willing") had cropped up in Clark's writing.

But lymphoma was something else again—cancer, the crab, is what the ancients called the malignant organic enemy within the body, at once parasitic and ravaging—and, given the position of the lymph glands, it could be compared to an assassin's knife at the throat. Quite possibly the perverse vitality of the malignancy was triggered by a case of blood poisoning Clark contracted on a trip to the West Indies in 1959. But even though the body was in difficulty, the heart, despite insurance company judgment, remained stout. Clark found some amusement in, and even repeated in jest, the unfeeling comment of a London specialist on his lymphoma: "If you were a younger man, it would be serious, but at your age a lot of other things could happen."

Other things did happen, but not the intervention of a morbidity assuring a quick and painless passing. Only the postmortem would reveal how much of Clark's urbane and vital exterior was veneer, covering up a sense of agony and desolation within. External data are scant, but his cousin, Senator Joseph Clark, recollected a dinner at the Hanover Inn during which Grenville bravely contended with his lymphatic and throat condition by having an unprecedented duo of cocktails.

In an interview with historian Richard Hefner in the last months that were left him, Clark disclosed what drove him on:

> . . . when I ask myself why I have spent many years of work and considerable money in the effort to prevent future wars, I feel that my dominant reason is a sense of shame at the incapacity of the human race to summon enough intelligence and will to solve this problem, when the knowledge and means to solve it are at hand. And since this failure offends me so deeply, I feel the necessity to attempt to educate enough people to the ways and means to achieve world order that the result can actually be achieved in our time.

An event which Clark knew would not be achieved in his time was the cause of justice and opportunity for the Negro. He hoped for a few more years of active service and to use them well. He was not to get them.

By the mid-1960s the evidence of ravage was simply too strong to ignore. After a reprise of the Dublin Conference in New York City in May 1966, held in connection with a commemoration of John XXIII's encyclical *Pacem in Terris,* Clark virtually withdrew from active participation in the movement, and by August was writing to James Conant (whom he had been unable to see) that he was "staying right here quietly in Dublin in an effort to regain my health." By September, the need for more radical measures was evident, and he wrote his cousin Senator Joseph Clark from Cambridge that he was "taking strong drug treatment for my lymphoma . . . staying here at 85 Brattle Street."

By late fall, it was apparent that the ravages of the disease were beyond remission by chemotherapy, and Clark was admitted to and then discharged from a Boston hospital. "They're sending me home to die," he told his secretary, Ruth Wight, who promptly relayed the melancholy message to Mary Kersey Harvey, a *Saturday Review* associate of Norman Cousins.

Mrs. Harvey had other ideas on the point, and determined to offer her own therapy—the Nobel Peace Prize for 1967—in the hope that the lift to Clark's spirit might keep him alive for a while. In fact, nominating Clark as Nobel laureate had been the brainchild of Henry J. Friendly, who had been in Norway in 1958, the year of the unveiling of *World Peace Through World Law*, and had become intrigued with both the prize and the criteria. The result had been a joint nomination, with which Clark went along. Shortly before his death, he wrote W. M. Sheehan, an official of the World Transport Association and prominent world federalist:

> I had, quixotically or not, joined Sohn's name with mine in the authorship of the book even though its conception and basic ideas had, of course, been mine. Therefore, again perhaps foolishly and quixotically, I told Friendly that Sohn had better be put up together with me and he fell in with that, recruited some sponsors and had our names nominated for the 1959 prize.

Now the time was short, and Mrs. Harvey moved with the energy of desperation in effecting the administrative requirements involved in submitting the nomination for 1967. An appreciation of Clark on his eighty-fourth birthday, entitled "Aristocrat of Peace," was to be carried in *The Saturday Review* (which Norman Cousins had brought to front rank in American intellectual life). As part of the campaign, Mrs. Harvey also procured an in-depth interview of Clark by historian Richard Hefner for *McCall's*.

Given Clark's patrician self-assurance, the Nobel itself meant little. But, unquestionably, the international prestige involved might be the impetus for which he had been searching for two decades, and it would obviously help the cause. On the issue of single or joint nomination, where Mrs. Harvey was almost adamant on singularity, Clark showed that, even dying, he was every inch the *grand seigneur*. As he wrote Sheehan:

On this question I want to make it crystal clear that I do not want to give any advice or make any comment to you or Mrs. Harvey or Norman Cousins or anyone else as to what should be done. I am sure that is the only possible position . . .

The point is that it was I who was really responsible for having Sohn's name joined with mine and I feel very strongly that I simply must not and will not say a word to go back on that whether or not it was a foolish mistake.

On the other hand, I do not wish to say a word to discourage anyone whatever who wants to have me nominated by myself. I consider that is entirely their affair as to which I should make no comment whatsoever.

This letter sounds rather cold and ungrateful. The contrary is the case. I am profoundly grateful to you and Mary Harvey and Norman Cousins and anybody else who has or will take any interest in putting me up for the prize either with or without Sohn . . .

Mrs. Harvey rallied her task group and, in a burst of determination, caused the efforts to be directed for a solo nomination: "By the beginning of the new year, 1967, a torrent of nominating letters and endorsements from public figures had rained on Oslo. But within twelve days, Mr. Clark was no longer ours . . . No Nobel Peace Prize was awarded in 1967."

Death had come in Dublin on January 12, 1967, at twenty minutes before midnight. The death certificate attested to both the ravages of the cancer and the quiet heroism of the last year. The body was cremated at Boston's Mount Auburn Cemetery and Clark's daughter, Mary, committed his ashes to the Dublin farm he loved so well. The formal funeral services were held in the small Unitarian church in Dublin which Clark had supported in his later years. An appropriate epitaph was later spoken by a black judge and longtime friend, Judge Francis E. Rivers: "When I joined the audience in their singing, in the most spirited fashion, 'Onward, Christian Soldiers,' I felt Mr. Clark was there and still trying to urge us on to meet bigger challenges."

19
Evening Star

*There the common sense of most
shall hold a fretful realm in awe,
And the kindly earth shall slumber,
Lapp'd in universal law*

—Tennyson, *Locksley Hall*

Clark's isolation in retirement was probably the reason that his death was not reported in *The New York Times* until January 15, 1967. The story included an epigraph which would have pleased him: "Publicly inconspicuous, Grenville Clark was privately a man of uncommon powers of persuasion."

Other tributes were to follow. One was a dinner in New York City on November 19, 1967, hosted by Clark's daughter, Mary Clark Dimond, to discuss the public causes Clark had served during his life. There, Paul Freund of Harvard, distinguished constitutional scholar and Loeb University Professor, felicitously caught the blend of public and private: "When I think of Grenville Clark, I think of the remarks of Justice Brandeis, who said that the requisites of success are these: brains, rectitude, singleness of purpose, and time. I also think of Brandeis' observation that the way to deal with irresistible forces is to resist them . . . I suppose one always says: Was it not Cicero who said it?, that 'in a democracy the most important office is that of citizen' Alas, it's all too infrequent that that office is adequately filled. But surely if there ever was an exemplar of that truth, it was our friend, Grenville Clark."

Another speaker at the dinner was Clark's close friend and duck-blind companion, John S. Dickey, president of Dartmouth College. In his typically forthright manner, Dickey stressed Clark's fiber and insistent moral instinct:

> My God, I've never known a human being, and I've known a lot of human beings, who knew the meaning of tenacity . . . as he knew it, and as he taught it, and as he bred it. Well, then, there was another quality, an old-fashioned quality, and it's not mentioned very much today, by God, it needs mentioning, rectitude. *Rectitude!* I don't care what the cause is, and rectitude is an entirely different thing from self-righteousness. Its essence is seeking, *seeking* the right, not having it, not possessing it, feeling that you have an obligation to seek it and serve it. Out of his *tenacity* and sense of rectitude; out of these came his special contribution to the causes for which Grenville Clark was greatly and wonderfully and thankfully as far as we are concerned committed.

Perhaps Felix Frankfurter's birthday greeting many years earlier also should have been read at the dinner:

> I have no doubt that you will be told in all sincerity and with ample felicity of your transcendental quality of moral courage. If courage, candor, and generous devotion to all that makes for sweetness and sanity in our national life are characteristic of you, as they are, you get no credit from me. The virtues of most men are achievements, something to be fought for. But you are what you are because you can't help being that kind of cuss—fortunately for all of those who have the great good fortune of being admitted to your friendship and for untold millions who know not their benefactor.

Dickey handsomely filled out his dinner tribute in acknowledging the gift of Clark's papers to Dartmouth College:

> Grenville Clark was a pragmatic idealist who worked for a more civilized and safer world in many ways, from the American Consti-

tutional system and the United Nations to the public schools of his community. He moved mountains without either the prestige or power of major public office.

Public plaudits and private praise alike had been rendered equally peripheral, in Clark's mind, by the possibility that their ultimate disclosure might come only to future Melanesian or Eskimo archaeologists poking through the radioactive ash of Manhattan. Far more important to him was that both people at large and the intellectual molders of public opinion have some comprehension of the ideas which beset him and the ideals for which he had struggled so hard.

Curiously, toward the end of 1981, there seemed to be some sign of such comprehension. On November 16, 1981, George F. Kennan accepted the Grenville Clark Award at Dartmouth College. The award is the laurel of the Grenville Clark Fund at Dartmouth College, Inc., established in 1971 to further the causes to which Clark had given such a full measure of devotion during his lifetime. It took considerable vision on the part of the Fund Trustees to offer the award to Kennan, and for him to accept it. A third of a century earlier, Clark and Kennan had been intellectual and political adversaries, separated by a gulf comparable to that then dividing the U.S. and the U.S.S.R. Kennan, architect of containment and possibly of the Cold War itself, was then perceived by Clark as an integral part of what he had labeled the "Truman-Leahy-Marshall-Lovett-Kennan-Forrestal-Harriman combination," whose "fixed ideas" were frozen in an icy Cold War carapace.

The trustees were on sound ground in tendering the award, for Kennan's recently published speeches had exemplified Clark's faith that, given time, sheer rationality would impel his antagonists toward his position. Indeed, in the spring of 1981, Kennan had sounded, not like a Cold Warrior, but like Clark himself, in accepting the Einstein Award at Princeton University and denouncing "the supreme sacrilege of putting an end to the civilization out of which we have grown, the civilization which made us what we are, the civilization without which our children and grandchildren can have no chance of self-realization, possibly no chance of life itself."

Kennan had then gone on to stress the admonition "to neglect nothing—no effort, no unpleasantness, no controversy, no sacrifices—which could conceivably help preserve us from committing this fatal folly." He reached the apogee of his thesis against nuclear weapons thus:

> I question whether these devices are really weapons at all—to my mind the nuclear bomb is the most useless weapon ever invented. It is not even an effective defense against itself. It is only something with which, in a moment of petulance or panic, you commit such fearful acts of destruction as no sane person would ever wish to have on his conscience.

Kennan admitted that his admonitions were not new, but rather restatements of what wise and far-seeing people had been asserting for thirty years. He named names, beginning with Albert Einstein and concluding with every President of the United States from Dwight Eisenhower to Jimmy Carter.

He did not name Grenville Clark. Later, in a *New Yorker* follow-up to his Einstein Award speech, Kennan edged closer to Clark in several planes of encounter. One was a plea for a less demonic perception of the Soviet adversary. A second insisted on the quantum difference between nuclear arms and conventional ones. The third could have been vintage Clark as far as it went:

> . . . there are people who consider it useless or even undesirable to try to get rid of those weapons entirely, and believe that a satisfactory balance can somehow be found . . . I believe that until we consent to recognize that the nuclear weapons we hold in our hands are as much a danger to us as those that repose in the hands of our

supposed adversaries, there will be no escape from the confusions and dilemmas to which such weapons have brought us . . .

His next public utterance, at Dartmouth College accepting the Grenville Clark Award, actually included a quote of Clark. Kennan said, ". . . if the various governments did not find a way to put a stop to this insanity, the awareness of the indescribable dangers it presented would someday, as he [Clark] put it, 'penetrate the general masses of the people in all nations' with the result that these masses would begin to put increasing, and indeed finally irresistible, pressure on their governments to abandon the policies that were creating this danger . . ."

Then, by providence or chance, something else happened, almost coincidentally, and from a most unlikely quarter—from the President whom Kennan had omitted from his list of postwar American leaders who were apprehensive about the nuclear dilemma. At a press conference in early November of 1981, Ronald Reagan, in a thoughtless response, used a metaphor of euphemism to assert that a tactical exchange of battlefield nuclear weapons could occur between NATO and Warsaw Pact forces "without bringing either one of the major powers to pushing the button."

The President had hardly bargained for the response he got. The following weekend, hundreds of thousands of people, finally comprehending the possibility of atomic war involving *them,* marched in spontaneous protest through the streets of Paris, London, Brussels, and Rome.

Slowly, intellectuals like Kennan were moving to Clark's grand view, and, as the anti-nuclear movement around the world attested, collective consciousness was also moving in that direction.

Another indication that Grenville Clark's plan for world peace will probably play a role in future world affairs lies in a remarkable tribute to Clark written by George Roberts, senior partner of the eminent law firm of Winthrop, Stimson, Putnam & Roberts, for the 1967 Memorial Book of the Association of the Bar of the City of New York:

> Grenville Clark was one of the leading lawyers of his generation with a great lawyer's ability to pick out the essentials in a problem. Yet his fame rests not on any particular work for private clients but on his public service. It may be summed up by saying that in a very real sense his client was the people of the United States. During his active lifetime occurred two devastating world wars, a world-wide depression, bitter controversies over civil rights and the invention and production of atomic and hydrogen bombs with a destructive power beyond belief. In all these matters Clark influenced the policy and thinking of the United States and the remarkable thing is that he did it as a private citizen without any portfolio or public office. How did he accomplish this? His greatest asset was his absolute integrity. No one ever thought of his having any kind of selfish interest in what he was doing. He had a most distinctive personality but, with his granite-hewed square jaw and powerful body, he radiated force. What he said, either to a small group or to a large audience, carried conviction.

At a later point in his article, Roberts said:

> The world is apparently not yet ripe for such drastic reforms as Clark proposed but with the thunder of cannons in Viet Nam and the Near East in our ears there can be no doubt that Clark was right when he said that the preservation of peace is the number one issue in the world.
>   . . . No new nor novel plan for the revision of the United Nations or for the creation of a new peace-making body has been put forth and sponsored by any of the major nations. But it is too early to say that Clark's work on the problem has proved fruitless. The need is so obvious. Somehow, somewhere an answer must be found. Although often in poor health, Clark never relaxed his efforts. In 1964 he made a world tour advocating world law. In 1965 he received the Publius Award from the United World Federalists. He was a born fighter! The fight will continue.

In the meantime we can all pay tribute to the superb idealism and unremitting work done by Grenville Clark in the interest of all those who seek a rule of law in world affairs.

Many comments on Clark in a similar vein are included in a book of recollections and appraisals written by fifty-one men and women who had worked with Clark or had in other ways had a special relationship to him. This book, published in 1975, is entitled *Memoirs of a Man: Grenville Clark,* and was edited by the late Mary Clark Dimond; Norman Cousins, editor and publisher of *The Saturday Review*; and J. Garry Clifford, a member of the history faculty at the University of Connecticut. Among the authors of the fifty-one sketches, in addition to the three editors, were Judge Friendly; John Dickey; Erwin Griswold, former Dean of the Harvard Law School and former Solicitor General of the United States; Joseph Clark, senator from Pennsylvania; and Alan Cranston, senator from California.

In May 1968, Dartmouth College announced the gift to the college of Clark's papers. The announcement indicated the importance of those papers and the probable future influence of Clark's work on public causes:

Hanover, N.H.—The personal papers of the late Grenville Clark, distinguished lawyer and citizen statesman who personified in his career the maxim, "First in peace and first in war," will be formally given to Dartmouth College Wednesday, May 29, at 11 A.M., in Baker Library.

Mr. Clark was the architect of American readiness in the two World Wars, a leading defender of civil liberties, social justice and academic freedom, and, since World War II, a champion of world peace through enforceable world law, several times nominated for the Nobel Peace Prize . . .

The collection was described by Dartmouth President John Sloan Dickey as the "legacy of a great American life."

In welcoming the collection to Dartmouth, President Dickey said, "Grenville Clark was a pragmatic idealist who worked for a more civilized and safer world in many ways, from the American Constitutional system and the United Nations to the public schools of his community. He moved mountains without either the prestige or power of major public office."

In 1953, at the time of President Eisenhower's visit to Dartmouth, the College awarded Mr. Clark its honorary doctorate of laws. In awarding this degree, Mr. Dickey said of Mr. Clark, "Perhaps no other man in our time so abundantly portrays the truth that a man can lead no better life than he does of whom it can always be said: 'He is a great citizen.' "

Notes

Unless otherwise noted, all references to correspondence involve material in the Grenville Clark Papers, Baker Library, Dartmouth College.

Foreword

xii. "Indeed I cannot consider" James Boswell, *The Life of Samuel Johnson* (Heritage ed., 3 vols., 1963), Vol. 1, p. 4.

xiii. "Peace, if it ever exists" Julian Benda, *The Betrayal of the Intellectuals* (Beacon ed., 1955), p. 147.

Chapter One

4. "inner-directed man" See David Riesman, *The Lonely Crowd* (1950).

5. "Had he been born in Jerusalem" Henry Adams, *The Education of Henry Adams* (1918 ed.), pp. 3–4.

6. "The punishment of each offending person" *Pace* v. *Alabama*, 106 U.S. at 583, 585 (1882).

8. "As the Latin School" Adams, p. 41.

8. "they united"   G. Clark, Transcript of Oral Reminiscences, Antigua, B.W.I., March 2, 1966. Mary Clark Dimond Papers, University of Missouri at Kansas City. (Hereafter cited as Antigua Tape.)

9. "Somehow or other"   Antigua Tape.

9. "not a very forceful character"   Interview, Mary Clark Dimond, Kansas City, December 11, 1980. (Hereafter cited as Dimond interview.)

10. "the theory of republican government"   LeGrand B. Cannon, *Personal Reminiscences of the Rebellion* (1895), pp. 221–24.

11. "Grenny writes"   Letter, February 27, 1945, from Felix Frankfurter to Grenville Clark.

12. "fight talk"   Antigua Tape.

13. "Great vigor of mind"   Transcript of NBC telecast "A Conversation with Grenville Clark," April 26, 1959. (Hereafter cited as Television Transcript.)

13. "The names of the professors"   Antigua Tape.

14. "slightly less disreputable"   *Ibid.*

14. "the year 1896 does not show"   Ralph Nading Hill, "Era of Opulence," *Vermonter,* November 14, 1976 (quoting corporate records).

14. "one could find most of the Groton, St. Mark's"   Richard Harrity and Ralph G. Martin, *The Human Side of FDR* (1960), unpaginated.

14. "since other"   Antigua Tape.

15. "SAVED BY BACK BAY MAN"   *Boston Evening Transcript,* June 29, 1901.

15. "I have only just heard"   Letter, July 3, 1901, from Theodore Roosevelt to Grenville Clark.

Chapter Two

18. "As to professors"   Antigua Tape.

19. "Austin Hall housed a family"   Gerald T. Dunne, "The Third-Year Blahs: Felix Frankfurter After Fifty Years," *Harvard Law Review,* Vol. 94 (1981), p. 1237.

19. "He [Clark] could not operate"   Mary Clark Dimond (ed.), *Memoirs of a Man* (1975), p. 82. (Hereafter cited as *Memoirs.*)

19. "I reviewed"   Antigua Tape.

20. "I got heavily involved"   *Ibid.*

20. "Gold Coast crowd"   Martin Mayer, *Emory Buckner* (1968), p. 19. (Hereafter cited as Mayer.)

20. "Grenville Clark, a great citizen"   Harlan B. Phillips (ed.), *Felix Frankfurter Reminisces* (1960), p. 27.

21. "a very powerful, high-tempered, and able man"   Antigua Tape.

21. "Roosevelt, you're drunk!"   Dimond Interview.

21. "I remember him"   Harrity, Ch. 1.

21. "That is to say"   Letter, June 10, 1907, from Edmund D. Paylies (of Carter, Ledyard & Milburn) to Franklin D. Roosevelt, in *National Law Review*, April 12, 1982.

22. "Where's that *paid* law clerk?"   Etling Morrison, *Turmoil and Tradition: A Study of the Life and Times of Henry W. Stimson* (1960), p. 64. (Hereafter cited as Morrison.)

22. "one little rut"   Letter, October 6, 1907, from Grenville Clark to Fanny Dwight.

22. "I get downtown"   *Ibid.*

22. "The work here"   *Ibid.*

22. "I went from office to office"   Joseph P. Lash (ed.), *From the Diaries of Felix Frankfurter* (1975), p. 4.

23. "Yes, that's his signature"   *Ibid.*

23. "You know, there's nothing the matter"   *Ibid.*

23. "There was one office"   *Ibid.*

23. "the modern corporate law firm,"   Louis Auchincloss, "The Legend of Henry Everett," in Ephraim London, *The World of the Law* (1960), Vol. 1, p. 541.

23. "genial, available"   *Ibid.*

23. "the most brilliant"   Mayer, p. 100.

24. "We hatched"   *Ibid.*

24. "Carnegie had the utmost contempt"   *Ibid.*

25. "Not that anybody"   *Ibid.*

25. "Andy" and "Mrs. Andy"   Letter, February 28, 1911, from Grenville Clark to Fanny Clark.

25. "Don't wurra, m'lad"   Interview, Robert Reno, Concord, New Hampshire, July 31, 1981.
26. "We have here"   Mayer, p. 101.
26. "the fellow I have to beat"   *Ibid.*
26. "Grenville Clark, as a practicing lawyer"   *Memoirs*, p. 79.
27. "I see you're having"   Mayer, p. 104.
27. "He prepares like a scientist" and "Grenville Clark: Statesman Incognito" (unsigned), *Fortune*, February 1946. (Hereafter cited as *Fortune* article.)
27. "Grenny was an impossible man"   Mayer, pp. 109–10 (Justice Proskauer).
28. "Let me be"   *Ibid.*
28. "Subtle . . . was a very inaccurate"   Letter, January 13, 1933, from Felix Frankfurter to Grenville Clark.
28. "[Clark] is an 'abler' "   Mayer, p. 105 (Emory Buckner).

Chapter Three

29. "As to girls"   Antigua Tape.
29. "A gentleman never"   Cleveland Amory, *The Proper Bostonians* (1947), p. 260.
30. "publicly useful"   *History of the Town of Dedham* (1859).
30. "No young lady or ladies"   Amory, p. 285.
31. "Beautiful balls"   *Ibid.*, p. 297.
31. "Marie is especially dear"   Letter, August 21, 1879, from LeGrand Cannon to Louis Crawford Clark.
32. "I'll get Mama or Mary to write you"   Letter, July 8, 1906, from Grenville Clark to Fanny Dwight.
32. "He was most kind"   Letter, August 24, 1909, from Grenville Clark to Fanny Dwight.
32. "small, small wedding"   Letter, August 23, 1909, from Grenville Clark to Fanny Dwight.
32. "we had a lovely day"   Letter, December 3, 1909, from Jane Dwight to Lady Peele.
33. "not too crowded"   *Ibid.*
33. "aired"   Dimond interview.

35. "She may not have played his public role"   James Dannel at Grenville Clark Dinner, University Club, New York City, November 24, 1978. (Hereafter cited as Dinner Transcript.)

Chapter Four

37. "too angry and horror-stricken"   John Gary Clifford, *The Citizen Soldiers* (1962), p. 54.
37. "utterly without fear"   *Fortune* article.
37. "inaction was intolerable"   Clifford, p. 54.
37. "a new movement for greater unity"   *Ibid.*
37. "The undersigned citizens of New York"   *Ibid.,* at pp. 54–55.
38. "national interest and honor"   *Ibid.*
38. "I really believe"   Letter, November 6, 1907, from Grenville Clark to Fanny Dwight.
38. "If I had been President"   Noel Busch, *T.R.* (1963), pp. 292–99.
38. "interventionist"   Interview with Henry Mayer, Summer 1978.
38. "we would be thrown"   Hearings, "Military Training and Service," House Military Affairs Committee (1940), p. 5.
39. "I have had a little scheme"   Letter, November 19, 1914, from Grenville Clark to Theodore Roosevelt, in *Memoirs,* p. 269.
39. "I could come"   *Ibid.*
40. "to get a crowd together"   Clifford, p. 55.
41. "most subtle engine"   Walter Millis, *Road to War* (1935), p. 94.
42. McCloy still remembered   Letter, July 14, 1977, from John J. McCloy to the author.
42. "As I was walking"   Letter, August 1915, from Grenville Clark to Fanny Clark.
43. "a first-class mediocrity"   Lash (ed.), p. 14.
44. "I heartily approve"   War Department Letter, March 16, 1916, in Hagedorn Papers, Library of Congress.
44. "the fact is that the incident"   Letter, January 23, 1931, from Grenville Clark to Herman Hagedorn, Hagedorn Papers, Library of Congress.

44.   "Plattsburg was not just"   John P. Finnegan, *Against the Spectre of the Dragon* (1967), p. 66.
44.   "Some of the most influential men"   *Ibid.*

Chapter Five

48.   "We have between us"   *Harvard Alumni Directory,* 1928.
48.   his first (and only) appearance   "Reform in Bankruptcy Administration," *Harvard Law Review,* Vol. 43 (1930), p. 1189.
49.   "Our roster"   Mayer, p. 105.
49.   "I wonder"   Jerold S. Auerbach, *Unequal Justice* (1976), pp. 87–88.
49.   "I hated litigation"   Mayer, p. 106.
49.   "Why did I start"   Interview with Judge Henry Friendly, New York, May 5, 1978.
49.   "Not true"   Interview with Leo Gottlieb, New York, February 20, 1981.
50.   "You don't have many options"   Dinner Transcript (Norman Cousins).
50.   "hard summer"   Letter, October 28, 1934, from Grenville Clark to Felix Frankfurter.
50.   "Harold, have you tried"   Telephone interview, Harold B. Kline, April 27, 1981.
52.   "It must be hard"   *Memoirs,* p. 90.
53.   "The result was not"   Dinner Transcript.
54.   "Did Bob Moses"   *Ibid.*

Chapter Six

55.   "We missed that one"   Dinner Transcript (John Dickey).
55.   "one thing that was intolerable"   *Ibid.* (Louisa Spencer).
56.   "Lots of good men say"   Henry James, Letter to the editor, *Fortune,* March 1966.
57.   "be damned"   *Memoirs,* p. 76 (Henry Mayer).

57. "Oh dear"   *Memoirs*, p. 177 (Mary Clark Dimond).
57. "Run like hell"   *Memoirs*, p. 76 (Henry Mayer).
58. "What fun"   Letter, December 6, 1966, from Elihu Root, Jr., to Grenville Clark.
58. "Now you must leave"   Merlo Pusey, *Charles Evans Hughes* (1951), Vol. 2, p. 539.
58. "Old Brushface"   *Memoirs*, p. 179.
59. "Old man Hughes"   *Ibid.*, p. 130.
59. "I did not know"   Letter, September 24, 1940, from Grenville Clark to Charles Evans Hughes, Jr.
60. "At the risk"   Telegram, September 30, 1930, from John Pope to advisees, Archives, New York Stock Exchange (Committee on Business Conduct).
60. "Clark's intellectual stature"   Interview, Willard Hurst, Madison, Wisconsin, August 1982.
62. "The first order"   *Memoirs*, pp. 212–13 (Edward P. Stuhr).
62. "Buy"   *Ibid.*

Chapter Seven

64. "CUT IN VETERANS' AID"   *The New York Times*, May 5, 1932.
64. "less than one per cent"   Talcott Powell, "The Rising Tide of Doles to Veterans," *Reader's Digest*, June 1932.
64. "I would never again"   Richard D. Hefner, "The Legacy of a Great American," *McCall's*, April 1967. (Hereafter cited as Hefner article.)
65. "If you expect"   *Ibid.*
65. "a terrible ear ache"   *Ibid.*
65. "[Lamont] has been telling me"   *Ibid.*
65. "I agree with you"   *Ibid.*
66. "one of the worst things"   *Ibid.*
66. "Please stick around"   *Ibid.*
66. "I can't"   *Ibid.*
66. "His veto"   *Ibid.*
67. "federal expenses"   Grenville Clark, "Federal Finances and the New Deal," *The Atlantic Monthly*, December 1934.

67. "The general level" Letter, November 9, 1937, from Grenville Clark to C. C. Burlingham.

Chapter Eight

68. "I have retained" *Harvard Alumni Directory*, 1928, p. 133.
68. "And let us resolve" *Ibid.*
68. "When I was a boy" *Memoir of Theophilus Parsons* (1861), p. 205.
68. "At Harvard" Television Transcript.
69. "You seem to be doing" Letter, April 12, 1921, from Grenville Clark to Felix Frankfurter.
71. "It is not easy" Letter, November 28, 1932, from Roscoe Pound to A. Lawrence Lowell.
71. "stood at the center" Max Freedman (ed.), *Roosevelt and Frankfurter* (1967), p. 117. (Hereafter cited as Freedman.)
72. "With regard to Frankfurter" Letter, May 5, 1933, from Grenville Clark to A. Lawrence Lowell.
73. "Would you like to know?" Lash (ed.), pp. 139–40.
74. "It was very sweet" Letter, May 16, 1933, from Felix Frankfurter to Grenville Clark.
74. "highly interesting" Letter, undated, from Grenville Clark to Felix Frankfurter.
75. "From all I have seen" Letter, May 16, 1933, from Felix Frankfurter to Grenville Clark.
75. "For years" Antigua Tape.
75. "Ah! But you see" *The New Yorker*, September 12, 1946.
75. "I meant to make it clear" Letter, May 23, 1933, from Grenville Clark to George Agassiz.
76. "Whatever people may say" Letter, January 25, 1933, from James Conant to Grenville Clark.
76. "Congratulations on the bomb" Letter, August 13, 1945, from Grenville Clark to James Conant.
77. "I don't know what to think" Letter, April 17, 1922, from Grenville Clark to Dr. Roger Lee.
77. "a university" *Memoirs*, p. 232 (William Eliot).

77. "to seek law's constant improvement" Grenville Clark (ed.), *The Future of the Common Law* (1937), p. 7.

Chapter Nine

78. "I have decided to vote for Mr. Roosevelt" Memorandum by Grenville Clark, "Notes on the Election," Frankfurter Papers, Library of Congress.
78. "Best congratulations" Telegram, November 5, 1936, from Grenville Clark to Franklin D. Roosevelt.
78. "ROOSEVELT ASKS POWER" *The New York Times,* February 6, 1937.
79. "If you voted" Circular letter, National Committee for Independent Courts, March 30, 1937.
79. "I have been unable" Letter, May 13, 1937, from F. Meredith Blagden to Grenville Clark.
80. "this bill" Hearings, "Reorganization of the Federal Judiciary," Senate Judiciary Committee, 75th Congress, 1st Session (1937), p. 1055.
80. "in a blue funk" *Memoirs,* p. 35 (Cloyd Laporte).
81. "(1) opposing the President's proposal" Circular letter, National Committee for Independent Courts, December 15, 1937.
82. "The situation in this state" Report letter, June 30, 1937.
82. the second proposal presented See *Supreme Court Historical Society Quarterly,* Vol. 2 (1984), p. 30.
82. "The Supreme Court proposal" Letter, June 30, 1937, from Grenville Clark to Senator Burton Wheeler.
83. ". . . taking a copy" Catledge Turner and Joseph Alsop, *The 168 Days* (1938), p. 278.
84. "COURT BILL DEAD" *Memoirs,* p. 25 (Cloyd Laporte).
84. "very confidentially" Letter, January 14, 1937, from President Franklin D. Roosevelt to Felix Frankfurter, in Freedman, p. 377.
85. "Even if you do not agree" *Ibid.*
85. "Dear Frank" Letter, February 7, 1937, from Felix Frankfurter to Franklin D. Roosevelt, in *ibid.*

85. "It was clear"   *Ibid.*
86. "It really bothers me"   Letter, March 4, 1937, from Grenville Clark to Felix Frankfurter.
86. "Candor about delicate themes"   Letter, March 6, 1937, from Felix Frankfurter to Grenville Clark.
88. "I was—and am"   Letter, July 20, 1937, from Felix Frankfurter to Franklin D. Roosevelt, in Freedman, p. 103.
88. "PRESIDENT'S SUPREME COURT"   *Harvard Crimson,* February 8, 1937.
88. Reportedly, Frankfurter sought   Letter, July 13, 1979, from Caspar Weinberger to Mary Clark Dimond, Dimond Papers, University of Missouri at Kansas City.
90. "The question is"   John Morton Blum, *From the Morgenthau Diaries* (1959), p. 329.
90. "The time has come"   *Ibid.,* p. 328.
90. "I want to name names"   *Ibid.*
90. "Why don't you call him"   *Ibid.*
91. "Under your hat"   Letter, May 27, 1937, from Franklin D. Roosevelt to C. C. Burlingham, in Freedman, p. 400.
91. "boldness and . . . ingenuity"   *Congressional Record,* Vol. 81 (75th Congress, 1st Session), p. 1013.
91. "at a discount"   *Ibid.*
91. "the letter of legality"   *Ibid.*
91. "the spirit of the law"   *Ibid.*
91. "to dodge the payment of taxes"   *Ibid.*
92. "Personally, I am unwilling"   *Ibid.,* p. 1610.
92. "ROOSEVELT ASKS"   *The New York Times,* June 2, 1937.
92. "INQUIRY BACKFIRES"   *The New York Times,* July 2, 1937.
93. "GRENVILLE CLARK, member"   *Ibid.*
93. "This is a very confidential letter"   Unmailed letter, July 7, 1937, from Grenville Clark to Douglas Arant.
94. "I enclose a memo"   Letter, July 7, 1937, from Grenville Clark to Douglas Arant.
94. "Assistant Chief Counsel Russell J. Ryan"   *The New York Times,* September 17, 1937. (Administration embarrassment was evident in the unexplained delay, duly noted in the *Times,* in announcing the resignations.)

94. "Lights burned late"   Randolph Paul, *Prosperity Through Taxation* (1946), p. 171.
95. "SENATE CHIEFS SHELVE COURT BILL"   *July 2, 1937.*
96. "Are you checking up"   Leonard Baker, *Back to Back* (1976), p. 281.
96. "EVADERS" OF TAXES   *The New York Times*, July 16, 1937.
96. none had volunteered   *Ibid.*

Chapter Ten

97. "read with delight"   Letter, July 1, 1937, from Felix Frankfurter to Grenville Clark.
98. "view of the Supreme Court"   *Ibid.*
98. "The fact of the matter"   Letter, April 29, 1937, from Felix Frankfurter to C. C. Burlingham.
98. "At the height"   Letter, undated, from Felix Frankfurter to Grenville Clark.
99. "I agree with the view"   *The New York Times*, April 28, 1938.
99. "American liberty"   *Ibid.*
100. "really and not nominally"   *Ibid.*
100. "the absence of arbitrary action"   *Ibid.*
100. "to . . . support"   *Ibid.*
100. "the free exchange of views"   *Ibid.*
100. "every other medium"   *Ibid.*
101. "a flagrant instance"   *Ibid.*
101. "notorious and unconstitutional"   *Ibid.*
101. "stimulating challenge"   *Ibid.*
101. "Liberty and Tolerance"   *The New York Times*, April 29, 1938.
101. "modern Babylon"   Letter, August 31, 1938, from Grenville Clark to Felix Frankfurter.
101. "BAR URGED"   *The New York Times*, July 12, 1938. The speech was also reprinted in full in the *Journal of the American Bar Association* (Vol. 24, p. 641, 1938) and inserted in the *Congressional Record* by ultra New Dealer Maury Maverick (Vol. 83, p. 2616, 1938).
102. "allowed to drift"   *Ibid.*
102. "the great rights guaranteed"   *Ibid.*
102. "I wish to make the point"   *Ibid.*

102. "But I suggest" *Ibid.*
103. "I venture to say" *Ibid.*
103. "beyond that" *Ibid.*
103. "what I want to emphasize" *Ibid.*
104. "We in Jersey City" John J. Gibbons, *"Hague* v. *CIO:* A Retrospective," *NYU Law Review,* Vol. 52 (1977), p. 738.
104. "JERSEY CITY" *Ibid.*
104. "a most perplexing" *Fortune* article.
105. "the callous disregard" *The New York Times,* July 12, 1938.
105. *Journal of the American Bar Association* Vol. 24 (1938), p. 883.
106. "I guess the appointment" Letter, August 31, 1938, from Grenville Clark to Felix Frankfurter.
106. "the legal problems" Gibbons, *"Hague* v. *CIO,"* p. 731.
107. *Davis* v. *Massachusetts* 167 U.S. 43 (1897).
107. "Do you think" Letter, November 14, 1938, from Grenville Clark to Felix Frankfurter.
107. "Most assuredly" Letter, November 16, 1938, from Felix Frankfurter to Grenville Clark.
107. "I know of no explicit repudiation" *Ibid.*
107. "Public order" Clark brief, *Hague* v. *CIO, Journal of the American Bar Association,* Vol. 24 (1938), p. 883.
107. *"Davis* v. *Massachusetts"* *Ibid.*
108. "cause of good cheer" *New York Herald Tribune,* December 23, 1938.
108. "stand as a landmark" *The New York Times,* December 23, 1938.
108. "How funny" Letter, December 31, 1938, from Felix Frankfurter to Grenville Clark.
108. "we cannot agree" *Hague* v. *CIO,* 307 U.S. at 515–16 (1939).
109. "stunning triumph" Gibbons, *"Hague* v. *CIO,"* p. 738.
109. "a very interesting" Television Transcript.

Chapter Eleven

110. "Logic and Fact" Letter, October 11, 1940, from Grenville Clark to James Landis.

111. "where there might be" Letter, May 3, 1940, from Grenville Clark to James B. Conant.
111. "I am quite concerned" Letter, October 11, 1940, from Grenville Clark to James Landis.
112. "CIVIL LIBERTIES" *The New York Times,* May 2, 1941.
112. "We utterly deny" *Ibid.*
113. "I must say" Letter, September 23, 1950, from Grenville Clark to Irving Dilliard.
113. "Z. Chafee, Jr." *Ibid.*
114. "Perhaps the most important" *Ibid.*
114. "The Committee believes" ABA brief, *Minersville* v. *Gohitis* (filed April 24, 1940).
115. "the great affirmative principle" *Ibid.*
116. "For nearly five generations" *Ibid.*
116. "The guarantees of civil liberty" *Minersville* v. *Gohitis,* 310 U.S. at 84 (Stone, J., dissenting).
116. Stone's clerk Telephone interview, Professor Alison Dunham, August 27, 1980.
117. "It may well be" William Douglas, *The Court Years* (1983), p. 46.
117. "Judicial review" *Minersville* v. *Gohitis,* 310 U.S. at 608 (1940) (Frankfurter, F., dissenting).
117. "F.F., who" Letter, September 23, 1950, from Grenville Clark to Irving Dilliard. (Rutledge was not appointed until 1943; Clark must have sensed his mistake and added the question mark after that name.)
117. flag salute issue *West Virginia State Board of Education* v. *Barnette,* 319 U.S. 624 (1943).

Chapter Twelve

119. "before the great attack" Television Transcript.
120. "In May 1931 Henry L. Stimson" Letter, November 14, 1966, from Grenville Clark to W. H. Sheehan.
122. "a peace-time conscription act" *Ibid.*
122. "he would have a program" Dinner Transcript (Judge Henry Friendly).

122. "Dear Mr. President" Letter, May 16, 1940, from Grenville Clark to Franklin D. Roosevelt.

123. "Dear Grennie" Letter, May 18, 1940, from Franklin D. Roosevelt to Grenville Clark, Roosevelt Library, Hyde Park, New York.

124. "without a sympathetic secretary of war" Letter, November 14, 1966, from Grenville Clark to W. H. Sheehan.

124. "eminently right" Letter, January 17, 1939, from Grenville Clark to Felix Frankfurter.

124. "Twenty-four years" *Ibid.*

125. "push it through" Morrison, p. 481.

125. "a very tired, decayed old man" *Ibid.*

126. "It was very sweet of you" Letter, May 3, 1940, from Felix Frankfurter to Franklin D. Roosevelt, in Freedman, p. 521.

126. "the hand which held" *Ibid.,* p. 533.

126. "an interesting illustration" *Memoirs,* p. 18 (Felix Frankfurter).

126. "the 'stab-in-the-back' speech" Freedman, p. 529.

126. "I've assured myself" Morrison, p. 482.

126. "an extraordinary thing" *Ibid.*

127. "I was called up" McGeorge Bundy (ed.), *On Active Service* (1947), p. 323. (Hereafter cited as Bundy.)

127. "Your preposterous plan" Morrison, p. 482.

127. "The Congress declares" Selective Training and Service Act of 1940, 54 *Stat.* 505.

128. "Why, Jim's" Personal recollection of the author.

129. "I compose my own statements" *Memoirs,* p. 15 (John J. Pershing).

129. "could have ended earlier" *Ibid.,* p. 19.

129. "My name is Grenville Clark" Hearings, "Compulsory Military Training and Service," Senate Military Affairs Committee, 74th Congress, 2nd Session (1940).

130. "Mr. Stimson said" Historical memo, February 6, 1948, by William Marbury.

131. "nothing miraculous" Letter, August 22, 1941, from Grenville Clark to Henry L. Stimson, Patterson Papers, Library of Congress.

131. "I don't imagine"   Letter, September 21, 1945, from Grenville Clark to Henry L. Stimson.

131. "After the appointment of Stimson"   Antigua Tape.

132. "the best team"   Bundy, p. 341.

132. "From October 1940"   Antigua Tape.

133. "I happened"   Dinner Transcript (Judge Friendly).

133. "The officer problem"   Biographical memo, "Note on the Activities of G. Clark," Dublin, New Hampshire, 1960.

133. "Grenville Clark"   Bundy, p. 348.

134. "It looks, does it not"   Letter, May 23, 1941, from Grenville Clark to Felix Frankfurter.

135. "I have worked up"   Letter, August 22, 1941, from Grenville Clark to Henry L. Stimson, Patterson Papers, Library of Congress. (It should be noted that the so-called Espionage Act constrained interference with military recruiting as well as spying.)

135. failure to mention   See biographical memo, 1960.

135. "the Japanese attack"   Bundy, p. 382.

136. "When the Japanese struck"   Hefner article.

136. "Oh, I guess FDR"   *Ibid.*

136. "About this date"   Letter, December 27, 1944, from Grenville Clark to Franklin D. Roosevelt, copy in Patterson Papers, Library of Congress.

137. "Now no cocktail party"   *Time*, May 17, 1941.

137. "lust for combat"   Bundy, p. 496.

137. "You may have forgotten"   Letter, September 21, 1945, from Grenville Clark to Henry L. Stimson.

138. "I was intending"   Letter, February 14, 1942, from Grenville Clark to Felix Frankfurter.

138. "there was nothing"   *Ibid.*

138. "Recently, I have been"   *Ibid.*

138. "Last winter"   Letter, August 7, 1941, from Grenville Clark to Felix Frankfurter.

139. "national service legislation"   Bundy, p. 482.

139. "I'm hoping"   Letter, December 27, 1944, from Grenville Clark to Franklin D. Roosevelt.

139. "It's a real tragedy" Letter, September 29, 1944, from Grenville Clark to Felix Frankfurter.
140. "Secretary-Treasurer" *Harvard Forum,* March 18, 1942.
140. "For the past 4 months" Letter, September 29, 1944, from Grenville Clark to Felix Frankfurter.

Chapter Thirteen

141. "I became cognizant" Autobiographical memo.
142. "The result might have been" Interview with John J. McCloy, New York City, October 26, 1984.
142. "Go home" Hefner article.
143. "If you are driving" Irving Dilliard, "Grenville Clark: Public Citizen," *American Scholar,* Vol. 33 (1963–64), p. 97.
144. orbit of . . . Dartmouth Clark's Dartmouth association was enhanced when poet Robert Frost undertook a Dartmouth appointment notwithstanding a conflicting Harvard contract; Clark forcefully presented Harvard's case, and the unhappy Dartmouth president acquiesced "for the cultural uplift of Harvard." Lawrance Thompson and R. H. Winnick, *Robert Frost: The Late Years,* Vol. 3 (1976), p. 111.
144. Saint-Gaudens' classic statue See Lois Marcus, "Augustus Saint-Gaudens," *Arts Magazine,* Vol. 54 (1979), pp. 144, 145.
145. "It should require" Grenville Clark, "A New World Order," *Indiana Law Journal,* Vol. 19 (1943–44), p. 189.
146. "Speaking of quotations" Letter, June 28, 1946, from Grenville Clark to Felix Frankfurter.
147. "Do the Dumbarton Oaks proposals" Letter, October 15, 1944, from Grenville Clark to *The New York Times.*
147. "With regret" *Ibid.*
148. "It requires" *Ibid.*
148. "subordinate to" *Ibid.*
148. "unanimity" *Ibid.*
149. "Under this formula" *Ibid.*
149. "The underlying defect" *Ibid.*
150. "a city whose atmosphere" *Ibid.*
150. "Let us raise a standard" *Ibid.*

150. "an anachronism" *Ibid.*
150. "Finally, I emphasize" *Ibid.*
151. "The writer" *Ibid.*
151. "the whole of it" Letter, October 24, 1944, from Felix Frankfurter to Grenville Clark.
151. "I feel about accuracy" *Ibid.*
151. "Next time you quote" *Ibid.*
151. "By the way" Letter, October 27, 1944, from Grenville Clark to Felix Frankfurter.
152. "1. 'Authoratative'" Letter, October 29, 1944, from Felix Frankfurter to Grenville Clark.
152. "Finland, Poland" Letter, June 2, 1945, from Grenville Clark to President Harry Truman, in *Memoirs*, p. 276.
152. "But what seems" *Ibid.*
152. "hard as it may be" *Ibid.*
153. "as you know" *Ibid.*
153. "Sometimes" *Ibid.*
153. "On this subject" *Ibid.*
154. "3. I know Justice Roberts" Letter, October 29, 1944, from Felix Frankfurter to Grenville Clark.
156. "It became clear" *Memoirs*, p. 255.
156. "unforgettable experience" *Memoirs*, pp. 247–48.
156. "He was looking ahead" *Ibid.*
157. "We cannot start" *Memoirs*, p. 5.
157. "effort to establish" Cannon, *Personal Reminiscences of the Rebellion*, p. 9.
158. "some pretty biting remarks" *Memoirs*, pp. 247–48.
158. "Mr. Clark flushed" *Ibid.*
158. "Let us raise" *Ibid.*, p. 254.
158. "Whatever may have been" *Dublin I Report*, privately printed.
159. "We do not join" *Ibid.*
159. "Grenville Clark served" *The New York Times*, October 16 and 17, 1945.
160. "cognizant" Autobiographical memo.
160. "But my dear classmate" Felix Frankfurter, Address to the Harvard Law Society of Illinois, April 22, 1955, p. 13.

161. "I will be happy" *Memoirs,* p. 244 (I. A. Richards, quoting Einstein).
162. "Will the effort" Letter, June 23, 1946, from Grenville Clark to *The New York Times.*
162. "The essence" *Ibid.*
163. "We should not be misled" *Ibid.*
163. "It would be folly" *Ibid.*
164. "I noticed" Letter, June 28, 1946, from Grenville Clark to Felix Frankfurter.
164. "(1) In the quote" *Ibid.*
164. "I am staying" *Ibid.*
165. "Actually" Samuel Spencer, "Cornerstone of Defense," doctoral dissertation, Harvard University (1951).

Chapter Fourteen

167. "The question is in fact" Letter, January 6, 1947, from James Conant to Harvard Board of Overseers.
169. "Ordinarily, I do not trouble" Letter, May 9, 1949, from James Conant to Grenville Clark.
169. "You first state" Letter, May 27, 1949, from Grenville Clark to Frank Ober, in *Memoirs,* p. 279.
170. "Both . . . meetings" *Ibid.*
170. "On this basis" *Ibid.*
170. "It is hard to believe" *Ibid.*
171. "Concerning your broader proposals" *Ibid.*
171. "A great university" *Ibid.*
171. "We must have" *Ibid.*
171. "The professor's right" *Ibid.*
172. "What sort of a place" *Ibid.*
172. "I am under no illusion" *Ibid.*
172. "I hope, though" *Ibid.*
172. "It is a superb" Letter, May 31, 1949, from William Marbury to Grenville Clark.
173. "PRESIDENT CONANT" *The New York Times,* June 20, 1949.

173. " 'I have done" Letter, July 5, 1949, from Felix Frankfurter to Grenville Clark.
173. ". . . Grenville Clark" Letter, October 31, 1981, from John Ciardi to the author.
174. The reverberations The author is indebted to William Marbury for the account which follows.
175. "Richard Field" Letter, March 25, 1949, from Alger Hiss to Grenville Clark.
176. "Thanks for your note" Letter, March 31, 1949, from Grenville Clark to Alger Hiss.
177. "22 Lawyers" *The New York Times,* October 15, 1952.
177. "We as lawyers" *Ibid.*
177. "Grenville Clark" *Ibid.*
178. "There seems to be" Letter, May 21, 1948, from Grenville Clark to Felix Frankfurter.
178. "definite intention to retire" Letter, February 2, 1949, from Grenville Clark to James Conant.
179. "That the Harvard Corporation" Letter, September 18, 1953, from Grenville Clark to Bradford Washburn, in "Correspondence in September–October 1953 between Grenville Clark, Chairman of the Finance Committee of the Arnold Arboretum, and Bradford Washburn," pamphlet privately printed at Clark's expense. (The substance of the exchange is contained in parallel letters to the editor in "The Arboretum Controversy," *Harvard Alumni Bulletin,* December 12, 1953, pp. 264–67.)
179. "long experience" Letter, September 23, 1953, from Bradford Washburn to Grenville Clark, *ibid.*
180. "troublemaker" Letter, October 7, 1953, from Grenville Clark to Bradford Washburn, *ibid.*
180. "any further correspondence" Letter, October 9, 1953, from Bradford Washburn to Grenville Clark, *ibid.*
180. "responsible persons" Letter, October 14, 1953, from Grenville Clark to Bradford Washburn, *ibid.*
180. "HARVARD ALUMNI" *The New York Times,* December 13, 1953.
180. "legal breach of trust" *Harvard Alumni Bulletin,* December 12, 1953.

180. "frivolous"   Letter, December 13, 1953, from Judge Learned Hand to Thomas Rankin.

180. "B's intervention"   Letter, June 8, 1955, from Felix Frankfurter to Grenville Clark.

181. "dirty pool"   *Memoirs*, p. 170 (James Conant).

181. "the punctilio"   *Meinhard* v. *Salmon*, 164 N.E. 545 (N.Y., 1920).

182. "I can personally bear witness"   *Memoirs*, p. 13 (John Dickey).

183. "Grenville Clark"   Letter, August 19, 1982, from Dr. George H. Williams to the author.

183. "A few hymns"   *Ibid.*

183. ". . . if this undertaking"   Letter, November 4, 1954, from John Lord O'Brian to Reinhold Niebuhr.

Chapter Fifteen

185. "By free institutions"   Grenville Clark, *Federation of Free Peoples* (1940), p. 1.

185. ". . . as a practical matter"   *Ibid.*, p. 11.

185. "This emphatically"   *Ibid.*

187. "No, I cannot stand"   *Memoirs*, p. 46 (Louis Sohn).

189. "Louis Sohn and I"   Letter, July 2, 1957, from Grenville Clark to Felix Frankfurter.

190. "In the past"   *The New York Times*, July 27, 1958.

191. "Can the authors"   *Ibid.*

191. "In all the history of mankind"   John F. Bantell, "Perpetual Peace Through World Law," doctoral dissertation, University of Connecticut (1980), p. IV-147.

192. "Secretary Dulles and I"   *The New York Times*, July 3, 1958.

193. "There's no point"   Herman Kahn, *Thinking the Unthinkable* (1962), p. 148. After Clark's death, Professor Sohn followed the 1958, 1960, and 1966 editions of the book with a 1973 version (published by World Without War Publications, 421 South Wabash Avenue, Chicago), which reflected changing times, particularly the explosion in UN membership following the dissolution of the British and French empires.

Chapter Sixteen

195. "I was persuaded"   Cord Meyer, *Facing Reality* (1980), p. 44.
195. "The truth is"   Grenville Clark, *A Plan for Peace* (Condensation) (1950), pp. 39–40.
196. "YOU WERE GROSSLY"   Telegram, March 15, 1948, from Grenville Clark to President Harry Truman.
196. "really nothing"   Letter, February 28, 1948, from Grenville Clark to Cord Meyer, in John F. Bantell, "Perpetual Peace Through World Law," doctoral dissertation, University of Connecticut (1980), p. 11-217.
196. "I believe there is"   Letter, May 10, 1945, from Grenville Clark to James Conant.
196. "We are faced"   Jerold S. Auerbach, *Unequal Justice* (1976), pp. 237–38.
197. "with less discussion"   *Ibid.*
197. "If nobody stood up"   *Ibid.*
197. "unfounded"   *Ibid.*
197. "I must confess"   *Ibid.*
197. "gratifying"   *Ibid.*
197. "supineness . . . appalled"   *Ibid.*
198. "Through his dedication"   ABA citation, *ABA Journal,* August 1959. Underlying the choice may well have been Frederick Bernays Wiener's suggestion that the honor go to someone besides a past president. Frederick Bernays Wiener, Letter to the editor, *Journal of the American Bar Association,* Vol. 44, 1958, pp. 1136–58.
198. "The American Bar Assn."   Letter, August 31, 1959, from Felix Frankfurter to Grenville Clark.
199. "Mr. Clark has been"   *The New York Times,* August 31, 1959.
199. "Isn't this wonderful!"   Undated superscribed original in Clark papers.
201. *Watkins*   354 U.S. 178, and *Sweezey,* 354 U.S. 234 (1957).
202. "Many thanks for sending me"   Letter, July 2, 1957, from Grenville Clark to Felix Frankfurter.
202. *Terminiello*   337 U.S. 1 (1949).
203. "revered the guarantees"   *Memoirs,* p. 116.

203. "black people being treated" *Ibid.*, p. 123. Beyond this there lay, quite literally, an ancestral commitment. Certainly the dinner-table declarations at 311 Fifth Avenue must have included Colonel LeGrand Cannon's memories of how he had effected the first successful emancipation in United States history some nine months before Lincoln's Proclamation. Interestingly, in effecting that action, "which practically and in direct immediate effect emancipated the Negroes sheltered in our lines at Fort Monroe," Colonel Cannon had combined the low visibility and intense personal persuasion which were to become the hallmark of his grandson's *modus operandi*. First had come the appointment of a commission of inquiry of which the colonel was not the senior member, but he was the draftsman of a report which went, not without difficulty, to the Secretary of War and received his sanction: "The paper was drawn by myself and required no little effort to have my associates on the Commission to sign it." (*Reminiscences*, p. 131.)

203. ". . . Like so many others" Letter, May 2, 1960, from Grenville Clark to Allen Chalmers.

204. "absolute minimum" *Ibid.*

204. "to the development" *Memoirs*, p. 122.

205. "You may ask" Letter, May 2, 1960, from Grenville Clark to Allen Chalmers.

206. "AN UNPRECEDENTED GIFT" NAACP release, May 27–28, 1964.

207. "It's a shame" *Memoirs*, p. 178 (Robert Reno).

207. "They're not" Interview with Robert Reno, Summer 1978.

207. "oddballs and idealists" *The New Republic*, August 18, 1960.

208. "patience; determination" *Memoirs*, p. 131 (Robert Reno).

208. "ON YOUR SEVENTY-FIFTH BIRTHDAY" Telegram, February 27, 1961, from Grenville Clark to Hugo Black.

208. ". . . you struck a strong blow" Letter, February 27, 1961, from Grenville Clark to Hugo Black.

208. "I cannot tell you" Letter, March 1, 1961, from Hugo Black to Grenville Clark. (Interestingly, Black came close to endorsing Clark's ideas of world order in a speech at Geneva, July 14, 1967, entitled "World Peace Through World Law.")

Chapter Seventeen

211.   "He began"   *Memoirs,* p. 5.
211.   "Accordingly, the overall East-West settlement"   *A Plan for Peace* (Condensation) (1950), p. 33.
212.   "We can be confident"   *Ibid.*
212.   "These provisions"   *Ibid.*
213.   "On the other hand"   Declaration, Dartmouth Conference, October 21–28, 1962.
213.   "Accordingly"   *Ibid.*
213.   "groovology"   *A Plan For Peace* (Condensation), p. 11.
214.   ". . . I find myself asking"   Letter, November 26, 1946, from Fritz Von Windegger to Grenville Clark.
214.   "We'll just carry on"   Dinner Transcript.
215.   "The rights of man"   Declaration of Second Dublin Conference, October 5, 1965.
216.   "The possession of nuclear weapons"   *Ibid.*
216.   "The highest sovereignty"   *Ibid.*
217.   "leading world citizens"   *The New York Times,* October 6, 1965.
217.   "I can certainly"   Letter, October 29, 1964, from Felix Frankfurter to Grenville Clark.
218.   "For such you are"   Letter, December 10, 1964, from Felix Frankfurter to Grenville Clark.
218.   "He seemed"   *Memoirs,* p. 51.
219.   "The reason I didn't answer"   Letter, June 13, 1964, from Grenville Clark to Felix Frankfurter.
219.   "You know how lonely"   *Memoirs,* p. 250.

Chapter Eighteen

220.   "erect of bearing"   *Memoirs,* p. 92.
221.   "D.V."   Letters, December 8, 1945, and December 12, 1946, from Grenville Clark to James Conant.
221.   "If you were"   *Memoirs,* p. 152 (John Dickey quoting unnamed physician).

222. ". . . when I ask myself"   Hefner article.
222. "staying right here"   Letter, August 6, 1966, from Grenville Clark to James Conant.
222. "taking strong drug treatment"   Letter, September 5, 1966, from Grenville Clark to Senator Joseph Clark.
222. "They're sending me home"   *Memoirs,* p. 217.
223. "I had, quixotically"   Letter, November 14, 1966, from Grenville Clark to W. M. Sheehan.
224. "On this question"   *Ibid.*
224. "By the beginning"   *Memoirs,* p. 218 (Mary Harvey).
224. "When I joined"   *Ibid.,* p. 119.

Chapter Nineteen

225. "When I think"   Dinner Transcript.
226. "My God"   Dinner Transcript.
226. "I have no doubt"   Letter, February 2, 1955, from Felix Frankfurter to Grenville Clark.
226. "Grenville Clark"   Press release, Dartmouth College, undated (circa May 29, 1968).
227. "Truman-Leahy-Marshall"   Letter, February 28, 1948, from Grenville Clark to Cord Meyer, in John F. Bantell, "Perpetual Peace Through World Law," doctoral dissertation, University of Connecticut (1980), p. VII-217.
227. "the supreme sacrilege"   George Kennan's speech accepting Einstein Award, partially reprinted in St. Louis *Post-Dispatch,* May 31, 1981.
228. "to neglect nothing"   *Ibid.*
228. "I question it"   *Ibid.*
228. ". . . there are people"   *The New Yorker,* November 2, 1981.
229. ". . . if the various"   *Congressional Record,* December 16, 1981, pp. 15467–69.
229. "without bringing"   *The Wall Street Journal,* November 2, 1981.
230. "Grenville Clark"   Memorial Book, 1967, Association of the Bar of the City of New York.
231. "The personal papers"   Press release, Dartmouth College, undated (circa May 29, 1968).

Bibliography

Amory, Cleveland. *The Proper Bostonians.* New York, 1947.

Anon. "Grenville Clark: Statesman Incognito." *Fortune,* February 1946.

Auerbach, Jerold S. *Unequal Justice.* New York, 1976.

Cannon, LeGrand B. *Personal Reminiscences of the Rebellion, 1861–1866.* 1895.

Chase, Stuart. "Principles for a Nuclear Age." *The Saturday Review,* May 6, 1961.

Clark, George B. *Clark, Dodge & Co., 1845–1945.* New York, 1945.

Clark, Grenville. *A Memorandum of New Effort to Organize Peace Containing a Proposal for a "Federation of Free Peoples" in the Form of a Draft (with Explanatory Notes).* New York, 1940.

———. "A New World Order." *Indiana Law Journal,* Vol. 19 (1943–44), p. 189.

———. "Conservatism and Civil Liberty." *ABA Journal,* Vol. 24 (1938), p. 640.

———. "Dumbarton Oaks Proposals." *ABA Journal,* Vol. 30 (1944), p. 664.

———. *A Plan for Peace.* New York, 1950.

———. *A Plan for Peace* (Condensation). New York, 1950.

———. "Federal Finances and the New Deal." *The Atlantic Monthly,* December 1934.

————. "Population Pressures and Peace." Dublin, N.H., 1962.

————. "Prospects for Civil Liberty." *ABA Journal,* Vol. 25 (1937), p. 741.

————. "Regulation of Outdoor Public Assembly." *ABA Journal,* Vol. 24 (1937), p. 741.

————. "Reform in Bankruptcy Administration." *Harvard Law Review,* Vol. 43 (1930), p. 1189.

————. "Solving the Inhuman Equation: Can Arms Control End the Population Crisis?" *The Saturday Review,* February 14, 1963.

————. (ed.). *The Future of the Common Law.* Cambridge, 1937.

————. "The Need for Total Disarmament Under Enforceable World Law." *Current History,* August 1964.

————. "The Supreme Court Issue." *Yale Review,* June 1937.

———— and Louis Sohn. *Peace Through Disarmament and Charter Revision.* Dublin, N.H., 1956.

———— and ————. *World Peace Through World Law.* Cambridge, 1958. (Translated into Norwegian, Swedish, Italian, Polish, Arabic, French, Spanish, German, Dutch, Japanese, Chinese, with proposed translation into Danish, Turkish, and Korean.)

———— and ————. *World Peace Through World Law: Two Alternative Plans.* 3rd ed., enl.; Cambridge, 1966.

Clifford, John Gary. *The Citizen Soldiers.* Lexington, Ky., 1962.

Daniel, James. "Grenville Clark and His Plan for Peace." *Reader's Digest,* May 1962.

deForest, Emily. *A Walloon Family in America.* 2 vols.; Boston and New York, 1914.

Dilliard, Irving. "Grenville Clark: Public Citizen." *American Scholar,* Vol. 33 (1963–64), p. 97.

Dimond, Mary C. (ed.). *Memoirs of a Man.* New York, 1975.

Dwight, Wilder. *Life and Letters of Wilder Dwight.* 2nd ed.; Boston, 1891.

Finnegan, John P. *Against the Spectre of the Dragon.* Westport, Conn., 1974.

Freedman, Max (ed.). *Roosevelt and Frankfurter: Their Correspondence.* Boston, 1967.

Gregory, Ross. *The Origins of American Intervention in the First World War*. New York, 1971.

Harrity, Richard, and Ralph G. Martin. *The Human Side of FDR*. New York, 1960.

Hefner, Richard D. "The Legacy of a Great American." *McCall's*, April 1967.

Lash, Joseph P. (ed.). *From the Diaries of Felix Frankfurter*. New York, 1975.

Leopold, Richard W. *Elihu Root and the Conservative Tradition*. Boston, 1934.

Lipset, Seymour Martin, and David Riesman. *Education and Politics at Harvard*. New York, 1975.

Mayer, Martin. *Emory Buckner*. New York, 1968.

Meyer, Cord. *Facing Reality*. New York, 1980.

Morrison, Etling. *Turmoil and Tradition: A Study of the Life and Times of Henry L. Stimson*. Boston, 1960.

Murphy, Bruce A. *The Brandeis-Frankfurter Connection*. New York, 1982.

Pusey, Merlo. *Charles Evans Hughes*. 2 vols.; New York, 1951.

Phillips, Harlan B. (ed.). *Felix Frankfurter Reminisces*. New York, 1960.

Sayre, Paul. *The Life of Roscoe Pound*. Iowa City, 1948.

Spencer, Samuel. "Cornerstone of Defense: The Selective Service Act of 1940." Doctoral dissertation, Harvard University,

Steel, Ronald. *Walter Lippmann and the American Century*. Boston, 1980.

Thompson, Lawrance, and R. H. Winnick. *Robert Frost: The Late Years*. New York, 1976.

Other

Clark, Grenville, *Frieden durch ein neues Weltreich*. Frankfurt, 1961.
———. *Varidsfred genom-varidslag*. Stockholm, 1960.
———. *Varensfred glemmon verdeslov*. Oslo, 1960.
———. *La Paix par le droit mondiale*. Paris, 1961.

————. *La paz por el derecho mundial.* Barcelona, 1961.

"A Conversation with Grenville Clark." NBC telecast, April 26, 1959.

Felix Frankfurter Papers. Library of Congress, Washington, D.C., and Harvard Law School, Cambridge, Mass.

Herman Hagedorn Papers. Library of Congress.

Robert Patterson Papers. Library of Congress.

Franklin D. Roosevelt Papers. Roosevelt Library, Hyde Park, N.Y.

Index